Getting Wrecked

CALIFORNIA SERIES IN PUBLIC ANTHROPOLOGY

The California Series in Public Anthropology emphasizes the anthropologist's role as an engaged intellectual. It continues anthropology's commitment to being an ethnographic witness, to describing, in human terms, how life is lived beyond the borders of many readers' experiences. But it also adds a commitment, through ethnography, to reframing the terms of public debate—transforming received, accepted understandings of social issues with new insights, new framings.

Series Editor: Robert Borofsky (Hawaii Pacific University)

Contributing Editors: Philippe Bourgois (UCLA), Paul Farmer (Partners In Health), Alex Hinton (Rutgers University), Carolyn Nordstrom (University of Notre Dame), and Nancy Scheper-Hughes (UC Berkeley)

University of California Press Editor: Naomi Schneider

Getting Wrecked

Women, Incarceration, and the
American Opioid Crisis

Kimberly Sue

UNIVERSITY OF CALIFORNIA PRESS

University of California Press, one of the most distin-
guished university presses in the United States, enriches
lives around the world by advancing scholarship in the
humanities, social sciences, and natural sciences. Its
activities are supported by the UC Press Foundation and
by philanthropic contributions from individuals and
institutions. For more information, visit www.ucpress.edu.

University of California Press
Oakland, California

Library of Congress Cataloging-in-Publication Data

Names: Sue, Kimberly, author.
Title: Getting wrecked : women, incarceration, and the
    American opioid crisis / Kimberly Sue.
Description: Oakland, California : University of
    California Press, [2019] | Series: California Series in
    Public Anthropology | Includes bibliographical
    references and index. |
Identifiers: LCCN 2019009256 (print) | LCCN 2019016406
    (ebook) | ISBN 9780520966406 (e-book) |
    ISBN 9780520293205 (cloth : alk. paper) |
    ISBN 9780520293212 (pbk : alk. paper)
Subjects: LCSH: Women prisoners—Social aspects—
    Massachusetts. | Opioid abuse—Treatment—
    Massachusetts.
Classification: LCC HV8738 (ebook) | LCC HV8738 .S835
    2019 (print) | DDC 365/.6672908209744—dc23
LC record available at https://lccn.loc.gov/2019009256

Manufactured in the United States of America

27 26 25 24 23 22 21 20 19
10 9 8 7 6 5 4 3 2 1

The publisher and the University of California Press
Foundation gratefully acknowledge the generous support of
the Barbara S. Isgur Endowment Fund in Public Affairs.

To Margie and Sam

Contents

Illustrations

Acknowledgments

Conducting fieldwork on addiction in prisons and jails certainly tested my mettle and dedication to the subject. Given the substantial institutional, bureaucratic, and systemic challenges that I have faced over the years, I realize that the contributions of many individuals other than myself have helped make the completion of this work possible. But it would not be possible without the women themselves, who have generously opened their lives and hearts to me. Incarceration, trauma, and drug use are sensitive topics to share with anyone, but I found a true generosity of spirit and commitment to the goals of this work among women who have used and continue to use heroin and other drugs. They gave me the encouragement to finish this work as I witnessed the truly difficult circumstances that they must navigate skillfully every day. I particularly want to thank the woman I call Tina for being such a kind and compassionate informant and friend. She took it upon herself to teach me about the complexity of addiction and incarceration in her life. Her ongoing work and commitment to serve others in similar situations is truly inspiring and gives me great hope.

From its inception, I knew that working in prisons and jails in the United States would be difficult, given the high level of concern surrounding prison research. Many people experienced with the prisons and jails in Massachusetts helped me with the necessary and critical logistics, including Dr. Warren Ferguson, Dr. Stephen Martin, Dr. Joseph Cohen,

Jennifer Johnson, and Rheana Kohl at the Department of Correction Research office. I also am indebted to Dr. Ken Freedman, Donna White, and the staff of the buprenorphine clinic including Ron and Jane. Thanks to Chris Jepson and Donna Clarke, who encouraged me to dream big about how to best take care of women on heroin and to make this project accessible to people working on the ground, one that speaks to real-life clinical quandaries and is grounded in patient experiences. I also wish to thank prison and jail administrators who made space and time for me at the prison and jail at the Suffolk County House of Correction as well as at the South Middlesex Correctional Center and MCI-Framingham. I thank the numerous caseworkers and program directors who allowed me to sit in on their programs.

At Harvard, Arthur Kleinman has challenged me at all levels to make this work both critical and accessible, encouraging me to believe that this project matters to many. Byron and Mary-Jo Good have been generous and inspiring mentors and friends, drawing on their vast and substantial fieldwork both in and outside of the United States. And Philippe Bourgois opened his field site and home to me, offering me many ways to think insightfully and critically at a grounded level about drugs and incarceration. Doing fieldwork and learning from the ethnographic team with Laurie Hart, Fernando Montero Castrillo, and George Karandinos was a great joy and is a continual reminder that this work can be fun, stimulating, and exciting. I have also benefited particularly from years of conversations and support from Allan Brandt, who is the true epitome of a thorough and kind scholar. From the moment I received a welcome email from him into the MD-PhD program in the social sciences at Harvard, he has been a great friend and champion of my work. He and I have had many important and inspiring conversations about studying and writing about addiction. I am beyond thankful for the stalwart mentorship of Paul Farmer, Salmaan Keshavjee, Anne Becker, David Jones, and Lesley Sharp, all of whom have been ardent supporters for many years; it has been my pleasure to learn and teach from them. I hope my work contributes to the body of global health knowledge and ideas that you all have pioneered. To Angela Garcia, Helena Hansen, Laurence Ralph, Laurie Hart, Jeremy Greene, Joao Biehl, Adriana Petryna, Jean Jackson, Susan Greenhalgh and Erica James, I thank you all for conversations and encouragement.

Graduate school is also a process of learning how to support oneself and one's colleagues, and my graduate school classmates have offered support quickly and often when I have been dispirited, discouraged, or stuck at a dead end. Marty Alexander has read and edited countless talks and papers, and we have had innumerable Skype conversations, the content of which is embedded in this entire book. Amy Porter has been my steady friend and companion in the MD-PhD process, along with my other excellent colleagues in this program, including John Heintz, George Karandinos, Sae Takada, Darja Djordjevic, Alison Hwong, David Kim, Zirui Song, Aaron Schwartz, and Tisa Sherry. Emily Harrison and Erica Dwyer have been my on-site historians and have walked with me alongside the research and writing. And I have benefited from the mentorship and friendship of so many in the program, including Felicity Aulino, Kate Mason, Seth Hannah, April Opoliner, Sa'ed Atshan, Andy McDowell, Maria Stalford, Janis Calleja and Marilyn Goodrich. I am inspired by joint-degree colleagues whose work shows both attention to academic scholarship and clinical medicine and who have gone along this path before: including Scott Stonington, Seth Holmes, and Carolyn Sufrin.

My friends and mentors at Harvard Medical School have helped me throughout my training with humor, compassion, and advice. Amy Cohen at the MD-PhD program has been an excellent cheerleader and source of support for social science research. I thank Ippolytos Kalofonos and Liza Buchbinder for our mutual support group in the final push and my dear friend Ling Tiong for her thoughtful feedback. I also thank my friends and family, who have witnessed and supported me through this entire endeavor and beyond.

Author's Note

The names of all my informants and their identifying information have been changed in this work to protect their anonymity. Many quotations are based on taped conversations, with permission granted by participants. I opted to leave officials in the prison administration nameless unless they were invoked as an authority or as a public figure. Since there is political sensitivity around this issue, I have endeavored to approach the topic delicately in order to access the opinions and experiences of people who work in prison and jail systems as well as individuals who have been incarcerated there.

The prison, the jail, and the clinic are public institutions, and I have identified them by name throughout the text. Their historical specificity, as well as their nature as public institutions, made an argument for the use of real names. In anthropology, context and history are critical. While this jail and prison have specific histories and orientations, I endeavor to show how the attitudes and policies they utilize are representative of a larger American cultural and political alignment toward drug use and deviance more generally.

1

Introduction

"It's Just Part of the Game"

Serenity woke up under the I-90 Copley Square bridge overpass in Boston to the uncomfortable sensation of Oscar's calloused hands closing in around her neck and squeezing. She couldn't breathe. He whipped her onto her back, jumped onto her chest, and pinned her down.

"I know what you're doing, bitch," he screamed. "You're making eyes at those dudes across the way. And I'll fucking kill you. I don't care. I'll go back to prison, because in jail I'm somebody, and out here, I'm nobody. Keep fucking with me bitch!"

When he let up his hands slightly, she screamed back at him. "What the fuck is wrong with you? I wasn't doing anything. I swear to God. You know I can be a flirt, but I swear to God I wasn't doing anything. I don't know if you need your meds or something, but you're having a lot of angry outbursts for nothing, Oscar. I didn't do nothing. You know I wouldn't. We're together. I'm not playing with you."

The next morning, she took her backpack and rolled out from beneath Oscar's heavy arm. She crawled out from under the bridge where they had been sleeping the last week—Oscar had been too jealous to allow them to continue staying in the homeless shelters—and made her way to the church in Copley Square. She had scraped together some money last night for their early morning fix, and she sat down in the cool darkness of the early summer morning, prepared herself some heroin, and prayed to God. *Send me back to jail, God.*

1

FIGURE 1. Suffolk County House of Correction, Boston, MA (photo by Emily A. Harrison).

I first met Serenity, a forty-three-year-old white woman originally from a small town in Vermont, in 2010. She had come to Boston eight years earlier seeking recovery from heroin addiction. After several month-long stints in and out of rehabs and detox programs, and after she had graduated from, failed, or dropped out of these programs, she had stayed in Boston. The drugs were plentiful, and to go home would have been to return to the source of her ongoing pain and grief. She could never stop blaming herself for missing the signs that her son was being sexually abused by his grandfather. She would sometimes hear his six-year-old voice innocently asking her, tormenting her, "Why did grandpa make me put his pee-pee in my mouth?"

There was something safe about being in jail, the Boston jail formally known as the Suffolk County House of Correction (figure 1). Maybe it was just that she felt safe from Oscar's hands on her neck or the constant threat of having her belongings stolen by other people in the shelter or on the street. Perhaps, most importantly, she felt safe from her own destructive drug use. Upon admission, users were forcibly detoxed from opioids. Like many other women, the longest amount of "clean" time she had ever accumulated was when she was incarcerated. Even though there was a fairly regular supply of heroin in the jail, she didn't have the money, or the desire, to use inside.

FIGURE 2. Shattuck Hospital, Boston, MA (photo by Emily A. Harrison).

Serenity tells me more when I see her in jail: "I feel calm here. It's crazy. I'm very institutionalized. I'm afraid that if I leave here that I'm just going to be in the spoon [using heroin] by noon."

As a fledgling medical student in the late 2000s, I became fascinated by the questions surrounding why and how women like Serenity had taken up heroin, or why a heroin habit had taken up in them, and their ongoing struggles with using and quitting drugs. When Serenity wasn't incarcerated, she was enrolled as a patient in the Lemuel Shattuck Outpatient Buprenorphine Opioid (OBOT) Clinic in Boston, Massachusetts, one of the community treatment sites where I conducted ethnographic fieldwork (figure 2). There, at weekly appointments, she received a medication called buprenorphine-naloxone (Suboxone) to keep her cravings for heroin at bay. Prescribed by certified primary care doctors, psychiatrists, or addiction specialists, the medication, if taken regularly, could eliminate her cravings and keep her off more dangerous opioids like heroin or fentanyl.

Yet taking buprenorphine couldn't erase the abuse Serenity's children had suffered, the neglect she felt that she had subjected them to, or the guilt that she felt for abandoning them in search of drugs. "Is grief a health condition?" she asked me once, in tears. Serenity would log onto Facebook every chance she could get—on the computers of homeless shelters or job readiness programs or at public libraries—in order to send them messages of love, birthday greetings, and other small reminders that she was thinking of them from several hundred miles away. She was thankful for access to medication, but it couldn't solve her problems of joblessness, homelessness, or multiple-drug-resistant HIV. What it could do was prevent her from being in opioid withdrawal (commonly known among people who use drugs as "dopesick" or simply "sick") and keep a needle out of her arm for that day, or at least for a couple hours.

As a medical student, I saw patients like Serenity in the community clinic where I was completing my third-year medical clerkship in the Roxbury neighborhood of Boston. Many of the patients there struggled with substance use disorders, mental health conditions, and other chronic diseases associated with poverty and lack of access to steady healthcare. Some patients wouldn't show up to their follow-up appointments and were dutifully marked "no-shows" by the clinic's secretaries. The office would call their phone numbers, which were often not in operation, as many patients lived month-to-month and were unable to keep paying their cell phone bills. Several months later, some would reappear saying they had been incarcerated and then released without medications or any assistance. They were arguably worse off after these stints in jail. What happened to them inside? What happened to Serenity as she was incarcerated over and over again, and how could she ever break this cycle?

Getting Wrecked: Women, Incarceration, and the American Opioid Crisis explores what happens to women with opioid addiction inside the prisons and jails in Massachusetts and in the aftermath of incarceration. I wanted to understand this world that was geographically so close to my life at Harvard Medical School in Boston and the Department of Anthropology across the river in Cambridge and yet somehow had such very different lifeworlds and experiences. Thus, I embarked on two years of difficult—at times, seemingly impossible—ethnographic research in the Massachusetts prisons, jails, and drug treatment community to understand how the prison had become a centralized node in the increasingly fraught politics of addiction treatment and recovery. During this time, I conducted semi-structured interviews with over thirty women at these three sites and followed them longitudinally forward as they moved in and out of jail, prison, and home.

Rooted in the methods and theories of sociocultural anthropology as a means to understand how inequality becomes embedded into physical bodies, I sought to explore how medicine, punishment, and drug use became bound up in politics and in the realm of the social. I learned, for example, that my ability to treat addiction effectively would entail addressing far more than what was at my disposal in the clinic as a physician and much more than any single prescription. I could give Serenity a medication to take away her cravings, but I couldn't stop the worlds she lived in from harming her or the ongoing harm she did to herself. My ability to effectively help someone like Serenity escape the cycle of problematic substance use lay rather in understanding and addressing deeper structural and social inequalities, deep-seated social mores and stigmas, and the punitive policing and legislation that contributed to her frequent bouts of incarceration.

Opioids, pain pills, heroin, and fentanyl seem to have dominated news cycles in the last several years as overdose deaths in the United States have reached new heights in fatalities, with over seventy thousand overdose deaths in 2017 noted by the Centers for Disease Control, with the numbers still rising or showing little sign of abating.[1] While opioids are not a new drug, there is newfound and rising awareness of their ubiquity and possible harms, as they increasingly are seen to affect white, suburban, and rural households. I use the term American "crisis" here (as opposed to other frequently used terms like "epidemic") in order to highlight this renewed attention and opportunity to address and intervene on the deaths of a structurally vulnerable group within our country. These deaths are preventable, thus tragic, as a result. But there can be significant harms besides death.

In the pages that follow, I explore the experiences of women on heroin and other opioids who are subjected to everyday violence, oppression, and inequality from many realms: within and from themselves, within their relationships, within their communities and within the judicial system. I followed them as they sought treatment in the community, as they tried to care for themselves in the prison and jail and after release, and as they cycled in and out of various regimes of care intermingled with punishment. These women have struggled mightily with self-care and caring for others throughout addiction, recovery, and incarceration while navigating various biochemical, spiritual, and socially prescribed forms of dependence and freedom.

Anthropologists Eugene Raikhel and William Garriott suggest that we might be able to learn much more about drugs, drug use, and historical and current moral orders by tracing people over time and across space and their substance use via *addiction trajectories*. As they write,

"Addiction cannot be reduced simply to a biological condition, a social affliction or the symptom of some deeper malaise. Rather, it must be seen as a trajectory of experience that traverses the biological and the social, the medical and the legal, the cultural and the political."[2] This is where anthropology's methods—of close and deep ethnographic investigation over time—can elucidate the complexities of a deep social problem like the American opioid crisis. Following the paths of women who used heroin, I kept finding myself at the gates of the local jail or the state prison. Reckoning with women's drug use in America meant reckoning with the carceral state.

This book takes readers through the epistemological orientations and practical applications of the treatment of women who use heroin or other opioids as in criminalization has become one of the primary social responses to the problem of opioid misuse and addiction. In the tradition of critical ethnographies of drug use that draw attention to the uneven playing field upon which the poor precariously build their lives, I use ethnography to interrogate what it means to treat others on a variety of registers. On the broadest level, how do we enact policies or legislation to treat the social problem of drug use? Do we have any means to understand the realities of these policies and practices when they travel behind bars? And what does it mean for the women at the center of such sociopolitical debates, as they dream of better lives for themselves and their families?

. . .

Heroin had been a presence in Boston for decades before Serenity found herself running its streets in the mid-2000s; it's presence dates back well before the current iteration of an American opioid crisis that swelled again in the mid-1990s. Like other large urban centers in the northeastern United States, Boston struggled with the problem of drugs and drug deaths during an early wave of heroin use in the 1960s and 1970s that was also called an "epidemic" at the time. In this context, President Nixon had famously declared drugs "America's public enemy number one," setting off decades of complicated and punitive waves of legislation around heroin, cocaine, and marijuana. And like other major urban cities, Boston also struggled with crack cocaine in the 1980s and waves of other substances including amphetamines, synthetics, and problems related to licit substances such as alcohol and tobacco.

In the summer of 1977, one of my informants, Jean, found herself scared and alone—only 14 years old—in the middle of Boston's infamous "Combat Zone," a small cluster of streets near Downtown Crossing and the Chinatown district. The Combat Zone ate up everyone who came to play. It was an equal-opportunity space for destruction or bliss. The Pussycats, the Naked I Lounge, and the Glass Slipper all promised ephemeral or forbidden pleasures. During its worst years, a Harvard football player was stabbed to death in a robbery gone awry, the House Ways and Means chairman Wilbur Mills was seen dancing onstage at a burlesque house, and a Tufts associate professor of anatomy murdered his mistress. In a profile of the so-called Combat Zone, two *Boston Globe* reporters noted that places like the Combat Zone always seemed to exist in big cities "as long as society, and life, has the ability to maim, and then ostracize the maimed, there will be a place for the maimed and the ostracized . . . a place where all acts and people who commit such acts, rejected by society, congregate."[3]

It was here that Jean first tied a belt around her arm and experienced the rush of intravenous heroin. Like many other teenagers, she had tried a couple of drugs before. When she was ten, she would occasionally sneak her grandfather's beers from the refrigerator when her mother wasn't looking. With an older boyfriend, she had smoked weed and even done quaaludes. But she had never done heroin, also known on the street as dope, H, smack.

Jean had recently run away from home, dreaming of getting into the fashion business. The reality she landed in was dismal and couldn't be further from a life in fashion: she was sleeping in the park and begging for food and spare change. One day, Jean was panhandling in a corner of Boston Common near the subway when a group of teenage girls approached her asking if she wanted to party with them. Too young to be properly scared, she followed them into an alley off the intersection of Beach and Essex Streets in Chinatown in pursuit of a good time.

The girls trooped down into a basement room that was dark and full of broken beer bottles and dirty mattresses on the floor. There were small clusters of people in various states of euphoria and consciousness lying around. Sugar, the ringleader of the group of teenagers, told Jean to offer up her virgin arm in the eerie candlelight of the basement. "It's fun," she said. "You'll like it."

Someone tied a belt as a tourniquet around her skinny arm. They told her to squeeze her fist tight and shut her eyes. Sugar saw a flash of blood return and knew she was in the vein, then she emptied the chamber into Jean's arm. Was it over, Jean wondered? She looked down at the needle in her arm and felt a wave of nausea rush over her. Then everything was black.

"Where's the bathroom?" she managed to ask. She ran toward the dirty toilet in the dark shooting gallery, hugging the bowl, her stomach churning in distress.

Jean was confused, wondering to herself: "What the hell? Why do people do this shit? Everyone else seems to like this, and I'm throwing up." Jean thought maybe she got a "bad bag," so the next day, she tried it again. This time, she told me, she became "hooked" on the feeling. The rush of physical and emotional relief it provided was like nothing else she had ever experienced in her life. Since Sugar had offered her a place to stay, acquiring and using heroin several times a day simply became part of their daily routine together.

Three weeks later, Jean recounted, "I started waking up craving it." She had no idea that she would become physically sick if she didn't have it, that she was now physically dependent on opioids, her brain chemistry already acclimated to the presence of the substance. Now her body would be wracked with the anxiety, nausea, and flu-like pains of opioid withdrawal if she was unable to access heroin.

In the beginning, it was hard for Jean to hit her own veins. She had to pay people to shoot her up by giving them some of her dope. But as generous as heroin addicts can be, sharing dope gets old. It always creates tension: "Who used too much?" "You didn't leave me any." The dope becomes all-consuming. Jean soon learned to find her own veins.

Money in the Combat Zone came fast and easy. The drugs were plentiful. Jean was able to wield her childlike, light-skinned African American features to chat up older men who would take care of her, set her up in apartments in Dorchester and Roxbury that they kept on the side, hidden from their wives. She was able to do it all: buy nice high heels, shop, shoot dope, go to a different club every night. These men paid for her car and her rent and gave her a little spending money on the side. But they were respectable, middle-class black businessmen in Roxbury with families, and they didn't like the idea of dope. Dope was dirty. They liked a little bit of danger but not that kind of danger.

They especially did not like needles. One of her sugar daddies found out about her secret habit at breakfast one day in a local diner. She went into the bathroom to shoot a speedball (cocaine and heroin mixed together in one injection)—because it was a "bad day" if she had to shoot just plain dope in the morning. When she came back to the table, her eyelids began to droop. She nodded out into her stack of chocolate chip pancakes. Two hours later she found herself homeless, again.

Sometimes Jean just thought she had bad luck because she stayed in bad neighborhoods, rife with street violence, drugs, and police officers eager to arrest drug users. One day, she decided to try to get away from her own bad habits and escape her local dealers. She picked out on a map a place she had never been to: Arizona. It seemed like a nice, warm place to someone coping with New England's long winters and heavy blizzards. Dopesick on the plane, and not knowing a single person in Arizona, she climbed into a cab and asked the taxi driver to take her to the worst neighborhood he could think of. She shot dope that very same day.

Jean's drug of choice, so to speak, was "more." The only time in the next thirty years she would stop using heroin was when she was in jail: "That was my detox. I'd go to jail. Whatever sentence I had—three months, six months, a year—I'd stay clean for that amount of time. When I'd get out, I'd go back to the same people, same everything and it would start all over again."

Jean thinks maybe she wouldn't have used heroin for as long as she had if she had had a family that actually cared where she was, that wondered if she was okay at night. Her mom never called to check in on her, and her stepfather didn't even care that she had run away. She thinks she was "addicted to the hustle" and wonders wistfully what her life would have been like if she had "seen a different way of life, since all I had ever seen was chaos and craziness." For Jean, just like Serenity, jail was "the only period of normalcy that I had, routine, wake up, you feel good, and you don't have to run and get some dope." Going to jail was simply a fact of life, since "you're going to get knocked eventually, it's just part of the game." For her last sentence she was actually sent to prison—MCI-Framingham, the sole women's prison in the state—and it was her longest period of confinement (figure 3). Prison, unlike jail, is where women are sent to serve sentences of generally greater than one year.

This time, the crime involved was more serious than using illegal substances. That particular day, Jean and her boyfriend were smoking crack in their tiny kitchen. Child Protective Services had just taken away their daughter, Kiara, because of their destructive drug use. Jean was on a tear. She had been accessing daily treatment with the methadone clinic to keep her off heroin, but she was continuing to smoke crack and drink alcohol in order to deal with the devastating loss of her daughter. Kiara

FIGURE 3. MCI-Framingham, the state women's prison, Framingham, MA (photo by Emily A. Harrison).

had been the only good thing about her life, and now she was gone. And then her boyfriend accused her of stealing the remainder of the leftover drugs. With the crack coursing through them, they both felt emboldened, aggressive, and violent.

Jean's boyfriend punched her in the face, knocking out her two front teeth, and then he put his hands around her throat. Backed up against the sink, Jean reached for whatever she could find, and stabbed him several times in the chest with a kitchen knife. She went to prison for three years for assault. The upside was that it was the longest time she had ever had, she said, to "clean myself out."

. . .

The prisons and jails in the United States are tasked with the problem of addressing, correcting, and treating substance use disorders in the wake of decades of legislation since the early 1900s that increasingly criminalized the consuming, selling, or buying of certain drugs such as cocaine, opium, and marijuana. Yet even the history of scheduling specific substances into the Controlled Substances Act and other such legislation, determining which drugs were most harmful versus possibly beneficial, was fraught, arbitrary, and often politically motivated by media portrayals of racialized fears of Mexican, Chinese, or black men tempting and tainting white women with substances like marijuana, opium or cocaine.[4]

Then it was not clear or consistent how these laws were enforced. According to the 2017 National Survey on Drug Use and Health, approximately 30.5 million Americans reported some form of illicit drug use in the previous month (or 1 in 9 Americans).[5] Clearly not everyone goes to jail for this use. As I continued in my research, I increasingly realized how fine the line was between behavior deemed normal versus pathological in our existential responses to suffering and quests for well-being. I wondered how, exactly, and in what specific ways, the consumption of certain drugs had been made into a criminal act. When my medical school classmates at Harvard traded or popped each other's benzodiazepines or stimulants in order to self-medicate against the mental anguish and physical limitations encountered on the arduous and stressful path to becoming a doctor, they certainly were not sent to drug treatment facilities or prison. They were applauded for staying up all night studying or working in the hospital. Or if they did psychedelics, like mushrooms or LSD, they were applauded for the creative writing or insights they produced in that context. As recreational or functional drug users of certain means, they were often protected from police. Even if they developed dysfunctional or problematic substance use, the societal treatment of so-called "impaired" physicians or nurses contrasts sharply with the entrenched system of incarceration for poor women.

Furthermore, examining the drug use of physicians provides evidence refuting the notion that people with substance use problems or drug dependency cannot make valuable contributions to society. Medical historian and physician Howard Markel chronicled the lives of two famous cocaine users in his book.[6] He explored the complicated lives of Dr. Sigmund Freud, one of the fathers of modern psychotherapy, and Dr. William Halsted, a famous surgeon at Johns Hopkins who is considered one of the founders of the modern surgical field. Halsted, who was treated for his cocaine addiction with daily morphine injections at Butler Hospital in Providence, Rhode Island, subsequently became physically dependent on morphine (a close chemical analog of heroin) for the next four decades of his life. And yet despite his substance use, at times very problematic, he still managed to make significant contributions to the medical field. So how are some lives deemed worth saving, handled with expensive and long-term interventions and treatments, while others, lacking a means to pay and a social network of support, face prison or jail?

Prison is a difficult and contradictory place to get better. People often lose private and public health insurance upon incarceration, and by law, prisons and jails must provide health care to people incarcerated within their walls. In fact, the incarcerated are the only population in the country specified in the US Constitution to have a right to adequate health care, as the Supreme Court ruled in *Estelle v Gamble* (1976); deliberate failure to provide adequate medical treatment was ruled as cruel and unusual punishment, a violation of the Eighth Amendment. Carolyn Sufrin, an anthropologist and an obstetrician-gynecologist, examined some of the tensions of providing care in these spaces in her recent compelling ethnography of the San Francisco County Jail.[7] For the women that Sufrin cared for, jail is a multifaceted, complex space, at times providing relief and respite, at other times trauma and isolation.

For Jean and Serenity, accessing health care and drug treatment in jail and prison were similarly fraught endeavors. For Jean, the experience of incarceration could be contradictory and sometimes conflicting. While she encountered occasional kind souls, brief moments of humanity from guards or other prison staff, striving for care and well-being within a place of punishment was an impossible contradiction. Yet it was, after all, the only place she was ever able to be abstinent from drugs. She was able to take her medications regularly and always would gain weight from regular access to meals. But she refused to talk to a counselor or go to a group regarding her drug therapy, asserting that it was her own business and not the business of some freshly graduated white social worker who would lecture her about her poor life choices.

The enormous size of the jail and prison populations and the complex effects flowing from the increasing reliance on prisons as a social solution within American communities has led sociologists, criminologists, social scientists, historians, and increasingly anthropologists to assess the sweeping impact of these institutions. Lorna Rhodes's seminal work on maximum security prisons, documenting the tasks and tensions of custody and treatment, questioned the underlying rationality of such a system.[8] James Waldman also interrogated these tensions in his study of a Canadian prison working to habilitate sexual offenders. Who were prisons for? Waldman argued in *Hound Pound Narratives* that the process of treatment, or therapy, is achieved by "glossing over the complexities of human sociality to make being moral seem as unambiguous as possible. Therapy is offered to inmates, not so much to make their lives better, as to make our lives better."[9]

For women like Jean and Serenity, what happens after they are marked as dangerous, bad, and criminal, has largely gone unwitnessed. This book builds on the expanding body of critical prison ethnographies in the tradition of the anthropologists noted above in order to understand how such women move across carceral spaces and time during what is now called America's opioid crisis, as they represent the feminization of the American "War on Drugs." Their stories are just a few out of many thousands. In this country, rates of incarceration of women have increased 834 percent since 1978. As the nonprofit research group Prison Policy Initiative notes, this growth is fueled by mostly state prisons as well as county jails, and efforts at decreasing or decarceration have benefited men disproportionately (the total number of men in state prisons from 2009 to 2015 fell by 5 percent while the number of women in state prisons over the same period fell by only 0.29 percent).[10]

Jean and Serenity's heroin use exposed them to a criminal justice system that did little to treat their underlying disease processes or cure them of the purported immorality that led to criminal behavior. They are part of a social story in which some substances and the people who use them became symbols of danger, contamination, and evil, posing threats to ideals of safety, virtue, upright living, and public morality. What does the current dominant policy response of criminalization actually look like for the women most directly affected?

The law intercedes in the lives of most people in the United States, but among poor women who use drugs it especially rears its head in a myriad of violent, jarring ways, adding to the many forms of violence they have experienced throughout their lives. While people of all classes engage in the purchase and consumption of a staggering array of pills, potions, and charms in search of health, happiness, and well-being, only the consumption of the poor is heavily policed, regulated, and viewed as pathologically excessive and out of control.

Heroin in particular is often still linked with crime in the American public imaginary as part of decades of concerted efforts by the Drug Enforcement Administration and partnerships with parent groups to link the two notions. In a forum on the implementation of medical marijuana in Massachusetts, a group of concerned mothers from the South Shore suburbs of Boston spoke of the dangers they felt existed regarding the increasing availability of marijuana. One woman stated that she was against a proposed medical marijuana law because she felt that, "with heroin there is a rise in drug-related crimes, fatal and non-fatal overdoses . . . and there is definitely a risk of home break-ins and that type of problems."

Drug use has been a consistently vilified and targeted proxy for the problems arising from poverty, racial discrimination, and perhaps most especially in certain populations and neighborhoods—largely African American and Latino American—what sociologist William Julius Wilson calls "concentrated disadvantage."[11] Instead of looking at complex historical race relations, at the systematic oppression of marginalized groups in terms of schooling, housing, and employment, at racist policing practices and subsequent social policies of systemic discrimination and exclusion, as Wilson and sociologists of poverty urge us to do, we instead think narrowly and myopically about specific issues such as the problem of heroin or fentanyl. Across various political cycles, politicians continually fall back on demanding "law and order" and "cleaning up" the streets—arresting drug users and dealers, locking them up and throwing away the key.

This mind-set has had a distinctly racial bent over the past several decades, targeting low-income communities of color.[12] Over decades in this country, the American War on Drugs has morphed several times (fears of heroin, crack cocaine, methamphetamines, marijuana, tobacco, and alcohol), yet people still continue to consume drugs—in largely the same proportion as they always have done—and communities of color have disproportionately been ravaged by the effects of the prosecutorial and policing apparatus that continues to police these substances and those who use them.[13] Anthropologist William Garriott has called the apparatus and mentality of drug war rhetoric in local, state, and federal governance in America "narcopolitics."[14] This deep entrenchment makes both analysis and subsequent action to change difficult.

The contemporary American opioid crisis is not our first, and not our first drug scare with concurrent misinformation, misguided law enforcement, and scare tactic efforts by the government. Waves of crises have occurred since the prohibition of alcohol, including heroin, crack cocaine, methamphetamines, and others, and such crises will continue to occur unless we see dramatic cultural paradigm shifts. This current crisis, though, is in many ways deadlier than ever before, because of the adulteration and contamination of street heroin with illicitly manufactured fentanyl.

. . .

As I sat in a downtown courtroom waiting for Serenity's case to come up at the Boston Municipal Court, I wondered what the process of criminalization of opioid use actually looked like. I mused about how "law and order" politics played out in the lives of the women I had met. At this point, I had known Serenity for over two years, following her in and out of jail and in out of treatment at the local state-funded buprenorphine-naloxone clinic at the Shattuck Hospital in Boston. This time, she told me, the charges against her were trumped-up ones from over a year ago, including drug possession and a "hand-to-hand" in a school zone. It turns out her case was part of what became known as the Hinton drug lab scandal, which revealed the vast state prosecutorial and political apparatus bearing down on women like her.

After waiting two hours, Serenity's case was finally called. Her young, harried female public defender shuffled through a set of papers, files of people like Serenity who were too poor to hire a private lawyer. Serenity had been brought up in her street clothes—tall leather boots and a jean jacket—not her jail jumpsuit, and she looked out into the galley, smiling at Steve, her on-and-off man—twenty years older, with whom she occasionally smoked crack. He had come to support her. Her attorney looked at the prosecutor and they awkwardly addressed each other using antiquated terms still used in Massachusetts calling each other "my brother" and "my sister." Serenity had told me before she didn't respect her lawyer (a "public pretender") but didn't know how to get another one.

The judge seethed with visible anger at the prosecutor representing the Commonwealth: "This case is a year and a half old," she said, referring to the February 2012 charge of selling in a school zone. "Have you received the discovery?"

The prosecutor pleaded for more time to get the physical evidence, or the discovery, saying, "We understand the final discovery was requested, but we understand this was a Hinton lab case."

The judge interrupted her angrily, "That doesn't matter. It's a year and a half later. Where's the discovery?"

The state district attorney asked for more time again, saying, "Your Honor, we're asking for another day to provide the discovery."

"You're not getting it," the judge said. "After a year and a half, they still don't have any bench drugs. You still don't have discovery?"

The judge then asked about the distance from the school; the DA pleaded that they thought they had measurements attesting to the school zone distance. The judge wanted to know about the drugs again: "February 2012? But you don't have the lab results? Why? Somebody's not doing their job here."

The Hinton drug lab in Jamaica Plain had been run by the Massachusetts Department of Public Health and ran the majority of police samples for identification and evidence. The scandal at the lab centered on the activities of a thirty-six-year-old chemist named Annie Dookhan and several of her colleagues, who had been caught violating numerous protocols during the summer of 2012. A more detailed investigation into her behavior revealed that Dookhan had been, among other things, mixing drug samples and even "dry labbing," that is, looking at a substance (a white powder, for example) and certifying it as illicit without doing the necessary chemical testing.[15] She also had processed several thousand more samples than her peers at the lab over the same period of time, possibly affecting twenty-four thousand criminal cases handled in some way by her between 2003 and 2012. In some instances, no name was attached to a test and some vials had labels such as "Fat Black Man CB#1." The lab itself was in disarray, with drug samples found in garbage cans, drawers, and even in manila folders marked "Quality Checks." Because of her "evidence," hundreds of people lost their jobs, lost custody of their children, were deported or sent to prison; they had convictions and served prison sentences for drug cases that were not reversed or altered.

The commissioner of the Massachusetts Department of Health at the time, John Auerbach, resigned over the scandal. The lab was shuttered. And perhaps most importantly, the case exposed the tragic vagaries of a deeply flawed criminal justice system and a failing War on Drugs in which thousands of people went to prison for possession or trafficking under mandatory sentences often based solely on what kind of substance they were said to have had and how much of it. The scandal exposed a nefarious system rigged against drug users hiding under a thin veneer of science, impartiality, and propriety.

While state officials tried to paint Annie Dookhan as an isolated outlier in a sea of otherwise upstanding and precise agents of the criminal justice system, it became clear she was connected with the state network of prosecutors in unsavory ways. In emails obtained by her prosecutors, she had discussed trial strategy with assistant district attorneys. In one exchange, Norfolk County Assistant District Attorney George Papachristos, who later resigned, told her he needed a marijuana sample of over fifty pounds to get a conviction of drug trafficking ("any help would be greatly appreciated!", he wrote). She wrote back two hours later, "Definitely trafficking, over 80 lbs."[16]

Over 21,000 cases were dropped in April 2017 after the Dookhan case. Several years later, another Massachusetts chemist at a separate facility admitted to using drug samples in order to get high at work, as well as tampering with evidence related to thousands more cases. The release of so many "convicted criminals" after the Dookhan scandal brought renewed fears of increased public safety risks. Drugs were tied so closely to crime in public rhetoric that it upset many people who were worried that "people convicted of drug crimes" (and often predominantly people of color)—albeit on faulty evidence—would be released back into their communities.

Yet the Dookhan case simply made clear what many people had already suspected: the War on Drugs in Massachusetts was a corrupt and deeply flawed apparatus of social control. The deck was stacked against poor people and people belonging to racial minority groups who had very little legal and social recourse (over 60 percent of the Dookhan cases were for simple drug possession). Many had been coerced into pleading guilty or taking time served, thus becoming marred possibly for life with felonies, which in many states limits people's ability to live in public housing, obtain benefits, get a job, obtain a driver's license, food assistance or even vote.[17]

The Dookhan case had briefly interrupted the usually shrouded "business as usual" by highlighting the structural forces fueling the phenomenon of mass incarceration. Serenity was freed a week after that court case was dismissed. While she had thought long and hard during her time in jail about how she was going to change her life and look for a job, when she walked out of court, getting heroin was the only thing on her mind.

. . .

It was August when I heard from her again. The clinic at the Shattuck Hospital had received a phone call from a social worker at one of the major Boston hospitals stating that Serenity was in the hospital with a cellulitis of her face. Her right eye had swollen shut with inflammation and Steve, her best friend, told me he thought it looked like she had gotten beat up.

Serenity stayed at the hospital for only one night. She left "against medical advice" (AMA) because she was transferred to a room where she could have no visitors. She had insisted that Steve be able to come in and be with her. Steve tried to talk her down, saying they could talk on the phone instead. She was enraged by the staff treating her "like a prisoner in the hospital," and she insisted, "I was a person before I was a patient." She demanded to leave, and the hospital sent her out with a prescription for oral antibiotics (a compromise that if she couldn't stay for a full course of intravenous antibiotics, at least she would have something working on the infection). Steve dutifully doled them out to her.

For Serenity, part of the problem with being hospitalized or interacting with social services was the stigma she faced as someone who used drugs intravenously. As she told me, it sometimes only fueled her use: "The defense mechanism for that is to be that. Okay, that's how you want to label me, that's what I'm going to be. I'm going to be the best goddamn junkie I can be. . . . It's easier to put up that front than it is to deal with those looks and things that people say about you."

Another two months passed before I heard from her again. I received a phone call from a different local hospital that Serenity was an inpatient again, requiring IV antibiotics for a different infection. She had ended up with another cellulitis after a jugular vein shot had gone awry when she had asked someone to shoot a speedball (an injection of cocaine and heroin) into her neck. She usually did it herself with a mirror, but she told me that she had a cold and couldn't hold her breath long enough to do it because she felt as if she were about to pass out. She told me that she thought the coke had numbed the area and the guy just pushed it up anyway, eager to get his share after helping her out. The syringe was dull because it had been used far too many times. It was like pushing a blunt sewing needle up into her neck.

Serenity had thought she should go to the hospital two weeks earlier, but she kept rationalizing why she couldn't. *I can't go to the hospital dopesick. Oh, I can't go to the hospital because it's the weekend, and they don't have an emergency room. Oh, it doesn't look so bad today.* All her friends from the street—seasoned at dealing with skin infections and other complications of drug use—had been urging her to go to the hospital. Finally, the pain was simply unbearable.

Serenity told me that she feels old now. "I don't bounce back after my runs," she concedes. "God does for me what I can't do for myself. He got me sick, he let me be stupid so I'd get sick." Her life on the streets was full of chronic despair: "I just don't have it in me anymore, I am so tired. I see people walking around, they're clean, they smell clean, they have a smile on their faces, they have a destination to go to, they have a life. I don't have to sleep in Port-a-Potties under the bridge, and I don't want to anymore." She yearned for a place to go, for a life that she once thought she could have but that had become an increasingly faded memory.

I asked her if she thought that her life would have been different if she had not been released from court right back to the streets. She told me that she felt like the jail had given up on her. She is critical of a system that exists to feed off her failures and relapses: "Because you're job security for them. That's money in their pocket. They really don't give two shits, especially for someone like me that's a frequent flyer. They just give up. Oh well. She's coming back; she's not going to go [to a program]. . . . I'm a lost cause. . . . I see it differently. I don't care if you fail a million times, maybe on the million and one times you're going to get it." She thought they throw up their hands because "the prison industries keep making more and more money off of people like me, because that's what we do."

Even as she recognized the profit motive involved in her chronic and cyclical incarcerations, she also internalized the sense of ultimately being the one responsible for her own sobriety and ongoing substance use despite the hardships in her life. This is consistent with predominant American values about one's body, with an emphasis on personal responsibility for one's health. The economics and philosophy of neoliberalism—with its worldwide effects on healthcare marked by privatization of state services, increasing user fees, and decreasing government health expenditures—has in many ways contributed to her subjective guilt and feelings of failure, while commercial treatment providers, community organizations, and recovery-based enterprises continue to profit off her ongoing failures to stop her destructive substance use.[18]

Serenity's conflicted perspectives reveal the various paradigms of the relationship between drug use and user subjectivity. Orientations toward drug use and addiction more generally have changed greatly over the past several years. As the definition of *addiction* has evolved, so has it changed the experience of being a person who uses drugs. These various paradigms—including but not limited to the medical, carceral, self-help, and spiritual—have significant consequences for Serenity and others: is she a bad person with a faulty moral compass, a sinner, a criminal, or is she a patient with an a neurobiological disease?

According to the American Society of Addiction Medicine, the term *addiction* can be defined as "a primary, chronic, neurobiological disease, with genetic, psychosocial, and environmental factors influencing its development and manifestations. Addiction is characterized by behaviors that include impaired control over drug use, compulsive use, continued use despite harm, and craving."[19]

This notion that addiction is a chronic disease that permanently damages the user by depleting dopamine receptors within the reward system in the brain is relatively recent and still contentious.[20] Yet is it actually a disease, a disorder, or a condition? Can it be "cured," overcome, or simply managed? Some, like journalist Maia Szalawitz, propose we view addiction as a developmental disorder or a condition of impaired self-regulation, much like attention-deficit or autism spectrum conditions, that occur when certain genetic and personality components meet with environmental and developmental conditions like poverty, adverse childhood events, or trauma.[21]

Yet, prior to these frameworks, and still a dominant perspective, is the idea of addiction as essentially a "bad habit." As historian David Courtwright writes in his informative history of opioid addiction in America, "Prior to 1870 the prevailing view of opiate addiction was as a vice, a bad habit indulged in by weak-willed and sinful but otherwise normal persons."[22] Only later on did opioid addiction become associated with "vice" crimes, such as prostitution and gambling. Meanwhile, the American Medical Association rejected the notion that addiction was a disease at least two times in the 1910s and 1920s, dismissing it as nothing more than a bad habit.[23] It was neither the purview nor the responsibility of doctors to "treat" drug use, physical dependence, or addiction.

Such perceptions of the addicted person as morally deviant or as inherently criminal continue to persist today. In many ways, the notion of addiction as a disease—or perhaps, even less pejoratively, as a chronic disease—was perhaps originally intentioned to counter some of this moral judgment. Such a depiction was meant to release a person from the moral culpability of drug use, but the very same notion also had the perhaps unintended consequence of robbing people who use drugs of autonomy and a sense of free will. Addicts were now seen as helpless in the face of the onslaught on their neuro-biochemical pathways.

Angela Garcia's 2010 book *The Pastoral Clinic* reckons with the now seemingly unending subjectivity of heroin addiction when reclassified as a medical or neurobiological disease process among communities in New Mexico.[24] It is disturbing to the people she works with there, who also feel that there are numerous power structures—prisons, jails, and treatment centers included—that profit off their ongoing relapses within the paradigm shift toward addiction as a disease process. In contrast to the biomedical teachings that suggest that addiction can now be seen as a kind of chronic disease, the Hispano locals in the Espanola Valley view heroin addiction as an escape from lives of melancholy and a history of land dispossession. For them, the seizure by the state of the common lands that had been used for farming and husbandry has resulted in the enforced and abject poverty of the younger generations of these families. The everyday landscape is a constant reminder of the loss of their lands, cultural identity, and economic livelihoods. Contrary to being a vice or an inherent personal weakness, heroin use was *medicina*: it allowed a despairing people to feel better, to imagine the possibility of an alternative future.

The implications of these paradigms on one's sense of self and ongoing navigations in the world are critical and complex. Which structures of power and institutions prevail when, and which approaches might have less or more harm?

Like many others, Serenity simultaneously identifies these institutions as problems but also blames herself. On the one hand, she wishes that hospitals and the jails and the judges would try a little harder: "If you look at somebody's record and you see they're there for prostitution and they have two misdemeanors: I'm chronically homeless, that's why I get trespassing. Prostitution, why don't we send her back there [to jail] until you find a program and your probation starts as of today, but you need to stay in South Bay detained until you can go to a program and you're stipulated to do a program. I think sometimes the system and the jails fail people. And sometimes you're going to hit the road anyways but why not give it a shot?"

. . .

Angela Garcia, Philippe Bourgois and Jeff Schonberg, Merrill Singer, E. Summerson Carr, Robert Fairbanks, and many other ethnographers of drug use have argued for new understandings of care within the structural violence that frames the lives of people who use drugs.[25] This book adds to this body of literature, taking its cue within a tradition of "critical medical anthropology," highlighting the myriad sources of structural violence that complicate the agency, decisions, and lived experience of women who use heroin in Massachusetts as they encounter the criminal justice system.

Furthermore, as a physician and an educator, I am fueled by the sense that we must teach a framework for others to be able to engage with these often invisible yet extremely powerful institutions and approaches. Many anthropologists and physician-anthropologists, headed by Helena Hansen and Jonathan Metzl, have been engaged in teaching the paradigms of structural competency and structural vulnerability—that is, teaching medical students and other health care workers about these social and structural, institutional, and political-economic determinants of health, including racism, and how to theorize them and how to think critically about addressing them in order to counter their deleterious effects on patient and community health.[26] I see this book as a means of getting students of many disciplines at many levels of training to engage critically with these powerful systems and structures.

Getting Wrecked contains two major arguments. First, conventional and current social responses to drug use with incarceration are ineffective and largely inhumane, violating commonly accepted biomedical standards of care toward the treatment of substance use disorders as well as more fundamental notions of how we should care for and value the other. At the time of my fieldwork, drug treatment was increasingly becoming appropriated by carceral institutions, and the presence of a variety of so-called treatment modalities now buttresses and legitimizes these institutions in what I call the "carceral-therapeutic state" at the expense of community-based alternatives for the care of people who use drugs. With this phrase, I am specifically referring to contemporary prisons and jails, ubiquitous across the American landscape, that have become dominated by therapeutic ideologies, language, and processes. Yet the carceral-therapeutic state is also much broader than that, having reached and instantiated itself in the structures of the community: including but not limited to drug courts, probation and parole, and recovery houses. While an estimated 2.3 million people are currently incarcerated in the United States on any one day, over 4.5 million people remain under the confines of community supervision programs such as probation and parole.[27] These are spaces that are similarly permeated by carceral-therapeutic dictates, ideologies, and processes. In the pages that follow, I document the complex and often damaging effects such a merging of criminal justice and therapeutic approaches has on people who often live in the shadows outside of mainstream discourse. Such discourses are dangerous in that they perpetuate these racist and oppressive institutions, ultimately harming our patients, their families, and communities. This is further complicated by the relatively and until recently very profound lack of access to medication-assisted therapy (commonly known as MAT, also known as medication for addiction treatment) that include the life-saving, evidence-based treatment such as buprenorphine or methadone (also known together as opioid agonist therapy, or OAT).

Second, we can also learn something important about American selfhood, narratives of redemption, and what it means to be worthy of health and, more broadly, belonging, by examining the prison, the punishment of drug users, and carceral systems' attempts at rehabilitation.

Why and how are women who use heroin still able to dream of better lives for themselves and their families despite the myriad of structural forms of social exclusion manifesting in stigma, oppression, and direct or indirect threats to their dignity and bodies? Put more simply, looking at the experience of drug users reveals many of the fault lines along which our society determines whose experiences and lives matter. These embodied tensions about self-determination and hope are magnified in examining the peculiarly American enmeshment of punishment and treatment. People who are dependent on heroin refer to the process of scoring or using heroin as "getting well"—preventing or staving off, even treating the symptoms of dopesickness. So, is there another way that we can reconfigure institutions and structures of care to actually foster the conditions to cultivate health and wellness? How can we envision achieving true societal wellness from the problems presented by opioid use disorder without carceral systems?

Throughout this book, I look directly at many paradigms of treatment and approaches taken to rehabilitating or curing damaged women with histories of heroin addiction. I also approach the problem of addiction and incarceration from several angles and alternate between a clinical gaze and an ethnographic one. This reflects the multiple sites in my fieldwork as well as my multiple roles and sources of training. In chapter 2, I examine the historical origins of the incarceration of women and notions of the rehabilitation of women on drugs, and how the prison became a central node in addressing the social problem of drug use and addiction. Looking closely at MCI-Framingham, I show how the prison historically responded to the problem of female drug use and illustrate in what ways modern-day treatment approaches remain constrained and often ineffective based on paradigms that are not entirely new. In chapter 3, I look at the everyday work of carceral-based drug treatment programs. I examine how prison-based drug treatment programs attempt to align yet conflict with the prison's primary orientation toward security and punishment. What is the aftermath of these programs? How do such programs ideologically function and then function in practice?

In chapter 4, I examine the space of trauma treatment in the prisons and jails as the women's prisons turn to notions of "gender-responsiveness" and seek to become "trauma-informed" institutions. Trauma is an emerging paradigm for conceptualizing and treating problematic drug use and I look at how these institutions adopt this language and orientation to instantiate their significance in the social response to the seemingly endemic trauma of poor women on drugs. How is the notion of trauma used in everyday practice by the carceral system and what are the implications of the popular rise of such a paradigm?

In chapter 5, I examine the ways in which pharmaceuticals and medications to treat opioid use disorder become both central to and side-stepped in narratives surrounding the American opioid crisis and incarceration. I explore how medications to treat this condition are either criminalized, becoming seen and seized as contraband, or alternatively, others have been welcomed, without much evidence of long-term benefit. How do prisons and jails respond to the increasing medicalization, and pharmaceuticalization, of opioid use disorder?

In chapter 6, I look at how the prison and the jails in Massachusetts attempt to get incarcerated women into the labor market upon release. Following the experiences of several women after release, I examine the rhetoric of making work for women upon release and align it with the stark reality of women's lives. Finally, chapter 7 explores life after jail, focusing on how incarceration participates in creating physical risks and social dislocation for women upon their release. Through the lens of "social death," I examine the fault lines along which our society condemns some to face lives of extreme suffering and risk of death and why others might be protected from such risks.

I conclude by offering new ways in which we might imagine and actualize treatments for women on heroin, based on what they have witnessed, experienced, and advocated for at various levels. We need to envision new ways to care for women long before they get to prison and much more cohesively and intensively when they get out. Perhaps not surprisingly, the answer lies not in improving or reforming prisons, but in altering conditions that long precede them. Is what "wrecks" women their own destructive behaviors and substance use, or is it the cultural and political systems that lead to incarceration and the harsh conditions of confinement themselves? Is it possible to simultaneously lift up structurally vulnerable people who are currently incarcerated into better health and wellness while trying to eliminate the structural forces that keep them contained?

But first it is necessary for me to take you to the prisons and jails, to witness what happens to women who use opioids, who become arrested and incarcerated. From there, as we leave the prison and reenter communities, we will see that the lives of women are still darkened by the prison's long shadow.

This work has many limitations, and I hope to be upfront with them. As physicians, nurses, healthcare workers, social scientists, social workers, drug treatment counselors, politicians, lawyers, students, activists, or just simply concerned citizens, we all hope to live in a humane and decent world. Why would we choose this work if we believed we were not, in some small way, making the world a kinder and more tolerable place? Yet the research this book is based on is only a small and incomplete window into the heterogeneous spaces of several carceral sites in Massachusetts. Like any ethnography, it is rooted in a place with its own time, history and political context. It accesses the lives of a small group of women as well as their treatment providers, prison administrators, and health care workers in incomplete moments in time.

I also believe, like others, that many people on the ground, including people who work for or administer these programs in prisons and jails, are people who intend to and struggle to do good work and see themselves as good people. But it is critical to recognize and struggle with our complicity in systems of violence as well as our varying levels of privilege and power that either indirectly or directly can harm others in our community.

As a physician taking care of people with chaotic drug use or substance use disorders, I am constantly apologizing to my patients for the stigmatizing language, behaviors, and attitudes of my medical colleagues in the hospital or emergency room. They come seeking help and are called "junkies" or ignored because their veins are too scarred or difficult for blood work. They get called "clean" or "dirty," moralizing terms that do not exist anywhere else in medicine. We must do better, in terms of our language and actions. I believe it is possible to belong to and participate in these institutions, which certainly can enact structural violence and harm, while recognizing that we must strive for a better practice, acknowledging our history of harm and complicity, and thus bearing the burden of being change agents within our own systems.

Like all ethnographies, this is a book written through the filtered lenses that reflect my training: my biomedical training as a physician, my orientation toward social justice and critical anthropology as a means to draw attention to and disrupt sources of oppression and inequality, my involvement in politics as an HIV/AIDS activist, and my ongoing work as the medical director of the Harm Reduction Coalition and a physician at Rikers Island to advocate for a philosophy of harm reduction for people who use drugs. This book is informed by these various positions and fueled with the hopes and dreams of many who imagine ardently that another way is possible.

2

The Beauty Shop and the Segregation Unit

The black-and-white checkered floors, the rows of hair salon booths with rips in the black seat covers patched over with electric tape, the hair straighteners, the clusters of brightly colored fingernail polish all make this place seem like just your average neighborhood salon, where the hairdressers are cheap and variable in quality. But this place is somehow decidedly unique: it is the Beauty Shop, a small space tucked away in one of the decaying buildings on the campus of MCI-Framingham, the sole women's prison in the state of Massachusetts. It is where twelve women a year take a cosmetology class, as they learn how to tease and treat all shapes and colors of hair, nails, and skin while serving out felony convictions.

The Beauty Shop in MCI-Framingham has birthed many physical and emotional transformations. The inmates taking the classes there hope to master a variety of techniques to pamper, care for, and attend to the desires of other women who want to feel pretty, to feel loved, and perhaps most importantly, to look good. Looking and feeling good is something difficult to accomplish in prison cells, where hair dye is fashioned from Kool-Aid and makeup is manufactured from crushing up colored pills or candies. The Beauty Shop allows women access to somewhat more formal skills. Both the women training to be cosmetologists and the women utilizing their services as customers strive for these brief moments of beautifying in lives often marked by structural violence and lack of self-care, where women always seemed to put themselves last after the needs of their children, their men, their families.

The Beauty Shop opened to 1959 as a place for vocational training for incarcerated women. Its main purpose was to equip women with tangible skillsets so that they could find work in the beauty industry upon release from prison. It fit nicely into optimistic notions of appropriate work for poor women, providing them with a means to support themselves and possibly avoid lives of crime. Betty Cole Smith, the Superintendent of MCI-Framingham at that time, noted in the prison's annual report that the administration had been struggling to create "an atmosphere . . . more conducive to getting on with the business of rehabilitation. As opposite as they both may seem, the establishment of both the Beauty Shop and Segregation Unit had good effect. In their own ways, they are perhaps symbolic of the new trend: unlimited resources for personal development; but with increasing limits placed on deviant behavior."[1]

The Segregation Unit, or solitary confinement, was also a new feature of the women's prison in 1959. In contrast with the Beauty Shop, the Segregation Unit was a place of harsh deprivation, punishment and anti-sociality. It was envisioned for the seemingly incorrigible women, the women too broken and downtrodden and downright bad to take advantage of the prison's other resources and treatment efforts. These were the women that spit and fought and got high off nutmeg and refused to take up sewing and other forms of proper feminine labor. There was nothing further to be done for them but let them see how bad prison could actually be. The Segregation Unit represented the abdication of treatment efforts, a recognition that some forms of deviance could not be changed. These women could not be coddled or trained out of their badness.

Taken together, the Beauty Shop and the Segregation Unit represented the extremes and contradictions of life in a women's prison and the business of rehabilitating deviant women more generally. Today the women's prison continues to be a place bound up in, even defined by, these philosophical contradictions. In large part, the prison's policies in the 1950s were dictated by and reflected evolving community mores and notions of proper femininity. Early in the history of American prisons and jails, incarcerated women were an aberration, a rare anomaly in a harsh environment conceived by men and built for men. Later on, as more women were sent to prisons and jails for crimes of morality, and increasingly related to alcohol and drug use, prison programs began to evolve specifically for these sub-groups of socially deviant women.

Women, especially women who consumed drugs like heroin, were not surprisingly treated differently than their male counterparts in American culture. This chapter seeks to understand when and under what circumstances these notions of female difference informed our understanding of addiction itself as well as its various treatment modalities, particularly in the prison. These notions of gender difference—that women who used drugs had weaker constitutions and more moral purity than men—are critical in understanding the contemporary phenomenon of the mass incarceration of poor women who use drugs.

Historically, women only comprised a small fraction of total drug users, yet what their drug use represented tended to unsettle and disturb the general public much more than the drug use of men. The problems posed by female addiction were myriad in a society where difference was dangerous: as ethicist Carol Gilligan has written, "One problem in talking about difference . . . lies in the readiness with which difference becomes deviance and deviance becomes sin in a society preoccupied with normality, in the thrall of statistics, and historically puritanical."[2] White women's drug use, accordingly, invoked xenophobic- and class-based fears, stirring up latent obsessions with women's societal and physiological roles as potential or actual child-bearers and keepers of the domestic realm. Treatment of women with substance use problems, not surprisingly, tended to work within these prevailing societal attitudes.

In many ways, the prison refracted these community concerns, forming a kaleidoscope of the social by reflecting primal and resonant values. A close analysis of the annual reports from the commissioners of correction in Massachusetts from the 1930s to the 1960s helps us to better understand what prison superintendents—themselves important representatives of contemporary thinking—thought about prison treatment and their role in enacting mandates to treat women with alcohol or drug problems. Their writings largely reflect dominant cultural narratives about crime and punishment, personal responsibility, citizenship and femininity. Using MCI-Framingham as a case study I examine how this state prison in particular attempted to intervene upon the bodies and minds of the women sent there both to endure punishments and to be healed. I place this in the context of ongoing societal debates regarding the merits of incarceration versus community treatment, and then trace more recent changes in addiction treatment at MCI-Framingham, through which women's overall well-being was reconceptualized and reenacted in the setting of increased privatization of prison services.

At its core, this is a story of an important, gendered double standard, in which the women's prison became the central player in the both *treatment* of women on drugs and the *punishment* of women for their deviance. Intriguingly, MCI-Framingham largely fumbled its way into providing drug treatment over the decades. For the better part of the twentieth century, the numbers of women with drug or alcohol problems in the prison was low. Yet with ongoing "tough on crime" legislation and the criminalization of substance use in the 1970s and 1980s, the prison began to fill up with women. Currently the United States, while having 4 percent of the world's population of women, has approximately 30 percent of the global population of incarcerated women.[3] Notions of female difference and epistemological orientations toward the drug use of women would lead to differential treatment and lengthier prison sentences—the so-called "feminization" of the contemporary War on Drugs. And even though the prison's treatment methods were never particularly effective, the prisons somehow became one of the largest sites of substance use treatment in the state.

TREATMENT OF THE "DELICATE FEMALE"

Historically, women who used opioids were seen as decidedly different from their male counterparts; H.H. Kane was quoted in 1880 saying "a delicate female, having light blue eyes and flaxen hair, possesses, according to my observations the maximum susceptibility [to opium problems]."[4] Because of their painful reproductive physiology—including but not limited to giving birth, menstruation, and menopause—women were frequently prescribed opioids such as morphine and laudanum by general practice physicians. They comprised a significant percentage of habitual users in the early twentieth century, estimated at between one-half and three-quarters of all users, and were thought to be particularly vulnerable to subsequent physical dependence or addiction, which was seen as a regrettable side effect of a necessary medical treatment.

Some physicians called for special precautions for women seeking to shake off the physical dependence, as they would undergo painful withdrawal symptoms. As James Tyson wrote in 1900, "In the case of women, whenever possible, a special nurse should be assigned to each case" given the female tendency to lie and exaggerate symptoms.[5] Alexander Lambert and Frederick Tileny, writing in 1926 on their treatment of opioid withdrawal with an experimental patented solution of proteins and vitamins known as Narcosan, concluded that women tended to be more difficult to treat, as "the women . . . are more likely to become wildly hysterical under these circumstances."[6]

Not only were the temperaments of female drug users understood to be more difficult than those of their male counterparts, the work of treatment entailed inciting them to different kinds of preoccupations and daily habits. M. Mignard, a French physician writing on the problem of *toxicomanes* (addiction) in 1924, felt that this was primarily an affliction that demanded "moral medication against despair and discouragement."[7] According to Mignard, physical labor was necessary to combat indolence that bred vice. The most salutary environment for women was the domestic sphere while the most therapeutic labor for men was in the field or garden.

Yet soon the problem of opioid use shifted from a matter of the home—between a patient and her private physician—to the prison. In the 1920s, women who used opioids became increasingly equated with a criminal status. Prior to the Harrison Act of 1914 (which was tax legislation that laid the legal groundwork for the future criminalization of specific substances and their use, sale, and possession), women were typically categorized in physician Lawrence Kolb's categorization of the five types of addicts as "Type 1," or those "normal individuals accidentally or necessarily addicted in medical practice," but over time and as heroin became more widely available on the street, they increasingly belonged to other types (including so-called "pleasure-seekers," Type 2, and "habitual criminals," Type 4).[8] In many ways, the Harrison Act of 1914, a tax legislation on illicit drugs, contributed to driving women toward consumption of street opioids such as heroin, with subsequent incarceration for possession and use of these drugs. This is because after Harrison it became increasingly difficult to obtain opioids from physicians or pharmacists and both women and men turned to the so-called "underworld" or street markets to access opioids.

However, there was a brief moment where it seemed possible that individuals with opioid addictions might be able to procure opioids legally and safely from physicians. From 1919 to 1923, approximately forty heroin maintenance clinics were operated by physicians at the initial urging of the Institutional Revenue Service and were promoted as a potential solution to drug dependence. Women comprised a significant part of the population of these "narcotic clinics": The Worth Street Clinic in New York had 7,464 registered addicts in 1920, including 1,600 women.[9] Eventually the government shut down these clinics, as drug enforcement officers were convinced that the clinics were giving opioids to people who were not genuinely physically "sick" and only were seeking a pleasurable high. This Puritanical stance against would continue to influence and resonate in contemporary debates on drug use, how opioids were obtained, and where people could seek treatment.

THE LEXINGTON "NARCO FARM" PRISON-HOSPITAL

As the medical community lost the social mandate to treat opioid dependence in the wake of failures of community treatment programs like opioid maintenance, incarceration began to rise as a dominant social response to perceptions of crime and deviance. Violators of the Harrison Act increasingly ended up in local jail systems that were ill-equipped to handle the symptoms experienced by withdrawing drug users or to provide them treatment. In response, Congress passed the Porter Act in 1928 to allow for the creation of a new kind of institution, the "narcotic farm," a hybrid treatment-research facility for addiction that might ostensibly ease the burden on other carceral facilities.[10] The act was a nod to the relatively new discipline of public health, with two new facilities run by the United States Public Health Service in Lexington, Kentucky, and Fort Worth, Texas. Yet it was complicated by its hybrid status.

The Kentucky facility, also known as the Lexington "narcotic farm," was largely an institution that contained men. The facility had both voluntary and involuntary patient-inmates, the former were people who had heard about the facility and sought subsequent detoxification and/or treatment, the latter were court-mandated to these facilities as sentences for criminal charges. Only a small percentage of the people at the Lexington facility were women. Not surprisingly, women suffered from the policies at these facilities. Administrators perceived of women largely as nuisances and generally unworthy of treatment, and they systematically excluded them from participating in existing federal addiction research efforts there. Furthermore, the program's long waiting list deterred many women from entering treatment there in the first place.

Part of the Lexington facility contained a research wing known as the Addiction Research Center, where federal public health scientists experimented with different potential treatments to better understand the physiological effects of drugs on humans. Within this facility, only men were allowed to volunteer for experimental research on addiction and addiction treatment methods. Addiction researchers thought women were unreliable self-reporters of their internal states and feelings. They were also just considered plain nuisances, flirting with and distracting the men from the serious work of their treatment. As the historian Nancy Campbell detailed in her history of the center, "By the late 1950s, administrators perceived voluntary patients as thorns in their sides, regarding women housed in the "Jenny Barn" as especially troublesome."[11]

Janet Clark, whose 1961 autobiography recalled her life of drug addiction, wrote one of the few known firsthand accounts of a woman's experience at Lexington. Clark had driven down from Ohio with her husband to "attempt the cure" there within the context of a voluntary admission. This entailed a mandatory period of hospitalization for eighteen days for her body to physically withdraw from the heroin she had been using. It was mostly a time to share tips and tricks about new ways to use drugs; as she recalled, "What can you do? You can only take so many baths a day, and you're weak. I mean, that was at least a diversion, you know and there's nothing to do—nothing—except talk about junk."[12] The singer Billie Holiday, who was in Lexington in 1940 struggling with her own heroin addiction, confirmed Clark's description of the treatment: "There was no cure. They don't cut you down slow, weaning you off the stuff gradually. They just throw you in the hospital by yourself, take you off cold turkey and watch you suffer."[13]

She wondered why people who had heroin problems were sent to prison and jail in the first place. As Holiday wrote in her autobiography about the response to her opioid use disorder: "People on drugs are sick people. So now we end up with the government chasing sick people like they were criminals, telling doctors they can't help them. . . . Imagine if the government chased sick people with diabetes, put a tax on insulin and drove it into the black market, told doctors they couldn't treat them, and then caught them . . . and then sent them to jail."[14] She had learned, to her great distress, while touring in England that doctors there could prescribe morphine as medical maintenance. The inequalities in access to medical treatment for heroin dependence, with the subsequent expansion of policing of black people and others who were forced to the street to buy heroin, maddened her.

The treatment components at Lexington after physical detoxification were also sparse. Clark insisted that she needed to see a psychotherapist, having seen one occasionally in the community. Her treatment providers laughed and refused, suggesting she might be able to get some in three or five months. Clark's expectations of psychotherapy reflected the predominance of this treatment modality for addiction in some elite circles, yet it was withheld from Lexington patients under the premise that the short-term patients did not possess adequate "level[s] of emotional maturity" to sustain intensive psychotherapy.[15]

A major part of the treatment at Lexington was what was known as "milieu therapy," which had patients engage in various kinds of labor as treatment, including farming, animal husbandry, common chores, and vocational activities as well as mandatory group and individual therapy meetings. Clark herself graduated to mopping the facilities until she signed herself out against medical advice and relapsed to heroin use with her husband within several days (Clark eventually died of a barbiturate overdose).

Women, not surprisingly, continued to cycle back to Lexington, as there were few places to go for treatment. In 1971, researchers at Lexington noted that four out of every ten admissions in the 1960s was a re-admission; these researchers worried their program was both expensive and not very effective, citing numerous "social costs" of female drug addiction, including "damaged self-image; deterioration of personal health, productivity and creativity; personal degradation from criminality and prostitution; high death rates; family disorganization with the resulting damage to the marriage partner, the children and extended family members; and aggression against individuals and their property, producing a climate of general insecurity."[16]

What they were doing at Lexington just didn't seem to work, particularly for the growing number of young African American women on heroin.[17] How could the Lexington prison-hospital treat the chronic conditions of poverty and trauma that led women into lives of sex work and drug use? The "treatment" they offered consisted of very few medications, if any at all, and little or no psychotherapy; mostly, it provided a strict, abstinence-based environment encouraging patients to take hot baths and perform physical labor to ameliorate the physical discomfort of withdrawal even though the medical community knew that gradually decreasing doses of morphine would actually treat these symptoms in a more humane manner. Furthermore, once individuals returned to their home environments, it was difficult to stop using, as a multitude of psychological, environmental and social cues to keep using heroin continued to be present in women's chaotic lives.

MCI-FRAMINGHAM: SAVING FALLEN WOMEN

While the research and practices conducted at the Lexington facility set the tone for national debates and research about drug addiction, local prison facilities also were attempting to address the problem of alcohol and drug use that led both women and men to their facilities. In Massachusetts, the sole women's prison, MCI-Framingham—originally known as the Reformatory for Women in Sherborn, Massachusetts—administrators crafted drug treatment programs within the specific late nineteenth-century reform tradition that endorsed the belief that female offenders deserved to be treated differently than men.

Prior to the advent of dedicated female reformatories (prisons), women were generally held in local jails that mostly housed men. Women in these mixed facilities, given their small number, tended to receive little to no treatment and lived in squalid, neglected parts of the facilities. They were generally seen as distractions to the work of incarcerating men or as downright trouble: in the words of one prison official in Illinois, "One female is of more trouble than twenty males."[18]

The Reformatory for Women was something innovative then, the product of the upper- and middle-class reform advocacy efforts by women who had been involved in other kinds of social crusading movements, including abolitionism and the social purity movement against prostitution, also known as "white slavery." Nationally, a convention of prison reformers decided in 1870 that they should focus on treatment rather than punishment. Reformatories like MCI-Framingham, designed in 1877, focused on the moral education of poor and working-class women at the hands of their upper-middle-class counterparts—"through sisterly care, counsel and sympathy of their own sex"—as prison official Zebulon Brockway of the Detroit House of Correction exhorted.[19] This was enacted through the dominant correctional and legal philosophy at the time: the so-called "indeterminate sentence." Brockway pioneered this in Michigan with women convicted of prostitution; he convinced the Michigan legislature to hold women convicted of prostitution in prison indefinitely up to three years.

Such a move legislated a gendered double standard and furthermore allowed states to regulate and interact with a wider range of poor women, including those who were not necessarily hardened criminals, women who appeared as if they could be saved from their immoralities. For example, in Massachusetts in the 1880s, a woman convicted of drunkenness could be held for one to two years, while a man convicted of drunkenness was held one year; the reasoning was that women's moral lapses were graver and therefore worthier of longer treatment programs than their male counterparts.

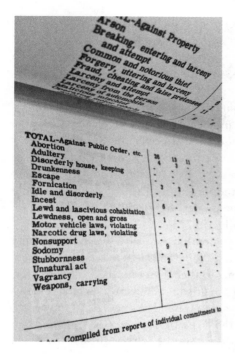

FIGURE 4. List of common offenses leading to incarceration of women (HS9/Series1318/Annual Reports Massachusetts Department of Correction [1951], courtesy of the Massachusetts Archive).

This approach likewise extended to parole. Parole, or conditional release to the community with the threat of revocation and subsequent reincarceration, was an integral part of indeterminate sentencing. In 1950, women who were on parole had their parole revoked for reasons such as failing to report to parole officers but also "leaving home, work, or state without permission, drunkenness, indiscreet conduct, failure to adjust."[20] Ongoing prison surveillance and power therefore extended markedly into the free lives of women who had been marked as criminals, enmeshing them in the surveillance of the carceral state.

Women in Massachusetts were historically incarcerated for three overarching categories of offenses. Between the 1930s and 1950s, these included offenses against persons (such as assault, manslaughter, murder, or robbery); offenses against property (e.g., arson, breaking and entering, forgery, larceny); and offenses "against public order" (figure 4). This third and last category comprised the majority of total offenses (90 percent of offenses during the 1930s and 1940s); in 1951 as the photo from the archives demonstrates, this included crimes such as "abortion," "adultery," "being a lewd, wanton and lascivious person in speech and behavior," "drunkenness," "escape," "fornication," "idle and disorderly," "lewd and lascivious cohabitation," "violating narcotic drug laws," "nonsupport," "stubbornness," and "unnatural acts." The chief offenders were poor and working-class women who could not easily conform to upper-middle-class ideals of domestic purity and femininity.

There was a strong sense that women who grew up in relatively deprived social conditions were in need of being "saved" by Christian women. Miriam Van Waters, who presided over the Reformatory for Women for three decades as the superintendent, had "great faith in the salvation of individuals . . . even a girl 'who has given herself to many lovers, has suffered disease, abandonment and rough handling' could become a 'healthy, charming woman, devoted to children and husband, if she could lose her delinquent identity.'"[21]

Philosophies of reforming incarcerated women stressed femininity and imparting beauty, grace, and hope to so-called fallen women. Women were meant to be reformed rather than punished. The smattering of "cottage"-style housing of the prison architecture (which remains to this day) was built to house women, intended to correct "the dearth of beauty and graciousness in the lives of so many of our youthful offenders,"[22] as Superintendent Smith wrote, although many women still perceived of these cottages as prison and could not "control their impulse to escape."[23] Michel Foucault professed in his now iconic work on prisons that architecture was one means of daily control and surveillance, it was "an architecture that would operate to transform individuals: to act on those it shelters, to provide a hold on their conduct, to carry the effects of power right to them, to make it possible to know them, to alter them."[24] The cottages were thus intended as surrogate houses, safe places for women to learn to interact and change their behavior toward societal expectations of good housewives, mothers, and women generally.

Within the Framingham cottage facility, there were separate cottages for women who had voluntary commitments as well as those committed to prison by the court for drug addiction as well as alcoholism. Much like the federal treatment facility in Lexington, Framingham had a system that allowed for the treatment of both voluntary commitments and mandated (women sent to prison from the court system). Thus, even the voluntary community-based treatment had the prison at its core. Yet the number of women involuntarily committed to the "Drug Addict Department" at Framingham remained relatively small, often in the single digits, from the 1930s through the 1960s.

The majority of the women's treatment during these decades occurred within these small, unlocked cottages situated around a common grassy yard. In the cottages they took classes on the "homemaking arts" and learned how to sew and cook. The cottage architecture was designed to create a healthful "milieu" (mirroring the processes going on at Lexington) for the young women based on the goals of seeing "each girl as an individual and whole person, for whom the open cottage situation might serve as an emotionally maturing, vocationally useful, and socially enriching experience in terms of the coming, broader challenge of the outside community," as Superintendent Betty Smith wrote.[25]

Physical labor was thought to be essential to the moral rehabilitation of the female prisoner, and within the ideology of the Protestant ethic, work had always been raised up as a means to salvation. Most of the state prison facilities were attached to farms and industries such as power plants, flag-making, and other endeavors that made a profit for the facility. Prisoners provided much of the labor that ran the actual day-to-day operations of the institutions. Women in the reformatory often worked as servants, training for lives in domestic service for well-to-do women. In this scheme, they were either equipped, perhaps unrealistically, for middle-class lives as housewives or as servants or maids, befitting their actual low- and working-class status.

MCI-Framingham's Superintendent Smith felt that this program helped the women, arguing that "day work is a vital rehabilitation step before returning to the community. It is an excellent therapy for our girls to observe how well homes function in the community."[26] This program appealed to prison administrators because it blended their treatment ideologies of providing both spiritual uplift and beauty with seemingly practical skills.

Yet despite all their efforts and optimism in prison-based treatment and rehabilitation of women with addictions, there was still doubt among the leadership as to whether the prison was the appropriate place for treatment for this population. As Superintendent Van Waters told a reporter in 1935, "More than half the people here should not have been sent here. There are chronic alcoholics. To send them to prison is absurd. Likewise prostitutes."[27] Some prison officials felt that a legal remedy was inappropriate: in a letter to the Massachusetts State Legislature, Commissioner of Corrections Elliott McDowell wrote that he believed that "the rehabilitation of this type of offender . . . primarily needs medical care."[28] This tension over the appropriateness of incarceration as a social policy to deal with crimes of morality or largely psychosocial and medical concerns—a concern expressed by administrators over fifty years ago—persists to this day.

PSYCHOTHERAPY, PROFESSIONALIZATION, AND THE CUSTODIAL CARE OF THE PRISON

In the 1950s, prison facilities for both women and men struggled with creating programs that could successfully rehabilitate women with drug or alcohol problems and prevent the revolving door of these individuals in and out of prison. This reflected more general epistemological uncertainty about etiologies of drug addiction as well as controversies about optimal treatment methods. In 1955, there was a concerted attempt to develop what prison officials called a "treatment oriented program within the department of correction."[29]

With psychotropic medications in its infancy, putting a patient-inmate on a medication for life was simply not a paradigm for treatment as it is today. Instead, the mainstay of the prison treatment program was largely oriented around psychotherapy and social work efforts. Following the success of a treatment service at two men's facilities, a program called the Division of Legal Medicine was expanded to MCI-Framingham in 1955. The Division of Legal Medicine was established to provide psychiatric services, social work, and self-help groups, including Alcoholics Anonymous which had been offering meetings in the prison since the 1930s.

Norman Neiberg, a clinical psychologist who founded the Department of Legal Medicine at Framingham in the 1950s and remained there for several decades, felt they were in the business of saving women from their own bad habits related to substance use. The treatment philosophy, according to Neiberg, followed a basic formula: "At the time drunkenness was a crime. And if you got soused and were a nuisance, you got sentenced to Framingham for six months. During which time we probably saved half the lives of people. Because they were well fed, they had a bed at night, they had a good doctor. . . . So, for the six months that they were there, they were all cured. That's cured by not having access to alcohol."[30] Treatment, at the time, according to Neiberg, predominantly consisted of "food, shelter, kindness, group discussions, contact with the outpatient therapist, and a lot of contact with the in-house social service staff at Framingham." Neiberg was convinced that individual long-term psychotherapy and group psychotherapy were critical to the short- and long-term success of these women, but that meant that the treatment team was routinely stymied once a woman left the facility. Importantly, the prison could provide some basic needs of women that often were not met when they were on the streets. Yet similar to today, the effect of being removed from a pathological environment was in and of itself what "cured" most women.

One of the main treatment problems facing the prison staff, therefore, was the relative inability of the prisons to establish a continuum of care that would help assist the inmates upon their release in dealing with the structural conditions of their lives that had led to incarceration. Neiberg actually created a prototype program to try to address this issue: he organized physicians from the Peter Bent Brigham Hospital in Boston, Massachusetts, to staff two half-day sessions a week to treat the women with alcohol disorders while at the prison, hoping to establish patient-doctor rapport to engage the women in community treatment upon their release. Yet few women showed up to their outpatient appointments at the hospital upon release. As the superintendent of Framingham in 1957 reported, "There have been 84 released and each has been referred in compliance with the law. The Clinics are asked to report to us when women report to the Clinic and only three so far have reported attendance at the clinic."[31] They were furthermore concerned that the most vulnerable women had nowhere to go. Thus, the halfway house developed by Friends of Framingham was seen as a critical innovation—a community-based extension of treatment initiated in the prison.

Yet women on heroin and alcohol often returned to prison or jail. Women who drank comprised over half the total admissions to the prison in 1960, and the prison hoped to "expand this [group therapy] program, to include some occupational skills, training, more groups and individual therapy, to an AA Sponsorship and help in obtaining room and jobs upon release."[32] In Neiberg's view, heroin addicts were particularly recalcitrant, frequently reinstitutionalized and disproportionately African American, possibly reflecting early racial disparities in arrests and policing.

Neiberg recalled that most of the women who came to the prison for heroin addiction did not actually enter by violating drug laws, but more commonly for prostitution or petty larceny. He characterized these women as tough, smart survivors, growing up in inordinately harsh circumstances: "The older ones I came to respect. . . . You're black, you're young, you're brought up by your grandmother . . . and if you survive, being on the streets, being addicted, having a pimp who maltreats you, which is not atypical, and you make it to forty or menopause, you gotta be smart." He became convinced that the only formula for effectively treating these women was to encounter them inside and then accompany them with social work on the outside, but few of the women once released seemed to want any help from his team or the prison staff more generally.

In attempts to address the social issues facing women, the prison's Social Services Department multiplied. The staff at the Social Services Department made efforts to document numerous characteristics about the inmates, even taking "occasional field trips to patients' homes either to gather data or help solve some of their community problems."[33] This was based on a genuine desire for the prison staff and administrators to know if the treatment they had provided for women worked upon release. Yet they found it difficult to actually measure outcomes, as do the prison programs today. As Smith wrote, "It is at the present time not possible to measure the effectiveness of our program in terms of a decrease of recidivism rate of people that are in treatment and those that are not in treatment. We are at best only one factor involved in the social controls of these persons when they leave the Institution."[34]

This was a period of intensive subjectification of women in prison. Their lives became case studies of wayward femininity for the prison social workers; the prison was, as Michel Foucault observed in his classic work *Discipline and Punish*, "a sort of permanent observatory that made it possible to distribute the varieties of vices or weaknesses" where prison officials and social scientists together strove to assess "the potentiality of danger that lies hidden in an individual."[35] Psychotherapy emerged as a key orienting principle to assess criminal women and treat their aberrant thinking and behaviors; it was, in many ways, the foundation of other methods of rehabilitation, including modern-day counseling sessions in the prison.

Yet the inmates did not view their treatment as favorably as the optimistic staff did. They continued to use drugs or have outbursts of anger or bad behavior. Neiberg once responded to the "rash of disciplinary problems within the institution" by "chronic troublemakers" with mandatory group therapy in the cottages. One of the reports from one of the Framingham cottages, Wilson Cottage, noted that the "clientele . . . is a lethargic group, with inner seethings rather than healthy outer aggressions."[36] The women appeared lackluster in their participation in treatment regimens.

The treatment staff just could not seem to achieve the benefits from holistic therapy and long-term psychotherapy that they hoped for. For example, the women who came to MCI-Framingham on cases of "drunkenness" stayed, on average, six months. Superintendent Smith felt stymied by the short length of prison sentences that could not achieve anything meaningful with women: "I feel that one definite element constantly appears as a hindrance to the most effective program of rehabilitation; the length of stay of the younger inmates seems cruelly short. These people are, in general, so damaged by the time they come to us that they need an extended period of time under control before they can develop any meaningful relationship—be it with a psychotherapist or a correctional institution."[37]

Yet, even in the face of such seeming failures to make significant changes in the women's life chances or circumstances, there was still great optimism among prison administrators that their efforts were valuable and that they could break the bad habits of these women. As Mary Clary, the Director of Hodder Hall, wrote in 1962: "If there is no accurate yard stick by which to measure lasting rehabilitative results from the foregoing projects, there is no doubt as to their immediate good. To plant a few seeds of referential potential and pleasure, to soften hardened concepts of authority and society, *to separate the sexes into their normal roles*, to give off a sense of personal worth and hope; these do count for something. They make, in fact, the difference between lethal custody and the truly therapeutic milieu [italics added]."[38] Thus, a gendered form of treatment and punishment slowly became enmeshed in the prison system for wayward women on heroin and alcohol. The difficulties the prison had treating these women reflected the still relatively sparse community treatment alternatives prior to the option for medication to treat opioid addiction with the advent of methadone maintenance in the 1960s and 1970s. Addiction was seen within the purview of prison mental health programs that were dominated by a psychotherapeutic orientation, where one had to cultivate "healthy outer aggressions" in order to get better.

At MCI-Framingham, the combination of professionalization of prison treatment efforts with a patronizing attitude toward poor women created a public image of treatment reflecting narrow, upper-middle-class, heavily racialized views of proper femininity. The increasing role of professionals in prisons during this time and continuing to the present day furthermore helped to consolidate and instantiate the prison as a proper, necessary, and inherently moralizing site for treatment of deviant women, even when programs showed little to no efficacy in substantively dealing with the underlying issues related to substance use and misuse.

ALTERNATIVES TO PRISON?

While the prisons and jails were somewhat reluctantly tasked with reha-bilitating criminal women, the 1960s ushered in community alternatives regarding the treatment of addiction and mental health with the election of John F. Kennedy. Community debates reflected new concerns that prisons were not the right place for drug users and additional questions about treatment modalities for both women as well as men.

In 1961, the Joint Committee of the American Bar Association and the American Medical Association assessed the effects of several critical laws (including the Harrison Law of 1914, the Porter Law of 1928, and the Boggs Act in 1951) that had effectively resulted in the criminaliza-tion of addiction with harsh prison sentences for drug consumption as well as the sale of many substances deemed to be illicit, including mari-juana and heroin. In a joint report entitled, "Drug Addiction, Crime or Disease?," Morris Ploscowe wrote that new methods of drug treatment and new research advances were sorely needed: "The statistics on relapse to addiction after attempted cures at narcotics hospitals like Lexington, Fort Worth or Riverside [Hospital] tell the stark story of the basic failure of the hospital centered approach in dealing with problems of drug addiction."[39]

At the same time, community-based physicians struggled to innovate new treatment modalities for opioid addiction. Methadone maintenance, whereby patients were prescribed a daily dose of a legal long-acting opi-oid, was being tested as a treatment modality in the 1960s by Dr. Vincent Dole, an endocrinologist, and Dr. Marie Nyswander, a psychiatrist at the Rockefeller Hospital. It promised the potential to curb addicts' desires and cravings for heroin and transform people who previously were being sent to prison into people living stable and functional lives in the com-munity. Because of its long half-life, the medication methadone could be administered once a day (as opposed to heroin, whose shorter half-life meant using approximately three to four times a day on average).

Women became very involved as patients in methadone programs. Early research suggested that women in methadone programs made pro-gress in metrics of both social stability and health. Frances Gearing, who evaluated the program at the Beth Israel and Harlem Hospitals in New York, found that women tended to leave welfare, return to school, and go back to work if they were able to stay in the program for twenty-four months.[40] Methadone programs gained ground nationally through a dis-course of reducing crime and Richard Nixon praised these programs.

The methadone clinics seemed as if they might benefit women in particular ways that echoed the potential benefits that drug maintenance clinics of the early 1920s had provided, such as liberating women from depending on men for drugs, preventing sex work that was traded or sold for drugs, and avoiding the negative health benefits of injection drug use. Some women reported regaining their menstrual cycles and a renewed feeling of well-being and health that came with it; other women reported that they did not have to steal as often. Others, however, claimed that the culture of methadone clinics was dominated by and for men, and retention rates of women in these programs declined by the early 1970s.

There was also a surging interest in abstinence-based programs, and such a position was embraced almost unequivocally by the prisons and jails. Programs such as AA and NA were spreading rapidly to many American communities. Additionally, an abstinence-based program known as the "therapeutic community" became popular after a recovering alcoholic named Charles Dederich started a drug treatment community called Synanon in the 1950s. In this particular form of therapy, individuals would confront one another about their bad habits, behaviors, and personality traits that had led to addiction and lives of deviance in a format that often involved yelling, shaming, crying, and public group-based humiliation. These methods were based on the philosophy that drug users were socially maladjusted, had deep-seated personality disorders, and had no sense of the world as rule-bound.

Even though therapeutic communities had widely published success rates, treatment effectiveness researchers noted that women were more likely to leave therapeutic communities than other types of programs. Women criticized these programs for being focused on restoring the self-esteem of men. In particular, they felt that the treatment approaches of criticizing their fellow patients' personalities and life choices stirred up feelings of shame, guilt, and victimization in women. The staff were typically all male, and some women reported having to perform sexual favors for them; male clients were admired for being "pimps," while women were degraded for being "sluts" and for being certain female stereotypes, including the "intellectual junkie, bad mother, and hypochondriac."[41] Like other kinds of drug treatment programs, women were encouraged to fulfill normative gender roles, such as cleaning or learning secretarial skills.

Studies of women who used drugs and attempts by researchers to create a model of female addiction simultaneously drew attention to the gendered aspects of drug use and its treatment but also served to enforce the notion of difference as deviance. Women deserved special attention, but much of the attention reinforced notions that women were somehow sicker and more difficult to treat than their male counterparts. For example, DeLeon and Beschner's studies of women in therapeutic communities found that women had more depression and tended to display in psychological testing more "externality," or the sense that their problems had external roots or, even worse, were simply part of their destiny.[42] In therapeutic drug treatment worlds, externality was viewed as a barrier to working on a troubled inner self that was the root of all problems; women were seen as blaming others—such as family, male friends and romantic partners, and life circumstances—for their behaviors and addictions. Addressing these external sources of structural violence was not within the purview of these treatment programs, which preferred to focus on the sick and deviant individual bodies.

Furthermore, women experienced many significant barriers to entering, staying in, and completing treatment programs, including bans on allowing pregnant women to participate in programs. Yet, even after programs attempted to address these issues related to women's health, childbearing, and motherhood, few of the programs were able to equip women to live independently and safely back in their home communities—much like problems that the women's prison encountered.

COMMUNITY OR PRISON: DEBATES ON DRUGS AND CRIME

The 1970s was a period of national upheaval and serious debates over the social problem presented by drug use more generally. In Massachusetts, the community discussion mirrored national discussions. With newspaper articles proclaiming that heroin was spreading to Boston's middle class and that it was "no longer a problem of the poor and the slums three years ago," a renewed and long-lasting moral panic about drugs began anew.[43]

Yet there was some controversy about how much rehabilitation was possible in prison settings. In the greater Boston area, the controversial Republican Middlesex County sheriff John Buckley argued that people who used drugs did not get better in jails, and he infamously traveled to London to learn about heroin maintenance programs. In 1973, he gave a talk at Northeastern University, where he said, "Drug programs in 'the devil's workshop', as the public insists on nicknaming our correctional institutions, have failed." Arguing that chronic opioid users should be maintained on pure heroin at public health programs, he said,

"At Billerica [jail] we've had more drug programs than any other prison in the state. Seven were started, but every one of them closed down."[44]

Some even pushed for decriminalization of drug use. House Speaker David M. Bartley testified to end prison sentences for simple possession of marijuana, heroin, and other drugs, proposing one hundred hours of community service work for a first marijuana offense and five hundred hours for a heroin violation. And the Narcotic Rehabilitation Act of 1966 mandated drug treatment as an alternative to incarceration, but the implementation of the legislation was slow, difficult, and imprecise.

On the other hand, many others argued that treatment was not enough, warning of the serious dangers of drug use and the need to take Nixon's 1971 "War on Drugs" speech seriously. In Boston, heroin use was depicted as dangerous and contagious: Dr. Dana Farnsworth of the Harvard Health Center said that "a heroin addict is handicapped beyond all possibility of cure." He warned that one heroin addict in a community "will produce five or six others very easily."[45]

In 1974, the Massachusetts House passed a harsh drug law in response to similar stiff New York State legislation known informally as the Rockefeller Drug Laws, with the fear that the tough law would drive New York drug dealers into nearby states like Massachusetts. The public clamored for harsh penalties for king-pin "pushers" or dealers. Throughout this debate, heroin became the iconic hard drug, linked in the public imaginary to criminal acts, even though legal drugs like alcohol and tobacco had far more widespread abuse and harmful implications for the public. Those knowledgeable about the drug treatment landscape claimed that a two-tiered treatment system had emerged; one for the wealthy user who could obtain private treatment and one for the street user who would be bounced to public drug treatment programs.[46]

Senator Ted Kennedy argued, "The idea that we should send offenders to jail to rehabilitate them must be eliminated from our correctional philosophy. . . . Prisons are for punishment."[47] Massachusetts at the time had one of the lowest per capita prison populations among the United States, but the newly elected Democratic governor, Edward King, had won office campaigning vigorously in favor of removing judicial discretion in sentencing drug cases. In 1980, another stiff drug bill passed, even though the governor's own correction commissioner, William Hogan, said that the state prisons could not house the number of people such legislation would affect.

The renewed emphasis on breaking and entering and petty crimes of property such as larceny (often a part of acquisitive crime related to substance use disorders) indicated the felt threat to public safety and a sense of security. Community-based drug treatment options, once so promising, receded as incarceration gained prominence. The City of Boston refused federal funds for methadone maintenance programs and instead decided to have a smaller, stricter program, arguing that they should only treat those who wanted to be "cured," stating that "the crime and violence associated with drug use . . . is properly a police problem, not a health function."[48]

The prisons saw swells of low-level drug offenders as a result of these legislations. During the 1970s and 1980s, the drug treatment offered at MCI-Framingham began to shift. The prison opened up a new modular building unit to house women who were detoxing from alcohol or opioids, and the women began thirty-day drug treatment programs there. Women who had committed no crimes were also increasingly being sent to prison, based on a 1973 state law said that alcoholics and drug users who posed a threat to themselves or others could be sent to MCI-Framingham for thirty days of detention in prison (while men would be sent to a community addiction treatment facility). When the state's twenty-person-bed treatment center in Jamaica Plain was full, women were sent to prison instead. One woman, Kathleen Neal, sued the state, asserting that she "received no treatment for her disease" and that it was difficult to access treatment elsewhere, as politicians had authorized treatment mandates but not the funds.[49]

Treatment providers for women in prison were also in flux, as community groups won and lost contracts when it became cheaper to outsource these services, but they were all generally of low efficacy. A popular drug treatment program run by an organization called Spring was canceled in 1987 for another program run by Social Justice for Women on charges that the Spring program lacked a diversity of treatment staff and could not speak to the experiences of black and Hispanic inmates. Defenders of the Spring program claimed "that 200 inmates a year attend drug and alcohol rehabilitation programs at MCI . . . [citing] success with 20 percent of that number, which is considered high in the field."[50]

POOR TREATMENT AND PRIVATIZATION IN MASSACHUSETTS PRISONS

The treatment of women with drug problems in state prisons increasingly came under scrutiny in the 1990s in the era of state prison health privatization. The Republican governor William Weld promised to reduce the state deficit, lower taxes, and cut unemployment during his tenure from 1991 to 1997. Part of this promise included privatizing the entire state's prison health care. Massachusetts then transferred its health care of 9,400 state prisoners to a Florida-based for-profit prison health contractor called EMSA Correctional Care, which had vastly underbid at $28.7 million, promising to provide extremely low-cost care. According to this new plan, EMSA had to reduce outside hospital visits for state inmates from five hundred a week to five hundred a month and EMSA would be penalized $100 for every visit above the set quota. EMSA became the first private firm in the country to provide prison health care for an entire state, presaging shifts around the country that are now quite common.

At MCI-Framingham under EMSA's care, several women incarcerated for drug use and coexisting mental illness died under the prison's purview. The physicians hired by the Health Services Unit by EMSA had no experience in women's health, HIV, or gynecology/obstetrics. Many nurses with prison experience left after EMSA offered them lower salaries and benefits, and nurses with no prison training came in. Scandal erupted after thirty-two-year-old Robin Peeler, an HIV-positive woman with a history of heroin addiction, died in the Health Services Unit of unknown causes. There was contention over the details of exactly how and when she died, but she was serving a one-year-sentence for shoplifting.

EMSA's head physician, Dr. Henry Phipps, claimed that they did not know that Robin had tested positive for HIV. He said that she died of a heart attack or a pulmonary embolism, even hinting she overdosed on drugs: "This is a prison. I hate to say I'm a suspicious guy, but it's a concern I have."[51] Her roommates told stories about Peeler vomiting blood in bed and when others stole bread for her because it was the only thing she could keep down, they were punished for it with disciplinary infractions. Outside physicians called it a case of medical neglect, but the Department of Correction claimed that all due diligence by the state had been taken. Soon thereafter, Donna Jean Hamilton, a thirty-one-year-old woman incarcerated at MCI-Framingham for "common nightwalking," died. She had told prison staff repeatedly that she planned to kill herself, but she was allowed to go back to the general population, where she committed suicide.

Community groups alleged that the prison health care for women was egregiously bad. The Neil Houston House for pregnant women under DOC custody had only five out of fifteen beds used, and they alleged that the Department of Correction would not transfer women out of

MCI-Framingham out of a "punitive attitude that these women shouldn't be sent here to detox and learn parenting."[52] After Peeler's death, the prison had inmates repaint the unit and they removed cages used for psychiatric patients. Community physicians found that tests were routinely ordered and not done; referrals were made, and inmates were never sent. Nurses could not get visits approved at outside hospitals.

MCI-Framingham was increasingly overcrowded with first-time, nonviolent drug offenders serving mandatory minimum drug sentences, rising from 2 percent to 26 percent between 1990 and 1995. A *Boston Globe* investigative piece found that violent offenders (convicted of rape and armed robbery) were often serving shorter sentences than nonviolent or first-time drug offenders.[53] The authors found that major drug dealers would trade information with prosecutors to reduce prison sentences; the legal system would then profit off significant amounts of drug forfeiture money and their ability to turn dealers into informants, while the nonviolent consumers had nothing to trade. These laws disproportionately punished women, who were often low in a drug-dealing hierarchy.

Even though drug laws were increasingly strict and widespread, the War on Drugs seemed to be failing. So-called "hard" drugs like heroin and cocaine were more plentiful and cheaper than they had ever been. The massive influx of poor, low-level drug offenders serving long sentences filled the jails and prisons. It also feminized the War on Drugs, indicting the mothers, sisters, girlfriends, and partners of men involved in the drug trade, since they were easy prosecutorial targets.

The feminization of the War on Drugs added further injury to poor women already subjected to attempts by the state at character retraining and rehabilitation. Was the prison the right place for them or their treatment? A careful examination of the historical record demonstrates how women's prisons historically struggled to achieve their stated goals of rehabilitation, including their mandate to discipline, punish, and uplift women to fulfill societally sanctioned feminine roles of domesticity and motherhood. The prison simply could not address the myriad forms of structural violence nor the attendant stigma of being a woman on drugs. Furthermore, clashing attitudes regarding whether women with addiction issues should be treated as victims who need training and structural support (as demonstrated by the Beauty Shop) or as moral deviants best removed from society and others (as demonstrated in the Segregation Unit) have a deeply rooted history. From examining the writings of prison administrators and clinicians within these prison treatment spaces, it is apparent how conflicted they were about being given the social mandate to cure and rehabilitate these women.

This pendulum of our approach to women who use drugs continues to swing between these poles of punishment and treatment. Women who use drugs continue to present specific moral anxieties and dangers that have long embodied histories of female exceptionalism based in fears of women's bodies and reproductive processes. Thus, prisons, with their promise of both rehabilitation and containment, have become one of the central societal institutions for addiction treatment, even in the absence of clear data that the women's prison was ever effective in treating substance use problems among women. As the debates raged on over whether substance use was a problem fit for either police and crime control or medicine, the prison became an increasingly sedimented social fixture in local, state, and federal policies, thus fueling the widespread criminalization and incarceration of women who used drugs.

3

Heroin Is My Counselor

Waiting in line to see the bank teller was the worst part of the process for Kaitlin. She had never been a patient person. No one in her large Irish American family seemed to have any patience. When she was growing up, it had been difficult to wait for her father to get out of prison each time he went away. It was hard for her to wait for the ambulance to arrive that time when she was a teenager and had walked into her family's apartment in the Charlestown housing projects and discovered her uncle's body hanging from the doorway. Many years later, it was hard for her to wait for her boyfriend to come back with the drugs he had scored for them to snort, so hard that she decided to shoot up the already-wet heroin glistening on a spoon in front of her that another friend had procured just several minutes earlier.

When she was in prison for a crime related to her problematic heroin use, it was hard for her to wait the entire week for her two-year-old daughter, Amber, to come to visit her on the weekend in MCI-Framingham. And it was especially hard to wait for Amber and her grandmother to make it past all the prison checkpoints—sometimes with a strip search for the adults and always with a pat down for the children, which Kaitlin worried could traumatize her young daughter—and to wait for them to finally gain clearance to spend time together in the family trailer. But when she was sick from opioid withdrawal, waiting for it to be over was the worst. It seemed like relief would never come for her nausea that progressed to dry heaves and her abdominal pain that proceeded to diarrhea, while her anxiety only built up to an unrelenting pitch.

When Kaitlin finally reached the front of the line at the bank that fateful day, she pulled a 38 mm handgun out of her purse and into the line of sight of the plump and smiling bank teller. She passed a note, which she had typed on her mother's computer. It read: "I'm not fucking around, I have a gun. Reach into the drawer quietly and no one gets hurt if you give me all your cash."

Kaitlin was slight of frame with long red hair, No one would ever have suspected her of robbing banks. She looked more like a suburban soccer mom than a dopesick heroin user.

On her sixth time robbing banks, she was finally caught. For Kaitlin, it didn't actually matter how much cash was on hand, as long as there was enough to get $100 of heroin to stave off the dopesickness for one more day. The most she had ever gotten was $3,200. The last time she robbed a bank she got $995.

Perhaps she should have known she would end up robbing banks; it was an occupation that ran in the family. Her father had been in and out of prison his whole life for robbing armored cars, and the family was, after all, from Charlestown, Massachusetts, one of the Boston neighborhoods notorious for producing gangsters, mobsters, and bank robbers. "If your family are all dentists, I guess you pull teeth," she shrugged.

Kaitlin attributes her bank robbing to the time her mother tried to force her into treatment for heroin use disorder against her will in a legal order known as a civil commitment. In Massachusetts, as in many other states in this country, women and men who are deemed a risk to themselves or others from alcohol or substance use can be involuntarily committed to drug treatment centers or even jail or prison against their will in the absence of any criminal wrongdoing. Passed in 1973, the Massachusetts law, known as Section 35, reads, "Any police officer, physician, spouse, blood relative, guardian or court official may petition in writing any district court or any division of the juvenile court department for an order of commitment of a person whom he has reason to believe is an alcoholic or substance abuser."[1] The court would then issue a summons for the person to appear with a warrant of apprehension. This proceeding is colloquially referred to as "being sectioned."

In the civil court, a judge has the option to commit a person for thirty days and up to ninety days if the person is deemed to have "a likelihood of serious harm as a result of his alcoholism or substance abuse" based on medical testimony by a physician or a psychologist. Until 2006, the majority of sectioned women were sent to MCI-Framingham, the state women's prison, reflecting a historical lack of community-based treatment options for women as well as a historical enmeshment of the prison with addiction policy, as described in the previous chapter.[2]

Kaitlin's mother had been worried that Kaitlin's drug use was out of control. Every night, she prayed that her daughter would not overdose or die. And Kaitlin had her one-year-old daughter, Amber, to think of, after all. Kaitlin's mother didn't know what to do, so she decided to section her. The judge facing Kaitlin's section decided to send Kaitlin not to the prison but to the Women's Addiction Treatment Center (WATC) in New Bedford, run by the Department of Public Health's Bureau of Substance Abuse Services. Created in 2006, WATC was composed of three separate but linked units: the detoxification unit, the Clinical Stabilization Services (Tranquility Inn), and then the Transitional Support Services (New Chapter), each unit gradually moving patients toward physical stabilization and more intensive levels of treatment.

Kaitlin spent thirty days at WATC, first detoxing off heroin with the help of increasingly smaller doses of opioid-containing medications administered by the staff, and then spending more of her time in group coursework. But she was still angry at her mother that she had been sectioned: "I came out in February and I was robbing banks by March." Her actions were motivated by a combination of defiance and rage; as she told me, "Now you're going to see me get high. I came out angry. I wasn't ready to stop."

No period of treatment and no amount of money spent on the most luxurious or comprehensive treatment, let alone a paltry thirty days of involuntary treatment, was going to stop Kaitlin from using heroin when she got out. It was so much better than the angel dust or the cocaine that she had used and tried in her teenage years. The first time she tried opioids was actually when taking oxycodone tablets prescribed to her after the birth of her daughter via caesarean section. Taking the oxycodone "just made me feel better, made me feel different than my normal depressed young life. It made sense to me."

As a young mother in her early twenties, Kaitlin started to sniff the pills, and she and Amber's father would do them together. He was a carpenter in the union, so they had a steady supply of money that flowed in to purchase drugs. I wondered what about Kaitlin's life—a combination of her genetics, upbringing, learned behaviors, lived experiences—

had predisposed her to want to use the opioids in such a way. Why did she report paradoxically feeling more energy, when heroin is traditionally conceived of as a depressant, or downer, like alcohol?

"I would think I was a better mother on drugs, because I was more productive," Kaitlin mused. "Everything was just great." She moved on to shooting heroin when Amber was one. Taking heroin intravenously was the best possible feeling in the world. "It was love," she declared. "It was the best thing I'll feel for the rest of my life." The heroin lifted her out of a life of depression and trauma that had started at twelve when she found her uncle's lifeless body after he committed suicide in their house. She just felt relief from the weight of the world, the constant burdens presented by everyday life. She professed that when she was using, she didn't need any other kind of treatment: "Heroin is my counselor."

. . .

One hot August afternoon, drops of water fell irregularly, yet steadily, from the ceiling tiles of the treatment unit at the Women's Recovery Academy (WRA) in MCI-Framingham. A small trash can placed under the leak had begun to fill up, threatening overflow. This leak was just one in a long line of structural and environmental problems the prison faced as it sought to cope with its ancient architecture and slow bureaucracy. The treatment program, located in the "Townline" cottage building, took place in the Day Room of one of the general housing units surrounding a small grass quadrangle. Women who qualified for the program, and who elected to participate, were all placed in this housing unit to undergo intensive drug treatment together.

In one corner of the Day Room, the WRA counselor confided in me, "Brittany's going to fail. She's not going to make it." It was a daunting task facing the prison drug treatment staff: to turn a drug dealer and daily heroin user into a reformed, abstinent, law-abiding citizen. Brittany, a chunky twenty-three-year-old woman with baby fat and piercing dark eyes and chestnut curls, just didn't want to and couldn't seem to stop using heroin. What could possibly be done?

This was Brittany's second time in prison for the same conviction: possession and operating under the influence. In short, she had been her town's oxycodone-acetaminophen (Percocet) dealer, and she had pleaded upon her arrest that she had so many pills on her because she was a raging drug addict. She told the judge that the numerous "perc30s" (containing 30mg of oxycodone) that she had tucked in her underwear were for her own use, even though, unbeknownst to the authorities, she had already moved on to injecting heroin, a much stronger and cheaper opioid, and that she sold the pills at a premium price and used it to obtain cheaper heroin for her own personal use.

Like Kaitlin, she had initially been sent to the state Women's Addiction Treatment Unit (WATC) instead of prison, but after thirty days of treatment, she was released back to the streets, where she resumed her heroin use. Because this was a violation of probation and she had "failed the treatment opportunity that had been given" to her before, Brittany was sent to serve three months in prison at MCI-Framingham. Brittany served her three months with relative ease but couldn't stop thinking about heroin. It was simply too pleasurable a sensation and a memory. During this time, she chose not to participate in any treatment plans that the prison offered.

Indeed, she had big plans that started the second she got into her boyfriend Aaron's car. They had driven only five minutes away from the prison before she was shooting up. It was even easier than usual, since her veins had partly recovered while she was in prison. Over the next six months that Brittany was out on probation, she kept getting high but tried to "piss clean" for her probation check-ins. This involved tucking other people's urine samples into her vagina—in this case, a child's urine placed in an alcohol nip bottle that she had bartered in a trade for some pills—so that she could pass her probation drug tests.

After she was released from prison, Brittany overdosed ten times by her own account. It was partly because she had lost physiologic tolerance (so when she used the same amount of opioids, it overwhelmed her system) but also because she loved edging to the point of unconsciousness by mixing heroin with additional sedating medications (including gabapentin, quetiapine, and clonazepam, to name a few). Her friends were able to revive her with naloxone, or called 911, and she was administered the opioid overdose reversal medication by paramedics and then discharged from the emergency room. The same physicians and nurses wagged their fingers at her. She felt fleeting moments of embarrassment and shame, but she didn't really see a way to change and she felt conflicted about stopping. In fact, she just didn't want to stop.

One day when her urine drug screen for probation was positive for heroin and several other substances, she told the judge that she finally wanted to go to a treatment program. She batted her eyelashes and looked down, praying she might get a softie. "No," he said, "You're going to do a year at MCI. Do the program there."

. . .

Any road involving heroin seemed to lead inevitably to the prison. Both Kaitlin and Brittany ended up there, either through civil commitment or for criminal offenses related to ongoing drug use (such as simple possession, possession of paraphernalia, or committing a crime like shoplifting or forging checks to obtain money for drugs). Many of the women I met in prison had also been sectioned, or involuntarily committed to treatment, either by family or themselves in order to avoid a potential criminal charge. Around 20 percent of the civil commitments each year were self-commitments, reflecting a dire lack of access to treatment on demand as well as a lack of knowledge of the public health system and resources for individuals and their families.[3] Many family members did not realize that sectioning their loved ones could often result in incarceration, especially in the case of women, since there were significantly fewer community treatment beds for them than for men.

Civil commitment has historically been governed by two main legal principles: first, *parens patriae*, which states that the government can act on behalf of citizens who cannot act in their own best interests, and second, the doctrine of police power, which gives the state the power to police their citizens in order to protect the welfare of the collective.[4] The procedure of involuntary commitment has been used as an intervention on a wide variety of disorders: most commonly, for mental illnesses such as schizophrenia, drug use, eating disorders, and even sex offenses. Out-of-control substance use disorders have been considered dangerous physical and psychological conditions posing a threat to both individuals themselves as well as the collective.

Civil commitment programs are widespread, existing in some form in at least thirty-three states in the country. Proponents of civil commitment argue that the potential harms of continued drug use outweigh the risks: in the worst-case scenario, individuals face imminent overdose, severe illness, or death. Detractors argue that until an individual is ready that the treatment will not firmly take root. As in Kaitlin's case, some people who are involuntarily committed feel as if they must retaliate against family members—they are "righteous dopefiends"[5]—and willfully defy the wishes of well-intentioned family and friends and society more generally.

In Massachusetts, the number of women civilly committed for drug addiction has increased significantly over time. In 2006, 346 women were civilly committed, in 2012, there were 1,557 and in 2016 over 6,500.[6] WATC had approximately ninety beds, but if WATC was full, many women went to the prison, as was the case often in the wintertime, when more people tended to seek treatment and shelter from the harsh weather. The Massachusetts Women's Justice Network, an advocacy group for criminal-justice-involved women, argued that there was an important racial distinction between the women sent to WATC for community treatment and the women sent to prison: according to their research, African American and Hispanic women comprised 31 percent of the civil commitments sent to MCI-Framingham versus only 8 percent of the civil commitments at WATC.[7] In short, black and brown women with substance use disorders were disproportionately sent to prison. This practice of sending women who had not committed a crime to prison continued until 2016, when the Massachusetts legislature banned it after ongoing community outrage and activism efforts.

During the era of sectioning women to prison for substance use, women described experiencing unhealthy and inadequate facilities there. They told me that they were housed in a giant dormitory gymnasium section of the prison called the "Mods," shorthand for "Modular Units." Kathy, who had been sectioned to MCI-Framingham for her drug use in 2010, explained that the women who were under a "section" were kept separately in the prison from women who had been sentenced: "I'm pretty sure it was eighty-something beds in there. . . . It's horrible. If one person isn't sleeping, no one is sleeping." By law, the prison was forced to house the civil commitments in separate housing from pretrial detainees or sentenced women. This meant, unfortunately for them and their families who might have thought otherwise, that the sectioned women were unable to participate in any of the regular programming on drug treatment, domestic violence, or additional educational opportunities.

Once women were sectioned to MCI-Framingham for drug use, it fell onto the prison to relocate the women into approved Department of Public Health community-based treatment programs. The staff at MCI-Framingham felt burdened by this task, telling me that they spent inordinate amounts of time on the phone trying to find available drug treatment beds for women when the state-run WATC was full. One of the correctional officers told me that they would deliver a woman to her program in the community only to hear from the program within hours or days that the woman had run away. "You can almost immediately tell who are going to be the runners," one prison staff member said.

"They want to get into any program possible and then they run away immediately. They're wasting taxpayer money."

Sectioning was sometimes used strategically by women on heroin, and some saw entering state-mandated drug treatment as a last-ditch effort to avoid going to prison or jail. Mae said that she sectioned herself after leaving detox because she knew that she would otherwise pick up heroin, having to ironically detox off the methadone used to detox her off the heroin. (Patients say that physical withdrawal from methadone is far worse—more protracted and painful than the withdrawal from shorter-acting opioids like heroin.)

The state civil commitment law for addiction presumes that involuntary treatment is necessary, effective, or at least overall more beneficial than it is harmful. This is not always the case. Many of the women in my study reported that when they were released from WATC, they were back to using within the week, often within the day or hour. The enforced abstinence of being in jail or being civilly committed to detoxification or treatment can beget vengeful and self-righteously renewed drug use and, in fact, increased risk of death. One seminal research study found that people leaving prison in Washington State were at 120 percent increased risk of overdose death compared to the general population, in part because of loss of physiological tolerance to opioids in combination with the chaos and disruption associated with release from carceral settings.[8] Another study proposed loss of tolerance as a reason for increased overdose mortality among a cohort of people who successfully completed inpatient drug treatment rehabilitation programs.[9]

Mae tells me that she had been sectioned twice by her mother, the first time when she started to shoot heroin instead of snort it, and then the second time eleven days after she was released from WATC. The first time, Mae thought she was going to court for a clerk's hearing, and her mother, who also used drugs, had given her a solidarity present for her courthouse anxiety: "Five Xanibars [street name for Xanax] and then she gave me three perc-30s and I shot two before I left the house." The court employees ambushed her with the Section 35 commitment order, and she recalls being too high to resist. Yet forced treatment by the courts did little for Mae. Mae tells me that when she went back to WATC the second time, she learned that two of the women who had been in the earlier cohort with her were dead: "The people that work there say that two or three of every group of girls dies as soon as they hit the streets." How could she be committed to a program that clearly didn't work, with so many people leaving and then immediately overdosing and dying?

Mae stayed twenty-five days at WATC the first time and twenty-two days the second time. The treatment consisted of group programming, education, and recovery-based skills, but they were useless against her drive to use: "I had just found shooting up a little before that and my time was not up with that. I was pissed, absolutely pissed. It was literally a newfound love. . . . I got out, and I caught three more [criminal] cases in that week, because I'm like I'm going to show you [Mae's mother]." The second time that her mother sectioned her, Mae thought it was retaliatory for her ongoing bad behavior. After she left WATC the second time, she vowed "to get wrecked . . . to come home and I'm going to put my face in my mashed potatoes because I can't get up [too high] and I'm going to show you."

Mae's story, one of the increasing number of civil commitments for women who use drugs in Massachusetts, reflects the dearth of community detoxification programs, transitional services, ducation for concerned families, housing and employment opportunities for people who use drugs. In fact, abstinence-based programs often lead to increased risk of death, especially when programs were not offering access to opioid agonist therapy (OAT), which includes both buprenorphine and methadone as evidence-based, effective options for the treatment of opioid use disorder.

Being sent to prison is not only no real solution to the problem of opioid addiction for women who have committed no crimes, but it also enmeshes women in a surveillance and police state that can harm them more than help them, instead of getting them what they need in the communities where they live. What it does provide is simple detainment, not so different from the alcoholics and drug users of the past, such as Dr. Neiberg advocating prison-based "cures" because women couldn't easily access drugs or alcohol there.

DOPESICK IN PRISON

Like many other American prisons, MCI-Framingham had historically provided drug treatment programming as part of an overall larger commitment to rehabilitating morally deviant women and decreasing recidivism. Proponents of prison-based drug treatment argue that the prison can be "rock bottom" for many people, and that hitting rock bottom is sometimes necessary for long-lasting attitude and behavior change. According to this logic, incarcerated women are at their highest motivation to change and are most amenable to making changes in their attitudes, their practices and their bad habits. Some drug treatment researchers argue that drug users might only ever encounter treatment in a prison setting.[10]

Brittany had tried her hand at community treatment programs (including both methadone maintenance and intensive outpatient programs with three days a week of treatment) but she had never completed anything that fully disrupted her daily routine of getting high. At the prison, she would have her first chance. The process of drug treatment process at MCI-Framingham begins with the painful process of forced detoxification. Brittany knows her body precisely, including exactly when she will start getting "sick" (dopesick), or going into physical withdrawal from opioids. For her, it all starts with an itchy feeling in her throat, a sense of coughing, a feeling of nausea. Then it's on to the goosebumps, a temperature fluctuation between hot and cold, restless legs and, oh, the sugar cravings on the second and third day.

Going through withdrawal is so unpleasant that many people will do anything they can to avoid experiencing it. The fear of getting sick is a fierce motivator to find drugs and money for drugs: people emphasize that they need to get "well" or "off e" (empty) with heroin before their brain and subsequently their body revolt with physical symptoms. At the point that they become physically dependent on opioids, most people who continue to use them are doing so simply to avoid the pain of withdrawal, to not be "sick," often not even achieving the sensation of being high.

In a hospital environment or a monitored clinical setting, physicians can administer a variety of medications to ease the physical symptoms of opioid detoxification to make the immediate process less uncomfortable over a period of three to fourteen days using an opioid substitution medication, often with a taper that decreases the dose gradually over a period of days. Yet the vast majority of criminal justice institutions do not administer opioid-based detoxification or offer opioid maintenance therapy even to patients entering prison and jail who are prescribed opioid agonist therapy by community physicians. Most offer "comfort" medications, which are other classes of medications that target secondary symptoms such as diarrhea or anxiety including antidiarrheals, analgesics such as NSAIDs, or antihistamines for off-label treatment of anxiety or for insomnia. Conventional practice within prison and jail settings is that opioid detoxification is simply uncomfortable, but not deadly.

Even though the United States has the means to alleviate suffering with opioid agonist medications, prisons and jail administrators typically refuse to utilize them. In a 2009 study that surveyed fifty-one state prison systems, researchers found that only 55 percent of the system offered methadone to inmates, mostly for pregnant women with opioid use disorders.[11] The most commonly cited reason for not offering an opiate replacement therapy for detoxification was that these institutions "prefer drug-free detoxification over providing methadone or buprenorphine." A more recent study examining national data from 2014 found that only 4.6 percent of justice-involved clients (including drug courts and diversion programs) received referral to opioid agonist treatment, which is now considered the gold standard of care.[12]

Despite this, women who use heroin are masters of ingesting a variety of pharmacological substances to achieve certain desired effects, and they share tips with each other to make a prison detox less painful. Mae tells how they all talk in the "paddy wagon" to the "girls coming in for the first time." They say to them, "Don't even say you're addicted to heroin because you're not going to get anything, tell them you're a severe alcoholic and you'll get Librium." This is because prison and jails are compelled to administer women a low-dose benzodiazepine such as chlordiazepoxide (Librium) to prevent possibly fatal consequences of alcohol withdrawal such as seizures or delirium tremens (DTs). One major exception to this forced detoxification protocol for some facilities is if women are pregnant and also physically dependent on opioids; in many cases, they can be maintained on methadone or buprenorphine maintenance therapy for the entirety of their pregnancies as withdrawal can be dangerous to the fetus and to the mother.[13]

At MCI-Framingham, the women who are detoxing are housed in a separate part of the medical building called the Health Services Unit (HSU). Most women want to spend as little time as possible in the HSU. Conditions there are fraught: there might be four to six women in one locked cell, each enduring a unique version of embodied distress, often involving insomnia, diarrhea, or vomiting. Allowed out of the cell for only one hour a day to clean up, many women would much rather be sent to the general unit where they can at least "walk it off."

All the women who come through HSU with a known opioid problem are sent to one of two cottages (known as Brewster 1 or Brewster 2), where a program called "First Step" is run. It is a mandatory twenty-day program run by Spectrum Health Systems, the external nonprofit vendor that runs all the drug treatment programming at Framingham. "First Step" is called a post-detoxification program and is intended to provide initial basic education about drug use and help women make plans for their discharge. The program is residential and largely group-based, with basic educational classes on overdose prevention, cravings and urges, HIV and infectious diseases, and general health.

Mae affirms that the First Step program is unpleasant because most women are still detoxing, and they are subsequently unhappy and irritable due to ongoing discomforts: "There's pretty much nine girls in every room and there's ten rooms. So, there's ninety girls in one unit, all detoxing, coming right off the street." All the physical sickness makes the programming at First Step difficult. It is hard for women to concentrate. Tina, an older woman who had endured many cycles of First Step, affirms that Brewster was out of control: "The girls were smoking crack, taking the toaster to light the straight shooter [used to smoke crack], doing stupid stuff like that, until they finally got caught, got hauled off to the hole [solitary confinement]."

After First Step, the drug treatment staff encourage women to move on to the next program, the Women's Recovery Academy (WRA). The WRA is related to the Correctional Recovery Academy (CRA) that is taught at all the male prisons throughout the state, and it is a "modified therapeutic community" (TC) drug treatment program that is "based upon what works in offender rehabilitation."[14] Within this program, the women live together in one of the cottages in a low bunker-like house of cells called Townline (although only about two-thirds of the Townline residents are participants in the WRA). They are required to participate in the drug treatment program "on a 24/7 basis" and participate "in all aspects of the program on and off the Unit," including doing chores and cleaning, providing duties useful to the whole community. According to Spectrum, the program's "therapeutic community functions as a distinctive community within the host institution, providing a highly structured and supportive learning environment in which to address criminal addictive behaviors" with particular "emphasis . . . placed on mutual respect, accountability and responsibility."

There are certain requirements for participating in the WRA program. It is partly a process of self-selection and partly a matter of meeting the requirements of the prison. In order to participate, a woman needs to have a certain length in her sentence as well as meet certain criteria in her profile and classification level. The prison uses a standardized instrument called the Criminal Offender Management and Profiling for Alternative Sanctions (COMPAS) to determine a woman's level of what they call "need" and "risk"; only those deemed at medium-or high-risk are offered treatment.[15] Interestingly, one program manager confided in me that she felt that who were deemed low-risk were actually made worse by treatment.

If a woman qualifies and wants to participate in the WRA program, she can then earn up to ten days of good time a month for participating, plus an additional ten for completing the entire program. "Good time" is the days taken off from a woman's sentence, translating into an earlier release date. The program only admits inmates who have a sentence longer than nine months, since the program takes at least six months to complete. One of the treatment administrators at Spectrum bemoaned the fact that the WRA program competes with other kinds of programming, including working around the compound as well as educational and vocational classes (the popular culinary arts program or the hair-styling course). These other forms of programming may appear more desirable and important to the women. Then there are some who are deterred by small details, such as housing assignments: they don't want to live in the drug treatment house or they have a girlfriend in another cottage.

Many women are uninterested in the drug treatment program offered. Jean, who first used heroin when she was fourteen in a basement shooting gallery in Chinatown and used for the next thirty years, told me, "I wanted to do my time and get up out of there." Over her thirty years in and out of the prison system, she witnessed the consistently short-lived careers of the case workers, counselors, and treatment staff, primarily young white women trained as social workers or teachers who had no conception of what life on the streets entailed. She did not find the treatment staff particularly compelling, nor did she trust anyone in the institution with her intimate and highly personal issues. For Jean, there were compelling race- and class-based reasons she had for not wanting to talk to a counselor or go to therapy. Was she going to tell this new social work graduate student intern about the time she was gang-raped by six men? Why? She questioned the adequacy of their training, their ability to relate to her life history and problems, as well as their overall commitment to her treatment in general. How could she trust anyone in the prison system, if their jobs were assured by her failure and lack of well-being?

THE WOMEN'S RECOVERY ACADEMY

When I first met Brittany in the old administrative building, she told me that she had never completed a drug treatment program before and that this was the longest time that she had ever been "clean" in the past six years, since she was seventeen. She is coming up on her Phase Test, and if she passes, she will move from Phase 2 to Phase 3.

The WRA is a modified "therapeutic community" program broken up into several phases of increasing responsibility and rewards. The original therapeutic communities in the 1960s and 1970s were based on the psychological theory that people facing drug addiction needed to learn how to function successfully within family and community hierarchies. In these programs, which often lasted two to three years, residents of therapeutic communities would take on increasingly more active roles and responsibilities in the house, including "acting doctor" and pointing out others' problems and "self-deceptions" via active confrontation, "ratting" in group meetings, and other humiliating public means known as "giving a haircut."[16] Spectrum describes the phase system of the WRA: "Program objectives seek to address known contributors of substance abuse and criminal behavior such as dysfunctional interpersonal relations, poor impulse control, and inappropriate responses to authority. Throughout sequential treatment phases, offenders' behaviors, attitudes, values and emotions are continually monitored, corrected and reinforced."[17]

The orientation of TCs to drug addiction aligns well with prison treatment-program philosophies because it works on the premise that individuals with substance use problems are socially and psychologically deficient; such programs work to "develop pro-social attitudes, behaviors, and values," as the WRA program book claimed. Dr. Judianne Densen-Gerber, a founder of the Odyssey House therapeutic communities in New York City in the 1970s, felt that their program was well aligned with the goals of a criminal justice system, claiming that "only with law enforcement and medicine working together can addiction be conquered."[18] At that time, TCs such as Odyssey House claimed to specialize in the seemingly recalcitrant deviance of specific subpopulations, particularly those of women (especially with histories of commercial sex work), Hispanics, and Native Americans, men who had served more than five years in prison, and institutionalized adolescents.

In the first phase of the WRA program in the women's prison, women are assessed and given orientation. Participants in this phase have to memorize the Absolute Rules and the Basic Guidelines of the program as well as develop an individualized treatment plan with a counselor (I met one woman who had been kicked out of the program for what was interpreted as threatening a staff member, which is breaking an

Absolute Rule). They must master the Morning Meeting philosophy that is recited every day, as well as use concepts including: redirects, Good Jobs, addiction, recovery, criminal addictive thinking, core skills, principles of recovery, the inner self, and the habit self. Then they must successfully pass the Phase Exam.

Phase 2 is the introspective portion of program, where clients closely examine their own lives, behaviors and the impact that their decisions have had on other people. To graduate, a client must show that she has developed "pro-social" thinking and behaviors and is able to handle high-risk situations, as well as negative or counterproductive thought processes and patterns. In Phase 3, the last phase, inmates work on relapse prevention and preparing their own discharge planning. They are expected to serve as mentors to new women in Phase 1. Graduating the entire program (and getting a final ten days of good time) requires an interview entitled the "Competency Review Panel" with the director of treatment of the prison, the head of the WRA program, and the regional director, as they evaluate whether a participant demonstrates understanding of the treatment concepts in regard to her own life. The twelve exit questions include things like "Define what humility means and how you express that behavior consistently" and "Name one time you have used a skill you learned in the program to cope with a personal challenge."

One morning I went to Townline with one of the correctional program officers (CPOs) to see Brittany in the WRA program. Each of the phase groups met at different times of the day, so I would be sitting in with some women in Phase 1. Here I encountered the prison in all its contradictions. Below is an excerpt from that fieldnote:

> The group is held in the "cottages" on the unit in the main living room are of the cottage. That area is set up with plastic tables with four chairs attached and the women are clustered near a fake fireplace where the facilitator is teaching. The CPO doesn't know who the CO [correctional officer] is at Townline, so we have to rap on the window in order to gain entrance. When I get there, my escort doesn't do a very good job explaining who I am and they are in the middle of a Family Feud style game ("Team Winning" versus "Team Divas") on health and wellness. I don't want to interrupt, so I just sit at a table at the back with two women. As they are playing their game, with questions ranging from gingivitis, plaque, and other kinds of health-related issues, I try to take notes about the unit and the program. The facilitator stands near the front near the fireplace asking the two teams of women questions. Near her is a white board that reads: "Goal: Share an experience that helped you stay clean. Word: Transcend. TC Slogan: Stop and think. Reading: Life is 10% what happens and 90% how we read it. We cannot change the inevitable!!!" . . . There are 12 women here not counting the facilitator, a

young white woman. 10 of them are white, two of them are black. I wonder if this represents the over-white-ness of prison programming; but Massachusetts also has a larger percentage of white people in prison than other states.

The game ends, with Team Divas beating Team Winning. During the break, one of the women comes up to me, shakes my hand introducing herself and talks to me about being in another Harvard-based sociology study of prisons. Another woman chides me about looking not a day over 21. Awkwardly, I tried to deflect attention from myself. The groups were switching, from Phase 1 to Phase 2. Brittany hears that I am around, so she comes to say hello to me during the break. We hug and she tells me that she is getting ready for release but is full of anxiety. She has been in touch with several of her ex-boyfriend-dealers who are vying for her attention and she is debating which one of them she should return to upon her release from prison.

We interrupt our conversation as the second phase's group begins to start. Phase 2 was significantly more inward-turning than Phase 1, whose activity was a health-related game based on knowledge. Today the session is on CRT (community recovery training). The theme today is "life is not fair." The women turn in their homework to the second facilitator, another young white woman. It's incredibly distracting to be the group in the main area because all around the other women who aren't in a program are doing chores, making a lot of noise. Two women almost get into a fight near the CO station where the guard peers out at everybody from the centralized control perch.

Finally, things seem to be settling down. One young white woman monopolizes the group conversation. She says, "Life is not fair" is like "Poor me! [another drink]."... Everyone laughs but the facilitator nods solemnly. The teacher writes up on the board: "Why can thinking this way lead to trouble? Seeing that life is not fair and that one may have been dealt a bad hand can be an excuse for not trying to make things better. The inner self must learn to listen and overcome the fears and grudges of habit self."

The program places a key thematic emphasis on defining the "habit self" and the "inner self" that are constantly in tension. According to the WRA, the "habit self" is "the part of you that is ruled by habits. . . . The habit self doesn't think. It just reacts on feeling and memory." In contrast, the "inner self" often loses out. It is "the part of you that is responsible, thoughtful, and reasonable. . . . The inner self doesn't get triggered into aggression or defensiveness like the habit self."

Philosopher William James, writing in a short treatise on habit, reflected deeply held American sentiments toward changing bad habits—namely, that it was largely one's own responsibility. He felt that one could not change one's habits by sheer desire to do so, but rather by endless grit and willpower and by altering one's neural circuitry with repetition. Every action, good or bad, was physiologically imprinted; as he wrote, "We are spinning our own fates, good or evil, and never to be undone. Every smallest stroke of virtue or of vice leaves its never so little scar."[19] The goal of changing one's habits included acting upon one's environment as well as one's internal forces, as the prison program emphasized.

If James's notion that we are constantly spinning our own fates is a consistent part of the American ethos, then Brittany's successes and failures to get off heroin could be seen as a logical consequence of her own bad habits and weak willpower. And what program could actually act on Brittany's force of habit for heroin and her inner and environmental cues to keep using? I wonder how, and in what ways, the Women's Recovery Academy will be able to instill moral fortitude in young women like Kaitlin or Brittany to ward off heroin use upon their release. The prison believes that emphasizing the awareness and power of one's inner self to make positive healthy decision is adequate treatment for opioid use disorder. At the same time, prison administrations refuse to begin or administer medical treatments like buprenorphine and methadone that both address powerful physiologic cravings that people have for opioids and that can protect them from possible opioid overdose death in the case that they do resume use.

GOING HOME OR GOING TO A HOUSE FULL OF DRUGS AND GUNS

The staff at the WRA program felt that Brittany was setting herself up for failure since she had decided that she did not want to go to a drug treatment program or a sober house upon her release. They recommend this option to most of the women, since the prison staff feel that an important part of succeeding after incarceration is having a stable place to go where they can possibly address some of the social factors that led to criminal involvement and incarceration. Where people return to vastly contributes to diverging outcomes, particularly between those who can go back to a place of stability and support and those who are forced back into a volatile situation or have no place they can call home.

Home can be a complex and fraught notion for women who struggle with addiction. In some cases, having family and simply a supportive place to go can provide a safe haven not only from drug use but also from the policing and supervision of the criminal justice system. Many of the women who leave prison resume drug use, but some are sheltered from being caught while others are bound up in systems of ongoing surveillance or exposure to policing and the criminal justice system.

The prison places a strong rhetorical emphasis on the importance of the programs that women attend in the communities after release. Once I attended a program fair at the pre-release facility where inmates milled about looking at a variety of drug treatment programs across the state. Some women look for places near home, while others try to flee their old stomping ground as part of their quest for sobriety.

Most prison discharge planning is centered on finding programs or sober/recovery housing for women. Traditionally, women have to be interviewed on the phone for admission to these programs, and there are many possible responses that could be disqualifying: a charge of violence; too many "mental health" issues; or simply not seeming serious or committed enough. Besides passing the interview process, ensuring that a bed at one of these programs will be available on the exact day you are released, with your "good time" factored in thus changing your actual release date, can be a difficult task. Being on medications such as buprenorphine or methadone can also be a barrier to living in a "sober" or "recovery" home, even if these medications are prescribed by a physician for you.[20]

In Brittany's case, she adamantly refused to go to a program or sober house after she left prison. When I see her a couple weeks before her "wrap" date (when she will "wrap" up her sentence), she is extremely anxious:

KS: The last time that we spoke you really wanted to go home and that's what you thought you needed to stay clean. Why can't you go home?

Brittany: She [her mother] is not letting me go home. Absolutely not.

KS: Why not?

Brittany: Because she's insane! I don't know. She's insane. She's stuck. She has it in her head that me coming home would just be horrible, a horrible idea.

KS: What does she think you're going to do?

Brittany: She thinks I'm going to use; she thinks I'm going to overdose; she thinks that I'm just going to be at the house getting nothing done. She doesn't want to have to deal with it. She doesn't want to have to be my taxi. She has a life, she doesn't want to have to "worry about me overdosing in my bed," those were her exact words. She's like harsh with it, she really does not care. "You've ruined my life for the past 6 years." She's kind of dysfunctional, we're going to fight.

Brittany mulls over the possibilities. She is currently talking to three different guys from her past. She half-heartedly asserts that she wants to avoid catching a "wicked bad habit." The wheels turn rapidly in her mind about who is the best positioned to give her a place to stay when

she is released. There is Corey, who is a drug dealer in one of the pros-
perous white Boston neighborhoods. He professes to love Brittany and
he readily supplies her drugs for free. He has been trying to cut back his
use, he tells her: "One shot of dope in the morning and he's not doing
ten more shots throughout the day, just one in the morning and taking
clonidine at night to sleep."

Then there is Nick, Brittany's most recent boyfriend. They haven't
talked for the last six or seven months while she's been incarcerated, but
they started talking now that Brittany is getting ready to leave. He lives
only five minutes away from her mom's house, so that would be perfect
for her. Nick isn't a heroin user ("he's an alcoholic and he'll eat benzos
sometimes"), so that is a potentially better option for her than going to
stay with Corey.

Finally, there is Paul who introduced Brittany to selling drugs when
she was sixteen. Brittany's mother hates Paul. Recently there has been
some tension, since Paul has been visiting her in prison and Brittany's
mother found out and threatened to no longer "take care" of her (stop
putting money into Brittany's canteen) if Paul kept coming to see her.
Paul had offered to get her an apartment upon her release.

Brittany's counselor in the WRA program is helping her look for
transitional living situations. Brittany protests, trying to explain why
she won't go to a sober house even though she has never been before.
She tells her counselor that she is sick of having rules and assigned beds
and no cell phone rules. Anyway, why does she need drug treatment
when she just completed a six-month residential drug treatment program at the prison? Brittany feels so anxious about her prospects that
she is having trouble sleeping and is having dreams about using drugs.
She tells me that she feels like everyone is "setting me up to fail and to
use and to go back selling drugs."

For one brief second, she levels with me instead of telling me what
she thinks I want to hear. "Honestly, I just want to get high," she tells
me. "I know it's bad." Even though she has to check in with probation,
she assumes she will use and then try to flush her system by drinking
lots of water several days before she goes to check in. She imagines that
she will eventually start selling drugs again "just to pay for probation
[fees] each month" that individuals must pay every month themselves.

. . .

Brittany is a successful graduate of the WRA program at the prison, so
I was particularly interested to see how much the program had been

able to change or help her. The next time I see her, I pick her up at a house "full of drugs and guns" in a far southern part of the state, a little bit over an hour away from Boston and past Gillette Stadium, where the Patriots play. She gives me the address of a house on a quiet street in a sleepy, working-class neighborhood, but it turns out this is not actually the house that she is staying at. I wait on the front porch of the wrong house while she straightens her hair several houses away.

On our way to a Dunkin' Donuts where she used to deal drugs, Brittany unleashes all of what has happened to her since she got out of prison. It's hard for me to absorb the torrent of unending, anxious speech that erupts. She tells me first that her dad picked her up the day she was released and got her a cell phone and paid for a hotel for her to stay in for two weeks. The plan was that she would then go live with Paul, who had offered her a place to stay but it wasn't ready yet.

The first night she stayed in the hotel, her ex-boyfriend Nick came over. According to Brittany, he seemed like a full-fledged heroin addict now, looking "all junked out," her derogatory term for the physical appearance of a strung-out, emaciated heroin user. They got high together, and the next day Paul came over with a friend, Johnny. Brittany began hanging out with Johnny, who also sold heroin.

The next night, Corey came over from his white, upper-middle-class neighborhood in Boston. It turned out that Corey was "still a raging addict, but not selling anymore like he used to because he's being watched. . . . He's only selling shit kind of, pretty much just to support his habit." Brittany was pissed because when Corey came over he didn't have any heroin on him to give to her and was "nodding out on benzos the whole time." She asked herself what good could he possibly be to her. They headed into Boston the next day, scored some drugs, and used them back at the hotel.

Johnny also pursued Brittany and, most importantly, let her stay at his house. Brittany was flattered by his pursuit, and she slept with him, despite the fact that he wanted her to be his girlfriend. She was irritated because she didn't want to be anyone's "girl." As she explained, "I just got out of jail, I need to get my shit together, I'm not going to be in any sort of relationship now. Mind you, I wasn't even attracted to him, so it's like, a dead issue."

She fussed with her straightened brown hair as she smoked a cigarette. I glanced over at her and realized that she was quite beautiful. I remember feeling despair recording her story about Johnny. She hated living with him, telling me, "I just wanted to be high the whole time, because I didn't even want to be there. I just wanted to stay high. He'd go out, make plays all day [do drug deals]. [He would ask] do you want to come, do you want to come? Nope, nope, I'm good. I just want to stay in this room, in a coma, please. I want to be comatose. I don't even want to be awake right now."

She was so unhappy with her living situation—essentially exchanging sex for drugs and a place to stay—that she reached out to a friend, Tracy, whom she met while she was in prison. She headed to Salem, Massachusetts, to stay with Tracy but quickly found herself "disgusted" by Tracy and her friends because they were "all junked out." The first night she stayed there they immediately asked her to go cash in her food stamps for money—an underground economy transaction often available at bodegas or convenience stores. Brittany protested, "I'm like, I don't do that. I actually use my food stamps for food . . . especially since I'm homeless and bouncing around." She left Tracy's to return to her father's house.

Her stepmother despised Brittany, so Brittany decided to reach out to an acquaintance, an older woman named Janet. Brittany's father gave Janet $400 to let Brittany stay there. She slept on a blow-up mattress in the same room as Janet's seventeen-year-old son. Janet was "jammed [high] on Perc5s," Brittany complained, even though "those are huge with Tylenol in them; it's disgusting to be sniffing them." She and Janet also fought over food stamps. Soon enough, Brittany was kicked out. While she was staying there, a two-year-old child also living in the house accidentally ate half of a buprenorphine-naloxone (suboxone) tablet off a coffee table that another girl had given to Brittany so that she could "get clean." They panicked and tried to slap him awake (following the common misconception that slapping or putting someone under a shower will reverse an overdose). No one wanted to bring him to the hospital, because automatically DCF (Department of Children and Families) would become involved. Every twenty minutes they frantically tried to wake him up until he finally vomited. Then Janet discovered a syringe in the house. She forced Brittany to leave.

Johnny drove over to pick her up from Janet's house and she was back to staying with him. She knew that it was dangerous for her to stay in Johnny's house, because if the police arrived, she could be rearrested and sent to jail, but she felt like she had limited options: "The cops, they want him so bad," she told me. "He has two open cases for Class A, and Class B, that are still open. They're non-stop partying, they're always fighting people in the parking lot. The cops show up here, they'll ask us about guns. They know we don't even have any guns. Well we do, but they don't know that we do." She told Johnny that he needed to take a break from dealing and get a new phone number, to not be so greedy when the cops were watching him. Brittany herself was taking a forced hiatus from dealing. She had lost her phone, had no contacts and no car. She couldn't sign on to her Facebook account because she forgot the password and had used a fake email address to sign up in the first place.

Much had changed in her town since her stint in prison: "Pills are hard to come by now; they're not as free flowing as when I went to jail. I was picking up a hundred a day, and eating all of them. . . . But everyone I know is shooting now. I pretty much got everyone hooked on [percs]. Everyone is shooting up now [a year later]." She laughed matter-of-factly.

Brittany planned to go live with her father in Vermont. He had gotten her a job in shipping and packing at his company. Even though she had to report to probation—which she felt kept her in line—she managed to work it out so that she would have urines taken at her father's company and send the results to the probation officer. One thing she felt was working to her advantage was that she was too poor to have enough money to get a serious habit (to use heroin daily would lead to physical dependence); her ability to get heroin was too erratic: "I should be dopesick right now, I haven't used in two days, and I'm not [dopesick]. I just can't afford it."

Brittany's outlook on life was dismal. When I asked her what she was most worried about in her life, she told me, "Probably that I'm not going to stay clean. At this point, I've already been to jail and done the whole thing. At this point, I think if anything's going to happen, I'm going to end up dead from it. . . . I don't see me going back to jail." She wasn't scared of dying, she just hated the feeling of being "clean and sober." But she also hated the life she was leading and subsequently was torn between worlds marked by divergent affects.

Many people in the throes of active heroin addiction simply aren't afraid to die; they risk dying every time they shoot up. As Brittany told me, "And [if] I'm selling drugs and I'm out of control, and I'm overdosing and stuff and if I go back to the point where I have nowhere to live and I'm bouncing around and I'm so dopesick and I'm poking myself a million times to try to find a vein because my arms are all fucked up, that is just such a bad fucked up place that I hope that I overdose and die."

When I later talked to Brittany, she told me she had developed another "wicked" habit in New Hampshire. She had gone over to Paul's house, overdosed there, and after waking up in the hospital, agreed to go to a detox program. She went from there to a twenty-eight-day treatment program for women in Boston, then to a halfway house for women. She left there and overdosed again, then spent ten days in a psychiatric hospital and entered another program.

Only 5 percent of people after a nonfatal overdose begin medication-assisted therapy in Massachusetts, according to state data from 2013–2014, even though they have been shown to decrease overdose and improve mortality.[21] Brittany was not one of this 5 percent. Brittany's experience with these medications was limited to detox programs, and according to NA and AA discourse, taking opioid agonist medications was not "clean"—rather, it might be known as "replacing a drug for another drug" as it frequently is claimed in these circles. AA has a powerful hold on most of the addiction treatment and recovery communities. It is free, and widely accessible in small and big towns alike as well as in prisons and jails. But it has an inward turning gaze, a religiosity, a fervor for abstinence, and a cult-like community atmosphere that can be off-putting for many.

Brittany's life after prison was staggering in its complexity, with its rotating cast of characters compounded by her own frenetic mobility. Neither life after prison nor life after treatment was by any means easy. The prison just could not account for her feeling of overall hopelessness, her desire to use heroin, and her unstable social situation. The prison had nothing to do with her mother's decision refusing to let her come home. How could they possibly treat a lifetime of bad habits and behaviors?

I wondered what might have happened if the prison had started Brittany on medication such as buprenorphine or methadone before she left prison or if they had set her up with a therapist or had even done both. If she had at least had one of these medications in her system, she certainly would have been protected against overdose, based on the psychopharmacology of the medications that serve as a protective mechanism in the brain. For example, buprenorphine binds more tightly to the opioid receptors in the brain, and if someone uses heroin or fentanyl after having taken the medication, the heroin and fentanyl are blocked from binding, decreasing risk of respiratory depression and/or fatal overdose. Could Brittany possibly have avoided some of her multiple post-prison overdoses if she had been able to access medication treatment?

I began to realize the enormity of the stigma against these medications that existed in jails and prisons. Medical staff would never cut someone off any other life-saving medications, but in many places, patients on buprenorphine or methadone who become incarcerated might be forced to withdraw. Would a doctor ever stop a patient's life-saving medication such as a statin, used to prevent a fatal heart attack, or insulin, pre-scribed to prevent a patient from life-threatening diabetic ketoacidosis? Only with addiction, I realized, is this ever the case.

WHAT WORKS?

Tina Stinson credits the WRA program for saving her life. I met Tina, a fifty-two-year-old woman hailing from the Midwest, at the local buprenorphine clinic where I was doing research on community treat-ment for opioid use disorder. With her oversized baggy sweatshirts, gray hair, and thin-rimmed bifocals, she appeared more like a frazzled grandmother than a former intravenous heroin user. She was smart, no-nonsense, and blunt. Even though she had lived in the northeast for many decades, she retained much of her Midwestern charm. Perhaps too trusting and friendly for Boston, she reflected once. Yet behind all her toughness, she was quick to cry, her expressive face softened by overwhelming emotion.

Tina related to me the unadorned facts of her life, including first and foremost that she was raped by her father from the age of nine until she was thirteen, at which point she became pregnant by her father and had a baby at fourteen. Originally from a sleepy town in Illinois, she started shooting heroin at age sixteen after her family blamed her for "trying to break the family up" and her older brother introduced her to the drug. Her mother either didn't know what was going on or looked the other way. Tina reflects on her mother now with pity, as her mother essen-tially couldn't read or write and was wholly dependent on her father for getting by in the world.

When Tina met a pimp in 1988, she traveled around the country for the next twenty years with a group of his "girls." She had five children by him, including two sets of twins. One of her twin boys was killed while leaving a convenience store in New York City in an attempted robbery for his $10 "gold" chain. Tina was incarcerated in MCI-Framingham at the time and the prison did not allow her to attend the funeral. It was just one more indignity heaped upon her by the carceral system that she knew all too well.

Tina had been incarcerated approximately thirty-two times, by her rec-ollection, all for non-violent addiction-related activities like shoplifting, larceny (over $250), and car theft. Her longest and most recent incarceration was at MCI-Framingham for four years for a "hand-to-hand" drug sale in a school zone, in which she received a sentence of three years and a day for the drug charge plus an additional mandatory year for being in a school zone. She had no option for parole, given the 1993 "Truth in Sentencing Act" that led to lengthier prison sentences for minor offenses. Tina admits she was involved in illicit deals, but in a minor way to fuel her habit. She had been a low-level part of a cocaine and heroin enterprise in a hotel in Revere, Massachusetts, yet the men she worked for actually signed statements saying she was the head of their operation and the state tried to prosecute her for fifteen years. Tina guffawed just thinking about it. Who could believe that a self-professed "junkie prostitute" could handle such an operation? The two men, Easy C and Big Chris, got less time than she did: two years and three years, respectively.

During that incarceration, Tina was "dopesick" when she first arrived. She was sent to the HSU and was kept for five days in a locked medical unit cell with five other women who were also "kicking it." While enduring her own physical discomfort, Tina vividly remembers the tortured cries of a young woman next door who was detoxing off methadone. It was around Christmas time and the girl was crying for help and crying out for her parents. Tina thinks that the guards disabled the woman's call button in in order not to hear her pleas. She and her cellmates called for the guards when that room had gone suddenly quiet. When the guards finally checked on her, they discovered that she had hung herself.[22] Tina shudders, recalling this still traumatic incident many years later. It is conventionally taught that withdrawing from methadone or heroin is unpleasant but not deadly. But the combination of emotional and physiological distress with the fraught circumstances of prison, including medical neglect, can obviously take a fatal toll. For many like Tina's neighbor, prisons and jails can represent a place of violence, not safety.

Tina vowed that she would get better from her heroin use, just as she had vowed many times before. Maybe this time would be different. Thus, she signed up to participate in the WRA program. She thought that many other women were taking the program for the seven and a half days of good time it offered per month (interestingly, men got twelve days of good time for taking the same class); her classmates were often unengaged, bored, or simply not serious. Class was also frequently suspended and interrupted by a state of lockdowns (where women were returned to their cells and not allowed to travel throughout the prison for any reason) that could happen for any minor matter out of place, for example, if the count of the spoons and forks in the cafeteria was off, or if there was a fight in the yard.

Tina recalls her teachers at the WRA program fondly, asking about them by name even though they are no longer there. She kept folders full of papers from that time and she gave me some of this literature to read. These included worn photocopies from the "12 Steps" series produced by Hazelden, a popular nonprofit addiction treatment recovery group; a guide to managing your cocaine addiction; and a guidebook for women's recovery and relapse. The literature exhorted having a positive attitude and taking responsibility for one's actions and thoughts.

Skimming over her papers, I read about triggers for drug use: "Getting paid; feeling stressed; bored, lonely, tired, angry, or depressed; feeling sexually aroused or deprived; holidays, weekends, and other celebrations; thinking or talking about using; being around other people who are using or talking about using." I thought about how hard, basically impossible, it was to avoid triggers if the entirety of one's life was made up of triggers. I recalled one woman who would get triggered driving down the highway and seeing the sign of the exit where she would go to score drugs. I recalled another woman who had to walk past a crack corner on the way to her doctor's office and another who simply felt guilty and bad looking at her son's face.

Tina enjoyed the education and treatment at the program, including a cognitive behavioral exercise she learned at the WRA program called "playing the tapes." Tina describes it this way: "We used to have to write out these things, what we did, what were the consequences, and how to, if it happened again, how to stop it again by playing the tape. You sit down and think about it before you act on it. You sit there and think about the consequences for selling drugs and getting caught. Instead of getting drugs and getting caught, get a real job, this way I have money, you know." She also liked the exercise of making life maps or using newspaper clippings to put together a timeline of one's life: "You got the using part, the part where you're at now, and where you want to see yourself in five years."

Tina graduated from the WRA program in Framingham and was reclassified to minimum security, so she was sent across the street to the prerelease facility where she participated in the graduate division of the same program. One condition of participating in that program was that they had to look for work or they would get written up for a D-report (disciplinary report). Tina found work at Bruegger's Bagels and accumulated over $7,000 in savings over three years.

When Tina was finally discharged from prison, she returned to the streets because she was actually released two weeks before her actual "wrap date" with her good time calculated in. Her caseworker at the prerelease had lined her up for a bed in a sober house on the date of her expected discharge, but there were no beds available the actual day she was handed her street clothes and the paltry few possessions that had been on her the day she was arrested. She begged the prison to let her stay until a treatment bed became available, but they told her that would be false imprisonment. There was no way she could stay.

Stressed and disgusted at an uncaring system, Tina was again on her own, as she always seemed to be. She had to fight the desire to use heroin. Heroin is what she had always used to treat her feelings of distress. After bouncing between friends' houses, she learned that an abusive ex-boyfriend was looking for her, so she hid from him by entering a three-month inpatient drug treatment program. From that program, she was introduced to the buprenorphine treatment clinic where she has been a patient ever since and where I met her many years later. She was stable; housed; happy; and, most importantly, alive, particularly proud that her life of incarceration seemed safely behind her.

Tina wonders if her successes were her own or if they were in part due to her prison treatment program. Did the prison drug treatment program actually deserve credit for "saving her life," as she remembers it? Sociologists of drug use might argue that Tina would have naturally aged out of drug use on her own as her ability to make money by hustling or prostituting diminished as she got older. Yet without early access to buprenorphine, she probably would have died. One longitudinal study of heroin users over the course of thirty years found that approximately half of a cohort of heroin users committed to a California civil program registry had died, and few were able to obtain abstinence from all substances, indicating heroin use disorder to be a chronic condition with high mortality.[23]

Tina is critical of the prison but also believes that it was part of her salvation. On the one hand, she feels like she was given no other option—no drug court, for example, that she would have certainly taken—and no options for treatment programs in the community, even though her lawyers fought for a program. "I think if I had went into a program and learned some of the stuff that I learned in jail, I think I could have been successful." It was hard to get treatment in the community and basically entailed getting on a number of waiting lists: "Even when people are out there seeking help, all the beds are full." Really the fastest way to access treatment was to get locked up and the longest period of "treatment" she had ever received in her life was while she was in prison.

What Tina valued most about the prison treatment program was its basic educational component, revealing the widespread dearth of health education for people using drugs in the community. She felt she was only properly educated about Hepatitis C and other health conditions she had when she was in prison in her forties. She also learned in prison that "for her opioid use disorder it took your body eighteen months to two years for it to get back right." She felt being incarcerated gave her an extended period of time to finally feel normal in her body after years of opioid use. She emphasized to me how important to her life that last time in prison was: "I think I wasn't arrested, I was rescued this time, for real. You know, I wish I could have got this time before."

Not surprisingly, many women like Tina embrace these dominant discourses of punishment and individual responsibility that dictate the course of their lives (recall that Serenity did as well, thanking God for sending her to prison). Sociologist Pierre Bourdieu suggests that this is the symbolic violence under which the poor live every day; they "regularly forget the economic and social conditions which make possible the ordinary order of practices."[24] People who use drugs are bad, as the dominant discourse states; therefore, they must be criminal, and punished for their crimes. In this sense, incarceration seems natural and inevitable. It is the natural order of things that preserves the existing hierarchy of power and the status quo. Yet what really saved Tina's life? Was it incarceration, the WRA program, or early access to the lifesaving medication buprenorphine upon her release? Or was it housing that she managed to obtain as a survivor of domestic violence, that protected her from the violence of men, the violence of the streets, or the criminalizing gaze of police?

Tina now rents a small one-bedroom apartment subsidized through the Boston Housing Authority. Prior to that, she lived for three years in a small, ten-woman sober house in Roxbury, where she was the house manager. She was voted in recently as the vice president of the community board of her building; she wants to clean up the building, starting with the front-desk officers, who sometimes have drugs or let drug dealers inside.

Yet Tina still struggles with a myriad of health issues, including kidney disease, Hepatitis C, high blood pressure, sleep apnea, chronic pain, anxiety, panic attacks, and PTSD that she felt were not well addressed in prison. She has also been shot in the leg, stabbed in the neck, and hit with a baseball bat by her ex-boyfriend. Perhaps even more than her physical conditions, she struggles with the ongoing trauma of her son's murder and not being able to properly grieve the violence of his death; she struggles with the knowledge that the daughter she had with her father, who was raised by her own mother and father, is now out in Ohio "drinking and doing drugs," refusing to participate in therapy with Tina about their distressing relationship.

Tina felt that the mental health care at the prison was poor at best, if not outright negligent, given the immense traumas all of the incarcerated women faced. Yet unlike many of the other women, who wanted any substance to help them ease the angst of simply living, Tina did not want "medications to numb me." She did not have easy access to a therapist even though she thought it would be useful. They told her after the murder of her son that "since you don't want to take the medications and stuff, you really don't need to see anybody [in mental health]."

Tina is by all accounts, to everyone that she encounters, a success, even though her quest for well-being is an ongoing project. Yet is she the prison's success? I presented Tina's case by interviewing Tina about her recovery at the Addiction Grand Rounds at our local public hospital before an audience of clinicians entrenched daily in the problems of substance use and misuse, in a place where drug use is ubiquitous and drug dealers run drugs up and down the floors to each other. The clinicians were inspired and impressed by Tina, but the question lingered: what individual qualities mixed with what structural aspects of health care were the formula for her success? It was a sad comment, someone said, that drug-using women would need a prison sentence of multiple years to recuperate from the violence in their lives on the outside.

Once Tina was released, she was one of the fortunate few to be able to find and enlist the help of a therapist, with whom she met at least once a month for five years. She also found strength in the idea of God and structure in the weekly NA and AA meetings that she attended. Importantly, she had received biochemical help with opioid agonist therapy in the form of buprenorphine, without which she might have had intolerable cravings. Luckily, the NA and AA groups she attended didn't mind that she was on medication to help her opioid use disorder, as many others reported they had been shunned or stigmatized for taking medications. She also has adopted two rambunctious young children, Julio and Amaya, and these children serve to keep her motivated. Their biological father is blind, on methadone for chronic pain, and barely able to play with them; their biological mother is out in the streets using intravenous heroin and now pregnant with her third child.

I spoke with a female senior-level prison official who told me she felt that women were particularly recalcitrant patients compared to male inmates: "The women," she explained to me, "Their problem is codependency." She continued, with increasing levels of frustration evident in her voice, "I wish these women would just stand up straight for once on their own. They are smart, they can do it, they just don't do it." She asked me if I was surprised how much programming there was available at the prison and in the community generally. Angrily, she said, "There is so much programming out there and the women don't go! They just don't go!"

I left her office slightly defeated by this attitude, which is endorsed by some officials. The prison refused to recognize the oppressive macroeconomic and sociological forces in the lives of incarcerated women. Instead, it was much easier for them to view women as decontextualized rational actors in which addiction was a bad choice, a decision to be a bad or absent mother, where not getting better was another failure in a string of bad choices.

This rhetoric of self-sufficiency is nothing new. It channels the American ethos of pulling oneself up by one's own bootstraps. It is echoed when Tina is told to play back the tapes in her mind before she chooses to engage in criminal behavior. Similarly, it echoes in the actions of the prison that largely left Tina to fend for herself upon her release. Only through an odd combination of lucky circumstances and resolve did Tina even make it through the first two weeks of release without using or overdosing.

Casting Tina's situation as essentially a failure of self-will also obviates recognizing the political economy of addiction and how addiction is a culturally mediated and produced affliction; her failures are her own moral responsibility and a reflection of low internal stores of strength and willpower, not a harsh, gendered outcome of trauma or multigenerational poverty. As the whiteboard in the group treatment common space of the prison cottage read, turning one's life of crime around entailed a mental shift in attitude: "Life is 10% what happens and 90% how we read it. <u>We cannot change the inevitable</u>!!!"

RECONCILING SUBSTANCE USE DISORDER TREATMENT
WITH INCARCERATION

Much of the drug treatment programming offered in prisons and jails just did not take. For example, at the WRA program, women did not necessarily embrace joining a metaphorical family of their peers and their largely upper-middle class counselors in a therapeutic community when the majority of them lamented for their own children or families on the outside. In fact, the very fact of being incarcerated was a necessary and always painful abdication of their roles as mother or wife or girlfriend or daughter. These ongoing failures to fulfill very real social roles caused them significant ongoing pain and guilt, which at times could fuel ongoing destructive substance use.

Incarceration, by its very nature, is about alienation and deprivation. The WRA drug-treatment programs stress freedom as a theme: women should free themselves from chemical constraints, from abusive relationships, from their traumatic pasts. Unfortunately, for the majority of women who are incarcerated, their lives after prison will not include such freedoms. This is partly a lack the structural opportunity to be free. It takes resources—financial, social, educational, community-based—to even possibly access the luxuries afforded from these freedoms.

Drug treatment programs in prisons and jails do little to address the structural violence that largely defines these women's lives. The fact of incarceration itself represents a further scarlet letter of stigma and shame that has not only social repercussions but also political and legal ones. Prison- and jail-based treatment programs cannot treat the desire to dissociate from the world that is the precise reason why so many women turn to heroin in the first place. And very few women are able to actually utilize their newly acquired cognitive-behavioral tools and techniques under the stress of homelessness, lack of income, or difficult family relationships upon release, as was the case with Brittany.

For the majority of women, the everyday vagaries of life—one's social status, relationships, and simply a sense of being-in-the-world—matter more than the big picture of their lives. Kaitlin, for example, was concerned with how she going to get enough money to get heroin for that day. In fact, by existing in the most present form of life for what appears to be short-term gains they defy middle-class normative expectations of future orientation. And for incarcerated and formerly incarcerated women, the isolated focus on drug use sometimes seems wrong. What would it look like to instead care about healing and spiritual and physical transformation and well-being?

Prison programs differ significantly in many ways from their community counterparts. One of the most obvious is that people engaging in treatment in the community can leave of their own accord. It allows them some agency, some sense of control, even to make bad decisions. Undergoing treatment takes some effort, prioritization, and attempts at little positive changes in one's life. In the prison, the drug treatment program has several coercive elements. It is a prison, after all. Making a bad decision (for example, to use drugs that are available in prison) can result in a disciplinary report, being sent to the Close Custody Unit (CCU, "the hole" or solitary confinement) and being dropped immediately from treatment (even though it is being taught in the program that addiction is a relapsing, remitting disorder marked by ongoing slip-ups).

Everything about prison treatment is a construct, an otherworldly reality in a space intended for punishment. The relationships that people have with staff or counselors, or even friendships or romantic relationships, are often fleeting and transient. Even if they wanted to, it is not considered professional for counselors to reach out to clients who have been released. Even if women seem to do well at treatment, like Brittany, who never used drugs once inside even though they tend to be available ("I was too scared," she told me once) and who successfully graduated the treatment program, her abstinence was a by-product of a combination of artificial rules and regulations that do not and cannot exist in the community.

Although community-based treatment programs can have their own seemingly arbitrary or harsh rules, they more closely mimic the reality of everyday life. One of the women I followed closely, named Jane, relapsed to heroin use after she let a drug dealer stay at her apartment and he accidentally left a large quantity of drugs known as a finger (approximately ten grams) in her house. She checked into a twenty-eight-day residential treatment program, but at that program she was not completely separated from her life. She could still attend court dates for custody of her children, she saw her children every weekend, and she could still go to her doctors' appointments. Her decision not to use was her choice and it was what she wanted at that time in her life. It was a much closer approximation of her actual life, including the constant possibility of day-to-day drug use and the circumstances that she would return to once she finished the program.

What do women hope for when they leave prison drug treatment programs? They measure their lives in hours and days, the rewarding smile of a child, the chance to reconnect joyfully with a friend from the streets. They prioritize handling the immediate stressors of homelessness, hunger, and not having clothes. Their health and often their drug use or lack thereof is understandably a fairly low priority. In fact, using drugs or accessing medication sometimes is a means of chemically stabilizing themselves so they can get some of these other priorities addressed.

While doing this research, I hoped that women would advocate for programs that would actually start them on opioid agonist therapy during their incarceration either at the initial intake or even a couple weeks or a month prior to release from prison. This would make the immediate aftermath of release less risky for overdose and was a critical component to the success of many patients like Tina. As a physician, this seemed like a humane and evidence-based approach to the problem of opioid use disorder, but it was seen as radical and costly and a shocking idea to prison administrators. Many women said they would have embraced such a program as a saving grace, but just as many thought that in doing so they would jeopardize their newly found, prison-based abstinence, consistently reflecting the American belief that total abstinence from substances was the only right course of action.

What women wanted most of all, desperately, was some kind of absolution. They wanted forgiveness for their sins, to be washed clean and able to start anew, as noted by many others in their work including anthropologist-physician Helena Hansen in her 2018 work on addiction in Puerto Rico.[25] Yet achieving this was easier said than done. Part of this meant a new orientation to their relationships with themselves. One program, called TIMBo, offered in the prison seemed to be a novel and possibly sustainable approach to self-care in a genuinely sustainable way. Developed by a community of yoga practitioners, the TIMBo program was "developed specifically for women suffering from chronic trauma, addiction, and/or abuse and offers women the tools needed to address the psycho-social, emotional, and physiological root causes, and enabling them to heal from trauma and to improve emotional regulation."

After completing the eight-week program, most women in prison noted significantly lower symptoms of anxiety and trauma as well as an increase in writing/journaling, meditation, and yoga practice. One participant told the staff, "I have re-found my faith in myself and my confidence. Life hasn't been as much of a struggle." The TIMBo program approached women as empowered and capable beings and gives them practical day-to-day skills for emotional regulation and cultivation of inner strength.

Yet emotional and spiritual growth in the context of ongoing structural violence is hard to achieve. The Women's Recovery Academy program stresses that "recovery is a growth process of overcoming both substance abuse and criminal behavior. Recovery is making lifestyle changes." They emphasize it "is possible for just about anyone who really wants it and works at it." Unfortunately, even undergoing the six-month treatment at the prison or even shorter stints of treatment at the jail just cannot erode years of habits and ways of adapting to lives of hardship. It cannot erase the fraught relationships to which people return that are simultaneously abusive, loving, and dysfunctional. The process of recovery is an individual one, but it is the norm, not the exception, to engage in treatment intermittently over the course of years before gaining what may seem like the trappings of clinical or individual life stability. Being incarcerated can make recovery even harder to achieve, posing a significant, irreparably damaging step backward for many, given the stigma, shame, and a demoted social status of being formerly incarcerated.

What women on heroin tell me that they enjoy most about shooting up intravenous drugs is the absence of psychic pain and distress. They tend not to define themselves by abjection, suffering, hardship, or trauma, although these are often integral components of many of their lives and routinely portrayed as such in the media. Rather, they seek out and cling to the small moments that make life worthwhile.

Tina, now with several years since her last heroin use, gets to hold Julio, a squirming two-year-old, in her arms and curl out his long locks. She delights in making a video on her phone of the two children doing a hula dance for the building's barbecue party. Full of childish ease, they force her out of her past sadness and her own dysfunctional relationship with her estranged daughter in Ohio. She worries about the children and not herself. How could she possibly think about anything else, when Amaya can't even spell her own name yet and she's already four years old? She needs to learn as soon as possible, Tina believes. She's going to do everything in her power to teach her how to spell her name.

4

Discipline, Punish, and Treat Trauma?

Mission Statement: The Massachusetts Department of
Correction's mission is to promote public safety by managing
offenders while providing care and appropriate programming
in preparation for successful reentry into the community.
Manage—Care—Program—Prepare

Vision Statement: The Massachusetts Department of
Correction's vision is to effect positive behavioral change
in order to eliminate violence, victimization and
recidivism.

—Spencer, *Massachusetts Department of Correction Strategic Plan*
  2013–2018

Alisha Hayes was tugging her curves into a red sequined mini-skirt
in the humid oppressive heat of Boston's Chinatown. She spent at
least two hours getting ready before work every day, with an elaborate
routine involving extensions, wigs, dresses, stilettos, and smoky eye
makeup. The competition among sex workers in the area known as the
"Combat Zone" was fierce. She was forced to compete with the Miss
America, blonde, blue-eyed wholesome-looking girl who had just
arrived on the block from Michigan. Alisha was hoping her extra curves
would give her the edge tonight. She also liked to act and look a little
bit crazier than everyone else to set herself apart, to keep her potential
customers' interest piqued.

Her pimp and lover, Dynamite, looked on, at times with disinterest
and occasionally with flashes of encouragement. "Baby, let's get this
money," he said encouragingly. She finished carefully applying purple

mascara to her long fake eyelashes. Alisha was only seventeen, but she had slept with more men than she could count on two hands.

Alisha got into Dynamite's new convertible. She didn't even know Dynamite's last name, even though they had been hooking up as a duo for over two years. She thought that he was maybe thirty-seven or thirty-eight. They were driving to their usual spot when a beat-up Toyota Camry accelerated toward them. Dynamite swerved away, forced to brake suddenly to avoid hitting the Camry and nearly slammed into a fire hydrant. Alisha heard heavy footsteps approaching and looked up to see her cousin Tommy and his girlfriend Cassandra.

Tommy dragged Dynamite out of the car and used a pistol to whip him in the head and chest. "How could you pimp out my baby cousin?" he demanded. "Who the fuck do you think you are?"

Tommy, who had just gotten out of jail, always referred to Alisha as "his favorite cousin." Alisha remembered growing up with Tommy in the Boston projects known as OP (short for Orchard Park) in Roxbury. When she was six years old, he used to throw her a five-dollar bill and command her to bury his guns in the scraggly shrubs of the housing project. She was expert at scraping out shallow holes for guns or drugs and covering them up with the broken tricycle and plastic pails that littered their small stretch of yard.

Alisha grabbed a small knife from her right boot and stabbed Cassandra in the arm. "How could you ruin this for me?" she yelled at Cassandra. "Dynamite and I aren't hurting nobody. We're in love!"

When the police showed up, Dynamite, who was already on parole for what was then known as "white slavery," was arrested and sent back to prison for assault. Cassandra lied to the police, telling them that Dynamite had stabbed her, so that Alicia wouldn't get arrested.

Alisha was then left on her own without a pimp—a dangerous situation known as "renegading." As she explained: "I got pimps trying to get at me, because they're like, her man's locked up, what the fuck is she doing down here. They're trying to rob me, since I was making thousands of dollars a night." Her one goal at that point was finding a new running partner, since being alone on the streets was not only uncomfortable, it was dangerous. So, when she met a beautiful woman named Jade, she felt lucky to hook up with someone so beautiful and powerful. Jade took Alisha into the world of high-end elite sex work, with clients paying up to $500 an hour for time with her in Boston's Back Bay hotels.

It was through Jade that Alisha was first exposed to drugs. Initially it was oolies (marijuana cigarettes laced with cocaine) and then simply the high-end powder cocaine that her clients procured and used. Alisha moved in with Jade until Jade was arrested and extradited to New York to do a four- to five-year bid in state prison for selling drugs. When Jade was arrested, Alisha, in desperation, used the entire stash of cocaine left in the house. Feeling panicky, with increasing paranoia brought on by the drug, she called a friend who brought over some heroin "to bring her down." Eventually, over the course of a month of continuous intranasal use, Alisha began to snub cocaine for heroin, as she developed a physical dependence on opioids: "I don't want any coke, I wanted dope."

The dope led her to dangerous places. She remains haunted by what happened in the Heath Street field of the Jamaica Plain neighborhood of Boston. Alisha recalled stepping into a van, assuming she was doing some $10 or $20 sex work. The man driving the van looked at her strangely, as if trying to place her in his memory, then he continued driving her over to a field. She looked up when he parked the van, only to see a gun barrel pointed at her.

The man grabbed a pillow from his backseat. "Alisha, it's gonna be quick. It's gonna be quick." She felt the sting of a cold gun on her arms and shoulders as she tried to fight off his blows. At one point, she bit him on his shoulder, on his tattoo of Jesus Christ. The last thing she remembered was waking up in the Heath Street field alone and naked, in the throes of opioid withdrawal.

She called out for help, and several passersby called the police. An ambulance arrived after five long minutes. But she refused to go to the hospital. She had to get rid of the sickness. Her skin was standing on end and the nausea was overwhelming.

Blood was pouring out of some gashes on her head, and the paramedics implored her to go the hospital for stitches, but she signed several sheets of paper absolving them of responsibility for her refusal to seek medical care. The police dropped her off in Orchard Park, at a "random house that I told them I lived at, and I remember asking at a different door for stuff because I was [dope] sick."

. . .

Alisha's counselors at the Suffolk House of Correction, the main Boston jail, taught Alisha about domestic violence and told her she was clearly a survivor, a victim of many traumas. At her twelfth stint in jail, Alisha heard, "You have a diagnosis of posttraumatic stress disorder, or PTSD." The former sheriff, an imposing African American woman named Andrea Cabral, had been a district attorney who devoted much of her energies to prosecuting domestic violence and professed that incarcerated women like Alisha had a special place in her heart. At a community meeting the sheriff attended, she interrupted presentations about the plight of incarcerated women to say that 70 percent of women in prison had been victims of sexual abuse or domestic violence before age seventeen. The sheriff demanded from the jail staff that there be substantial programs for the women who were survivors of so much trauma.

Trauma, whether it is explicitly called that or not, is at the core of prisons and jails everywhere. Prisons must confront, manage, and directly or indirectly address trauma on an everyday basis on multiple levels. In the past fifteen years in Massachusetts and around the country, there has been a shift in correctional trends toward explicitly responding to this trauma. In 2005, MCI-Framingham sought to become a "trauma-informed prison" as part of a "trauma-informed criminal justice system."[1] But why did this turn toward addressing trauma in the prison systems occur, and what were the implications of doing so?

I felt uneasy about Alisha's treatment in jail for several reasons. First, I wondered what such recognition of her own traumas did to her sense of self as a young African American woman who used drugs and engaged in sex work. But I also wondered about the political-economic and historical reasons that the prison had become a place for the treatment of traumatized, impoverished women facing addiction or substance use problems. What were the unintended consequences of situating trauma treatment into a carceral space?

. . .

In tracing the narrative of her life, it is difficult for Alisha to pinpoint where she thinks things went wrong. Perhaps it began when her mother, a woman struggling with a diagnosis of paranoid schizophrenia, tried to kill her as a newborn baby by stuffing bottles down her throat and then leaving her for dead. Or maybe it was when she was eleven, and had just gotten her period for the first time, and her fifteen-year-old boyfriend, Billy Soto, got her pregnant.

Alisha was thirteen when she got out of Division of Youth Services for her involvement in an armed robbery. At DYS, even though she had grown up around drugs for almost as long as she could remember, Alisha got high for the first time. This was where she first learned how to crush up and sniff pills of all varieties. It was fun, a genuinely pleasurable experience in a world of sadness and neglect. All her schooling was conducted at DYS, and she recounts sadly that the last time she was in public school was elementary school.

After she left DYS, Alisha returned to Orchard Park and sold drugs, mostly marijuana. She ran the streets, smoking cigarettes and weed and drinking 40s (beers). Then she met a nineteen-year-old man named Diego, who was originally from Honduras. When she got sent back to DYS for another infraction for possible participation in another armed robbery, Diego sent her little boxes of chocolate with long notes proclaiming his unending love. When she was released, she moved in with him. He was a doting boyfriend, and she had never felt that kind of intense love before. Growing up had been a lonely experience, since her mother had abandoned her to the care of her aunt, while her father—a "dopefiend," in her recollection—had fourteen children and did not concern himself with Alisha or any of his other offspring.

Diego became extremely jealous and would leave Alisha for days on end in their dark, one-bedroom apartment in Dorchester. "It got to the point that he was putting his cousin's dogs outside the doors because they didn't know me, so if I opened the door, they would bite me because they didn't know me." He would beat her for any reason—because he thought her skirts were too short or he thought it took her too long to come back from the store when she went out. She reasoned according to the bizarre logic of coexisting love and violence, "It's weird, I did know at some point, he did love me in a way, I just don't know if he knew how to show it. . . . He made sure I had clothes, that I ate, that I had sneakers; he took care of me."

Eventually, Alisha tried to leave Diego and return to her home in Orchard Park. Her sister and her aunt Rhonda (whom she thinks of and refers to as her mother) had arrived to help bring her things back to their house.

When Diego arrived home and found her packing with her family, he let loose a string of jealous epithets. He pushed Alisha's sister against the wall and punched her in the face. Alisha screamed for him to stop. Her aunt Rhonda, an imposing stately churchgoing woman, lunged at him, and he used a phone cord to tie up Rhonda's wrists. He grabbed Alisha, dragging her out in the yard by her hair and pummeled her with his fists. When neighbors heard the screaming, Diego jumped into his car and tried to drag Alisha in behind him. The all-too-common wail of police sirens approaching interrupted him and he drove off without Alisha. He was eventually caught and sentenced to four years in prison. "That was the end of that relationship," Alisha recounted simply.

Alisha herself was no stranger to jail. Getting beat up was a fact of life, just like getting locked up. For young African American men, and increasingly women, who grow up in Orchard Park, as sociologist Bruce Western has observed, incarceration is a more common life phenomenon than college.[2] All the guards at Suffolk House of Correction knew her by name. She had grown up alongside them, the baby-faced guards who policed her cells. Each time she became incarcerated, more of them had been promoted to lieutenants and sergeants and no longer did the stressful and time-consuming front-line jobs in the cellblocks. They had since become supervisors with coveted desk jobs now; when they saw her, they chastised her, "What the fuck are you doing here? Alisha, you look good, you're smart!"

None of her life circumstances were significantly different each time that she left jail (by her recollection, she has been incarcerated approximately twelve times), but this last time, she was coming to realize that her life is defined by trauma, by PTSD, which is "just from going through everything. . . . I've been stabbed, I've been in mad shit. Everything that I've been through I've been through myself, no family, nothing."

THE UBIQUITY OF TRAUMATIC EXPERIENCE

Alisha's life story represents the depth, chronicity, and magnitude of traumatic events in the lives of women with substance use problems. Sadly, Alisha's story is not atypical. Around 80 percent of women with substance use problems report a history of physical abuse, sexual abuse, or both, and rates of women with both substance use and PTSD range from 30 to 59 percent.[3] Women moved within many realms of traumatic experiences: physical traumas/accidents, rape, getting hit, having ongoing unsafe relationships. They were generally able to give a long litany of horror stories—in a shockingly matter-of-fact fashion—that constituted the plain reality of their ill-fated lives. There was the time Donna was fifteen and saw her mom get raped, or the time that Lydia saw her girlfriend murdered. Almost everyone had witnessed overdoses, some fatal.

Alisha told me that she had been "raped a lot of times [while engaging in sex work]. . . . Still, you know, it's traumatic to have, like, five guys hold you down." Others, like Alice, recounted getting beat up:

"My father was very abusive, and he would take rice and throw it on the hardwood floor and make us kneel on it for hours." Boyfriends were a constant source of precarious, sometimes transient, safety for many women who became homeless. Gabriella recounted: "He [my boyfriend] would hit me, burn me with crack stems, he raped me a few times. Stalked me, chased me with machetes, hid them under dumpsters all over [town]. . . . Some of the old little Spanish ladies used to hide me in their houses. They were all scared of him."

Jails have become collectively the largest providers of mental health in the American landscape.[4] Women often become incarcerated before they access any medical or mental health care services. Because of these lived experiences of violence, PTSD often becomes part of a long list of mental health diagnoses that they are given over the years (others include anxiety, depression, bipolar disorder, and borderline personality disorder). I found that women used the term trauma and PTSD almost interchangeably, even though PTSD is a formal psychiatric diagnosis with specific criteria. According to the *Diagnostic and Statistical Manual* (DSM-V), PTSD requires meeting specific signs and symptoms from different cluster categories, including experiencing a direct trauma, witnessing one, or aiding in a traumatic event; persistent symptoms and re-experiencing of the events; and duration of the symptoms greater than one month.[5]

Many incarcerated women that I spoke to often had physiological disturbances such as sleep dysregulation or nightmares. Yet it was difficult to tease out if the irritability and sleep disorders stemmed from PTSD symptoms or rather from the unique deprivations of liberty caused by incarceration: the lights were on all night or it was freezing cold or there were too many other women up making sleep impossible or you had to stand for count. For women in prison, the concept of trauma did not perfectly align with formal psychiatric definitions. Rather, it encompassed a sense of constant material and relational uncertainty in spaces of extreme marginalization. These symptoms they felt—of irritability and sleep disturbances—were precisely what incarceration had intended to imprint on women's bodies.

At the same time, prison and jail programming staff were becoming increasingly sensitized to the experiences of women like Alisha. There was a growing national awareness of trauma, especially after the federal agency Substance Abuse and Mental Health Services Administration (SAMHSA) sponsored a unique, five-year, multi-sited study in 1997 called the Women, Co-Occurring Disorders and Violence Study.[6] The study showed, not surprisingly, that the women and their children who received these trauma-informed interventions had significantly more positive outcomes than those who received services as usual.[7]

In Massachusetts, the Institute for Health and Recovery (IHR), based out of Cambridge, was one of nine national sites selected to implement the intervention arm of providing trauma-informed services. As a result of their work with community partners across the state, there was growing awareness of the importance and centrality of trauma to all ongoing treatment work and service provision.

The state prison system was additionally prompted to examine its own practices regarding trauma and violence within their walls after the murder of a high-profile inmate and former Catholic priest named John Geoghan while in Department of Correction (DOC) custody in 2003.[8] The governor at the time, Mitt Romney, ordered a review of eighteen areas of specific investigation throughout the state prison system; one of these areas included the state of women in prison. This resulted in a year-long investigation and a subsequent Dedicated External Female Offender Review.

The notion of female difference ran throughout the review. Their report noted that women in Massachusetts were sent farther away than men from their home communities to serve their sentences, simply because there were much fewer DOC facilities for women than for men. This had a detrimental effect on reentry efforts, since families were much less likely to visit and maintain connections with incarcerated women over these longer distances. The commission authors also noted inadequate screening of women with mental illness or significant medical needs.

Trauma was a central organizing theme in the report. Among the gender-specific medical needs of women, one of the major findings was the fact that the "majority of female offenders have trauma-related histories that negatively impact their health status and their successful utilization of health care services."[9] The recommendations of the commission were to train staff and change protocols to become "trauma-informed." The trauma subgroup found that 90 percent of the women in the mental health treatment at MCI-Framingham had known trauma histories and that the staff at the substance use treatment program in the prison reported similar prevalence of trauma among clients. The authors of the report wrote that "the absence of a trauma-informed environment and truly integrated health, mental health, substance abuse, and other support, puts women offenders at risk of under-utilization of needed health-related services, reduced benefit from services accessed, potential re-traumatization, and increased recidivism and behavioral and health risk upon return to the community."[10]

The trauma focus group also recommended a change in the largely fragmented ecology of care within the prison system. They argued for more coordination and communication across the various sectors of the prison, which largely did not happen because various medical and social services had been contracted out to a variety of vendors with their own record systems and their own staff. In MCI-Framingham at the time, substance use treatment services were run by Spectrum, an external non-profit agency, while mental health services were contracted to MHM, a vendor based out of Virginia. Additionally, some services were provided by the prison employees themselves or outside volunteers. The disparate groups of providers often only communicated with security staff after incidents such as fist fights occurred, not before.

SEEKING SAFETY?

Alisha was a fighter, and sometimes coming back to jail was a relief from the constant struggles in her life. When Alisha arrived back in Suffolk House of Correction jail for the tenth time in her life, she sighed as she heard the "trap" doors close behind her yet again. She hoped she could see the psychiatrist soon, since she felt she definitely needed a new medication. The last time she had been incarcerated, the medication they had tried (ziprasidone, an atypical antipsychotic) had made her mouth and jaw twitch out of place, a possibly permanent and stigmatizing side effect known as tardive dyskinesia. She hadn't continued any medications when she was released.

Alisha oddly felt safe coming back here, especially because of the familiar faces and names of staff who had watched her grow up over the years. Little did she know that the jail administrators were trying to make the facility safer by addressing the effects of trauma on and for women like Alisha. Yet could the facility itself be considered a "safe" space to address such sensitive subjects?

In Boston, the two local jails, the Suffolk House of Correction—known colloquially as South Bay—and the Nashua Street Jail, had been beset by recent scandals. The Nashua Street Jail located in downtown Boston, built to replace the historic Charles Street Jail, was a facility for seven hundred individuals awaiting trial. Suffolk County House of Correction, which opened in 1991 to replace the aging Deer Island facility (a jail facility located on an island in the Boston Harbor), had a capacity for one thousand two hundred fifty inmates but housed as many as nineteen hundred at any one time. The South Bay facility was equipped to hold both pretrial detainees as well as men and women who had been sentenced to time less than two and a half years, since the prisons were so overcrowded.

Both Nashua Street and Suffolk County House of Correction suffered from scandals within the first decade they were open under the leadership of the Sheriff Richard Rouse. At Nashua Street, a young woman named Katrina Mack came forward about being strip-searched after being arrested for driving under the influence.[11] On behalf of 5,400 women who had passed through the Nashua Street facility between 1995 and 1999—including Tina Stinson who recalled being strip searched there "at least ten times"—Mack sued Suffolk County, Sheriff Rouse, a female correctional officer, and the City of Boston, for her and others' injuries caused by unconstitutional strip searches, a violation against their Fourth Amendment rights prohibiting unreasonable searches. Suffolk County at the time had a policy that all women be strip searched, while men who were similarly detained after being arrested were not routinely searched.[12]

Federal Judge Nancy Gertner ruled in this case that the City of Boston and Suffolk County were guilty of violating the civil rights of these women and ordered restitution in the form of $5 million each from both the City of Boston and Suffolk County; the City of Boston paid in 2002 and the Suffolk County Department of Correction received $2 million appropriation from the State Legislature after it could not raise the money. The policy on strip searches was changed after the settlement to conduct strip searches of women only if there was probable cause (the same policy that was used for men).

As a result of the Nashua Street scandal, women were no longer detained there; instead, they were all moved to the $115 million modernized county facility at South Bay in Newmarket Square just off I-93 near Boston Medical Center. It perhaps was not a safer or better place for women to be. Almost concurrently as the Nashua Street civil lawsuit was being filed, a woman alleged that she had been sexually abused by a correctional officer there named David Mojica while she had been detained at Suffolk House of Correction. There was evidence that there was rampant sexual activity and corruption among the guards and health care staff. Inmates in sexual relationships with the guards could leave their cells and eat take-out Chinese food or obtain heroin from officers who would transport it for them from male inmates also housed in the facility. The jail facility unsuccessfully tried to keep the scandal internal.[13]

. . .

The deprivations of liberty and the extreme power differentials between staff and inmates caused by incarceration can lead to predictable consequences that stem from the lack of essential freedoms. It is the very architecture, process, and goals of incarceration that make these facilities sites of suffering and possible coercion.

Jail and prison staff ready themselves for potential flares of prior PTSD upon women's arrival; as one mental health caseworker at the prison told me, "A lot of that stuff [trauma] can certainly be exacerbated in a penal environment. . . . Any correctional institution is going to trigger people who are more vulnerable to PTSD just by the nature of the environment, so we expect a lot of that to surface." Thus, the mental health team actively seeks to work against unearthing trauma and minimizing potential damage caused by becoming incarcerated.

Jail and prison mental health staff begin the process of triage based on an initial intake nursing evaluation of all women who enter the facility conducted within twenty-four hours; they cannot treat everyone equally, so they must carefully assess a woman's risks and needs. They are particularly on the lookout for women with previous suicide attempts or self-injurious behaviors. These women pose a special risk to themselves—as well as to the facility's image as a safe, caring and rehabilitative space. The prisons have learned this the hard way. Every year, several women try to or succeed in hanging themselves at MCI-Framingham. Yet at the time of several deaths in 2009, two mental health positions had just been cut and two unfilled positions were eliminated from MCI-Framingham's mental health staff.[14]

Because prisons and jails are playing defense against potential suicides, the majority of the women entering prison suffer from the benign neglect of the triage process if there are no major red flags. One-on-one counseling tends to be rare, while group counseling is much more common and cheaply provided. Women can elect to participate in some kinds of programming once stabilized.

One of the trauma-focused groups at MCI-Framingham is known as Victims of Violence and is run by the in-house drug treatment vendor, Spectrum Health Services, using a widely regarded curriculum called Seeking Safety, written by Lisa Najavits, a trauma researcher at McLean Hospital/Boston University.

"Safety" became a popular buzzword in trauma treatment after the publication of psychiatrist Judith Herman's influential 1992 treatise on trauma.[15] In *Trauma and Recovery*, Herman argued that there were three stages of trauma treatment: (1) Safety, (2) Mourning (trauma processing) and (3) Reconnection. Najavits named her program Seeking Safety to represent Stage-1 work to specifically treat co-occurring PTSD and substance use. Najavits described the main goal of the program as establishing a sense of safety first and foremost: "When a person suffers from both substance abuse and PTSD, the most urgent clinical need is to establish safety. "Safety" is an umbrella term that includes discontinuing substance use; reducing suicidal and self-harm behaviors such as cutting; minimizing HIV exposure; ending dangerous relationships, such as with abusive partners and drug-using friends; and gaining control over extreme symptoms such as dissociation, or 'spacing out.'"[16] Along with colleagues at Brown University, Najavits assessed the effectiveness of the Seeking Safety curriculum in a small pilot based at a women's prison. They concluded that the treatment was a promising intervention for incarcerated women with PTSD and substance use disorders because it targeted "many of the deficits found in this population that may interfere with their recovery and place these women at risk for reoffending, such as impulsiveness, anger dyscontrol, and maladaptive life activities."[17]

This program particularly appealed to the prison treatment environment in which the deficits of women's thoughts and behaviors were the main target of intervention. And there was an emphasis on instilling and cultivating lofty ideals that female prison reformers had historically espoused. The program, comprised of twenty-five different topic areas, sought to restore hope among inmates and minister to their demoralization with a special emphasis on positive attributes and forward-thinking language, emphasizing respect, care, healing, and overall wellness.

Yet many women I met did not even try to enroll in the class, some professing that the prison was not a safe space for them generally to take any treatment at all. Perhaps they sensed that the prison was, by its very nature, antithetical to achieving the goals of Seeking Safety. Jean once told me that when she was at MCI-Framingham, she didn't "choose to share anything with my case worker." She elaborated, "I wasn't ready to deal with trauma, I had a nasty attitude and didn't want to be bothered. I wanted to do my time and get up out of there. . . . I want to deal on my own time with real, professional people [in the community] not these people that MCI-Framingham had working for them."

Prison scholar Megan Sweeney encountered similar narratives of mistrust and fear of therapy in her research on incarcerated women and their relationships to reading. She theorized that many women turned to books to contextualize, narrativize, and at times make meaning out of the suffering that they had experienced, reading stories with themes of abuse and trauma in the genre of "mis lit" (misery literature). As she wrote, "Several readers also argued that the maxim 'what happens in the house stays in the house' governs life in prison too, since penal employees fail to address women's histories of abuse and fail to understand how such histories can affect women's behavior."[18]

To put it simply, it is complicated to speak of trauma and abuse in a setting like a prison. In both male and female units, participating in therapeutic talk can actually be dangerous. Revealing your feelings, your background, why you use drugs, what you have lived through and endured on the streets and otherwise—all of these things can place you at risk of being preyed upon, emotionally, physically, sexually, or otherwise, either by guards or other inmates. One woman, Catherine, told me that if "you break down and cry in here, you just become a target for everybody else." This could mean enduring taunts, bullying, or even physical beatings. Therapeutic talk, in other words, can be highly dangerous in a prison environment.

One staff member at the South Middlesex Correctional Center, the unlocked, minimum-security prerelease facility for women stepping down from MCI-Framingham, told me that Framingham didn't "do" trauma treatment because "they have enough jumpers [suicide attempts] as is." She said that they didn't have much discussion of trauma at South Middlesex Correctional Center either, because they didn't have twenty-four-hour mental health staff and the facility was "too open." She insinuated that there was too much risk of being unable to handle the potential consequences of unearthing trauma at the prerelease facility, where the women had the comparative freedom to go to the track; use tools to garden; or, alternatively, to seriously injure themselves.

Doing trauma treatment, therefore, meant taking the risk that a person might attempt something desperate such as suicide or self-harm if feelings and memories were unearthed and difficult to control. These risks are generally deemed intolerable for prison administrators, who are responsible for constructing and maintaining the public's perception of prisons as a safe environment where the work of rehabilitation goes on. The public's perception of the prison as efficacious is critical to its very existence.

Inevitably, though, stories of past traumas slip through by inmates who are desirous of healing. Tina tells me a story of making life maps at her drug treatment class, where "a lot of girls wanted to talk about what it was like doing drugs while they were pregnant" or what it was like being raped or engaging in survival sex for drugs. They wanted to understandably process their life experiences as they tried to make sense of their pasts and their futures, but coordinators of such programs feel uncomfortable or undertrained to lead these discussions.

What is the use of learning about trauma and coping skills in prison and then being released back into pathological or dangerous environments in which violence, drug use, and certain kinds of relationships otherwise deemed harmful can actually be protective in the short or even long term? How can the goal of establishing a sense of safety be taken seriously in the context of a penal environment, where punishment and discipline are the main goals? In one of my interviews at MCI-Framingham, one woman was telling me about her anxiety and PTSD. When I asked her a follow-up question, she told me simply, "I don't really want to get into this now, because I'm just going to have to go back to my unit. . . . I don't want to fuck up [behave badly, like fight or act out]. On the outside, you have support; in here, you really don't have anybody you can lean on."

PSYCHOEDUCATION AND COPING SKILLS

The next time I saw Alisha, she was giddy about the possibility of getting released. Only eight more weeks until her parole hearing. The only thing she had to do to get parole was to complete an eight-week anger management class. This was in large part due to an incident several days earlier when she had gotten into a fight with one of her new cellmates—Shari Richards—after she was moved to a new cell because her toilet was clogged. Alisha was assigned a top bunk, and no one wants to have to climb up on a top bunk all the time.

Alisha had called in to her officer friends and told them that Shari had to move. Shari was ordered by the officer to switch to the top bunk, until the officer wavered and backtracked on the favoritism, and then tried to cajole Alisha to deal with the top bunk for one night.

Shari yelled out angrily, "I have seizures, I need this bottom bunk." Alisha reached out and tried to grab Shari's arm, then decided instead to just send a wad of spit down toward her. Alisha started climbing down from the top bunk, threatening to stomp on Shari's books, diary and assorted toiletries that were strewn across the bottom bunk mattress. Shari pulled at Alisha's dangling leg and tried to bite her.

Alisha's main intention in taking the bottom bunk was to beat down Shari, even though she had no true claims on a bottom bunk. Fortunately for her, the corrections officer broke up the fight, though not without writing up a "D report," which is what landed Alisha with a required anger management class.

Fighting was essentially second nature to her, since her aunt used to slap her for coming home crying if she didn't stand her ground and fight as a child. Alisha laughed when I told her I didn't know how to fight. I told her I imagined I might be good at it, in a sort of wily and unpredictable way. She giggled incredulously and clapped her hands together in delight, saying, "I actually met somebody that never had a fight. That is so wonderful!"

What Alisha wanted to do on her release was go to a domestic violence shelter since she had developed a newfound awareness of how trauma impacted her life. She had become convinced that her "whole lifestyle has been nothing but violence, and just like, being abused, whether it's verbally or physically or whatever, I've been through it all. . . . So that's a place that I need to be . . . a domestic place." There, she wanted to "focus on getting myself together, I want to be treated like a lady. . . [not] as no type of street person." She could always go stay with her latest boyfriend who had been taking care of her in prison (in jail lingo, this means he puts $50 a week into her prison canteen account to buy food and clothes), but this time, she wanted to "get on my feet, do my own thing . . . and work my way to the top." She hoped to get a job working with animals or becoming a motivational speaker about what life is like growing up in a rough neighborhood.

Through the various kinds of programming activities and her mental health casework at the jail, Alisha had adopted a "trauma-informed" lens through which she could examine her own life circumstances. Alisha told me that she thinks prison works "if you want it to work." So why is she back here again, I asked her? "The lifestyle." How does prison "work"? She explained: "Because prison lets you sit, think, plan, you know what I'm saying. And it gives you other opportunities like learning things about yourself, you have therapy, you have groups, you know, you can get your health checked out here . . . HIV test, you know, shit like that."

. . .

Shari agreed with Alisha that the way prison and jail work is that they give you a new lens through which to peer at your life. For both women, it was while being incarcerated that they confronted their mental health diagnoses and got a renewed awareness of their trauma. Shari, a baby-faced thirty-two-year-old African American woman, looked only half her age. Her plump cheeks were smooth and unlined and full, bearing no evidence of the chaos her life consisted of. She was involved in a complicated court process that meant that she had been incarcerated as a detainee for a little over a year at the Suffolk House of Correction awaiting a trial.

Like Alisha, Shari's main occupations were as a drug dealer and a sex worker, where fighting is second nature and a necessary part of survival. She had previously been arrested for threatening a woman with whom her man was cheating on her. Shari had prowled around outside the girl's house for three hours, yelling, "You want to fuck my man but you don't want to get your ass whooped?" I couldn't blame her. I would have feared Shari's imposing two-hundred-pound frame too. Turning to me, she explained, "I don't get that. If you beat me up, I don't care, but we're going to fight, and you can have him after that." But Shari is pleased with herself, because she's been currently incarcerated for a year now, and hasn't gotten into "one fight, so that says a lot."

When Shari was twenty, she was selling marijuana in one of the Dorchester subway stations when she met a man named Mike. She never thought that she would engage in sex work, and she emphasized to him: "I'm a drug dealer, I'm known for that. I'm just not that type of chick, no disrespect to you or anything. I rob guys, I sell drugs and shit like that. . . . I don't respect hos." But Shari and Mike hit it off, and she agreed to his offer of "$800 to do what you have to do and I just help you out and you help me out."

She told me that she was "straight sober" when she agreed to this arrangement. She and Mike began to travel, to New York City, Atlantic City, and finally D.C. After a while, she became scared of him:

He beat the shit out of this other girl. I thought somebody was like breaking in our house, you know, our hotel room, robbing us or something. Maybe, I didn't know what the hell was going on. So, I crept up the stairs, and I seen this girl, and I heard the fricking punch like boom [makes punching sound], and I'm like maybe he's fighting this dude, maybe he had to beat this dude for doing something to her, and like, he hits this girl. And she's like your size and he's fucking huge. I'm like, oh my god, my ex-fiancé was abusive to me, and I loved him. I don't know you, and if you're abusive to me, you could kill me. I'm like, oh my God, I'm like, all right. . . . I just came back to chill and the room was a mess, it was crazy. She's like fuck this I'm not making any money. I'm calling my sugar daddy at home telling me to wire me money.

I'm like all right, so I just stayed out the whole fricking night, we left and
went to D.C., and I'm like losing my mind.

Then that night went good; the night after that we weren't making any
money. It was 6:00 in the morning. . . . He's calling, how come you guys
aren't making any money out there? And I'm like, oh my God, he's going to
hurt us. And then he called me to come back and have sex with him, and I'm
like oh my God. I told him I am not going to sleep with him. Maybe if I don't
have sex with him, he's going to do something. So, I had sex with him, [and
while] he's asleep I took all the fricking money he had, all that money and I
left with the dude that I was getting high with.

Shari eventually managed to escape her abusive pimp, and through
various means, including stays at family shelters, she enrolled in a "rent-
to-buy" program for her own house to support and live with her two
children until she became incarcerated.

What Shari was perhaps most eager to tell me about was how she
was currently working through her traumas and mental health issues
that she feels now have defined her entire life. She tells me about how
she got diagnosed with PTSD while incarcerated at MCI-Framingham
awaiting trial:

Shari: I guess I've endured a lot of trauma, and it's like, with PTSD,
with any psychological diagnosis, the woman [mental health
counselor] is really good there. She's like, you need to be educated
on what you have so that you can talk about it. I knew I have
anxiety. I knew I was irritated, but I couldn't understand why. So,
taking this class at Framingham made me understand what's going
on with me, in that I'm irritated and anxious at people when the
littlest thing happened. It's just not that little thing to me, it's the
big thing that happened twenty days before that, and the little thing
sets me off. I can't just stay with that one thing. So, I'm coping with
that, I'm learning coping skills.

Kim: What was the name of the class?

Shari: DBT.

Kim: Oh, dialectical behavioral therapy?

Shari: I forgot the other name of the class we took before that. But I
couldn't even deal with it. It was just really hard for me, really,
really hard for me to sit and express and get deep, deep into me,
because I got frustrated.

The members of the Suffolk House of Correction, like their counterparts at MCI-Framingham, see the goals of their work with detained

and sentenced women as primarily stabilization and psychoeducation. Shari is a perfect example; the staff at the jail does psychoeducation with her, giving her the language to "understand what's going on with [her]." Doing psychoeducation in a carceral environment entails teaching women how to identify their emotions and their inner mental states, linking it with consequent substance use and coping skills, and identifying all these as psychopathological. Yet doing further trauma processing in carceral settings is frowned upon as bad practice, since the jail and the prison are such destabilizing environments. As Laurie Markoff, a trauma integration specialist at IHR, told me, "For people in prison, it's not the time for them to be going in depth in their stories, it's not a safe environment."

The staff at the jail felt they were constantly working at a time disadvantage as they tried to keep up with the movement in and out of the jail. The average time spent there could be anywhere from two to four days. They had to deal with a rapidly transient population. A woman might be there one day, receiving services and medications, and the next day, gone, if she made bail. If a woman has a court date in a week, she could be released that very day to the streets. Alternatively, she could be sentenced and sent to MCI-Framingham or be held waiting for another court date in the jail. It was nearly impossible to predict. Thus, trying to assess and treat the psychiatric and mental health needs of such a transient population was challenging. And providing programming and mental health continuity of care back in the community for a large number of women was thus an arduous task.

In this regard, to the staff, the psycho-educational piece felt like impactful work that could positively benefit incarcerated women's subjectivities by allowing them to both name their challenges and reshape their life stories. One of the staff mental health clinicians at the jail told me that engaging in psychoeducation was what was most rewarding for her in her daily work. She told me, "You know, I've had women say, my mind is drifting off and I don't understand what's happening. . . . I say, well, you know, this could be connected to things you've said you've been through. Some of them are just not—don't have the education about it. I'd say the psychoeducation can affect people [positively] sometimes."

Another staff clinician noted positive results working with a woman prisoner who happened to have been near the finish line of the Boston Marathon when the bombings took place there in April 2013: "Working with her in the immediate aftermath of that, and just educating her about the symptoms that . . . they're pretty common, and [that] you can probably expect them to get better with time. . . . And she did in fact see that nightmares and the hypersensitivity and stuff was declining over time, and I think it helped her to just have some education about what she might see happen over time."

Although it feels rewarding to mental health staff to educate impoverished women with life histories of neglect, abuse, and suffering about PTSD, there are unclear, perhaps unintended, consequences of doing so. In Shari's case, she was hesitant to engage in community treatment, largely related to feeling guilt about not being present in the community to raise her children:

> I think [this mental health treatment] is something that I want to continue, I think it's something that I need to make a part of my life. It's something that I am stuck with for the rest of my life, and I really have to take care of that. It's my responsibility to get up every day and address that issue. I have kids. So, when my kids do something that makes me upset, I can easily go into a fit and rage, and that's not how I am, I love my kids, I take care of my kids and I provide for them, I don't complain about taking care of them. . . . So it's very frustrating for me to have to step back and take the time away from her [my daughter] so that I can fix me, and that's something I wouldn't be able to do on my own, and being incarcerated is allowing me to do that; unfortunately, because of society too, it's my responsibility to take care of my children. I'm not going to say, you take care of my kids so I can go get help, that's not how I was raised.

Shari pointed out that were it not for her forced confinement, her incarceration, she probably would not have spent any time getting treatment in the community for her mental health issues. Like many women, she would rather be a caretaker for her children than a caretaker for herself. The mental health staff at the jail taught her how to construct and re-narrativize her life around the trope of trauma; as Shari told me: "What am I supposed to do? The trauma is coming there. That's where we get into trauma, because I start thinking of my life and every time something happens when I'm met with an obstacle, it immediately jumps back."

Part of her mental health treatment—for diagnoses she was given in prison of bipolar disorder, borderline personality disorder, PTSD, and a history of postpartum depression—was medication. The jail psychiatrist gave her different medications to try, including fluoxetine (Prozac), sertraline (Zoloft), valproic acid (Depakote), and tramadol. As she told me:

> I took Prozac and they upped my dosage and then I started taking Depakote and then I just got to a point where I felt stable and I didn't take it. I feel fine,

feel like I've accepted, I feel like I've come to terms with a lot. I feel like the only thing, I was explaining to the therapist, the psychiatrist yesterday, I'm peaceful naturally, you know. We're having a conversation right now, [but] if one of the officers came in here and was completely rude and disrespectful about us terminating [this interview], that would irritate me to the extreme, and my natural reaction would be to cuss them out. But I'm able to take that split second to think about it, but it would affect me, more than it probably would affect you, you know what I mean? And what is that called. How do I address that, how do I deal with that? They're telling me that I have to take medication every day for something, for some way that I might only feel for two seconds every day?

Like many other people do, Shari felt resistance to the use of psychiatric medications to make her feel calm and stable when her affect dysregulation was only a problem some of the time. She simply didn't want to take it when she felt fine for most of the time.

Shari was eventually found guilty and was sentenced to serve three to five years at MCI-Framingham. She now has criminal felony convictions for several violent offenses, including attempted murder, though she continues to insist on her innocence.

I wondered about Shari's fate. Would she leave prison better prepared when she returned to her children after three-to-five years of an interrupted life? Perhaps she would be able to find a medication regimen that truly works, but is prison really the place for that? The prison's efforts to raise awareness of her trauma—without sufficient community support and attention to the structural sources of violence in her life—may only contribute to ongoing guilt and shame over her separation from her children and a precarious life of economic and existential uncertainty after incarceration.

. . .

Many incarcerated women are encouraged to learn coping skills to deal with their embodied distress. Programs like Seeking Safety often place an emphasis on meditation and breathing and learning how to identify and regulate one's troublesome emotional states like anger or frustration or sadness. The prison treatment programs try to bestow self-care and self-soothing techniques on women who are often faulted for their crime as part of an overall inability to care for themselves or others. Such an emphasis on coping skills tries to teach individuals to deal with their present circumstances; in other words, it disarticulates the inmates from both individual past experiences as well as a collective history of social precariousness that all these women share.

Can such an empowering stance take root in people who have no choice about what to wear, eat, and do every day? It seems a difficult task, one that reflects the impossibility and the irony of treating trauma in a traumatizing place. Mental health staff at Suffolk House of Correction admit it is a difficult task to teach coping skills. As one case worker said, "This is a very artificial environment. So especially with trauma, a lot of the skills you might be able to use [on the outside]—to get up, get a warm drink, take a walk, things to calm yourself down—these are tools and skills that are not available in here that are available outside. But their outside lives are super chaotic." Another staff member chimed in, "Like deep breathing and warm drinks even touch any of this stuff [the traumas these women have experienced]. They look at you like, are you crazy? I'm shooting heroin to stop this and you want me to breathe?"

The insistent emphasis on coping, on regaining a sense of autonomy or control in a powerless world, is an important, perhaps noble, goal. It allows one to become the subject of one's own life, and to also be heard. But being incarcerated is also simply a disempowering life circumstance no matter what. Learning how to cope better with the daily insults of prison life and life after prison might be critically important in helping women preserve dignity and enable a sense of self-preservation as well as the ability to go on with life. But at the same time, such an approach de-emphasizes the conditions of power and the socioeconomic processes of exclusion and social abandonment that have led to women being in prison in the first place.

Both medical and penal systems have become sensitized and aware of the complexity of trauma in women's lives; in medicine, this is known as "complex trauma," extending beyond what is traditionally thought of as traumatic to the historical trauma of groups that have faced social violence or continuous oppression.[19] Trauma is thought of as cumulative or with a "kindling effect," so having experienced one trauma predisposes individuals to more.

Yet is the prison the right place to heal the complex traumas of women like Shari and Alisha? Shari struck me, at times, as downright dissociative, with significant mental illness and a life history consistent with complex trauma. I wondered about how effective community-based mental health treatment done well could have changed the outcome, given the complex calculus of risk and harm that she and others faced. Shari was what clinicians call "treatment-naive" until she became incarcerated, reflecting both the failure of community-based mental health treatment and the utter complexity and chaos of her life. In testament to the social precariousness of her life, it had taken thirty-two years and serious criminal charges for her to access mental health treatment in any form.

THE TRAUMAS OF THE TRAUMATIZERS

Alisha and Shari and Serenity all acknowledged feeling safe when incarcerated, but at the same time, they wished ardently that they weren't locked up. The tension between safety and violence is difficult to reconcile. On the one hand, Alisha praised the jail as a place where she could plan, sit, think, get therapy, and have her health checked out. It was a place where abusive partners like Diego couldn't get to her. In the era of the retrenchment of social services for the poor, the prison remains open.

On the other hand, the jail and prison can be a powder keg for women like Alisha. It's easy to blow up and get into a fight or sink under a flood of unhappy thoughts and feelings. With many women living in close quarters, it's difficult to share a space and find composure. In this regard, trauma can be found everywhere in the prison. The prison is simultaneously a site of women's trauma resurfacing—as they "seek safety"—and a place that can represent concrete threats to their physical and psychic well-being, such as prison rape or abuse by other women or staff. All of this makes the prison's recent turn to trauma and trauma-related psychoeducation all the more complex.

Laurie Markoff, the trauma integration expert at IHR, is convinced that the turn to trauma in the prisons is an essentially positive one that humanizes a place marked by many inhumanities. Markoff produced data for MCI-Framingham that showed that once she trained the staff about trauma, the number of incident reports for inmate-on-inmate assault, inmate-on-staff assault, and grievances filed by inmates fell by one-third. Orienting the prison staff, including the correctional guards, to trauma, it seemed, had tangible effects on the relationships and interactions between staff and inmates as well as among inmates themselves. But was the teaching of trauma only a way to construct a calmer, more compliant, more docile, and more easily managed prison population, as Foucault would suggest?

Markoff believes that research by Caterina Spinaris on the high rates of suicide, burn-out, and depression among correctional officers—what Spinaris has coined "corrections fatigue"— is the key to really getting trauma adequately addressed in penal environments.[20] She explains:

I find that if I start talking about the impact of trauma on the officers, suddenly they are much more interested in what this is really about. And then you hear them say, oh yeah, we're all traumatized. So, I think one of the ways into corrections, because they have a lot of power, the correctional officers, is through their own trauma, and once they understand their own trauma, they'll be less reactive because they'll get trauma treatment . . . but then they'll be able to recognize that what they're struggling with is what the women are struggling with.

Markoff admits that perhaps this is idealistic because correctional officers will always need to create psychological lines of difference between themselves and the people they guard. But Markoff's approach is also dangerous, appealing to the somewhat morally ambiguous logic that that the perpetrators of trauma endure the same psychological and physiological effects as those on the receiving end of traumas.

Anthropologists Didier Fassin and Robert Rechtman have voiced similar concerns in their work on trauma. They posit that conceptualizing of trauma as a great equalizer of human experience is a dangerous, slippery slope "by applying the same psychological classification to the person who suffers violence, the person who commits it, and the person who witnesses it, the concept of trauma profoundly transforms the moral framework of what constitutes humanity."[21] Not everyone is at equal risk for traumatic events and not everyone is equally predisposed to trauma. And only some people experience recurring traumatic incidents and exposures. This is not a level playing field: those who are more vulnerable to the vagaries of life, who have less social support, less financial resources, and less ability to shelter themselves endure a much larger burden of trauma in their lives than those who are more well-off.

Trauma is a compelling paradigm that links the macro level (historical, ecological and political disasters of both sweeping and small scales as well as their aftermaths) and micro (the clinical and biographical aspects of affected individuals). It can speak to a communal atrocity, such as violence and slavery, as well as the complex aftermath of memories and emotions experienced by an individual. As anthropologist Allan Young has pointed out, PTSD garnered such additional scientific credibility and plausibility that a wide range of actors and social institutions appropriated these discourses for their particular interests and means. This maneuver often elided both the role and effects on perpetrators and victims of trauma alike.[22]

Furthermore, taking such an approach to trauma means that the prison continues to be a central place for recognizing and addressing trauma. Movements toward "trauma-informed correctional care" or "trauma-informed services" in corrections settings are, on the one hand, arguable necessary and could have significant positive improvements on women's lives. On the other hand, these methods do not re-site trauma treatment; they do nothing to divert women with complex trauma toward places in the community that are oriented to healing and well-being. They still locate pathology in the damaged individual and do not recognize or articulate the violence of the state as well as the widespread neglect of these women by the state when they are not incarcerated.

While there is a general consensus that trauma treatment should be a community-based endeavor, the prison has increasingly encroached on this mission and adopted it as part of its rehabilitative efforts. How can the prison have appropriated trauma treatment and co-opted the language of care and healing for its own legitimization and perpetuation, when prisons and jails at the same time do much violence and harm to people within its walls? Teaching trauma symptoms and principles in the prison further legitimizes the very existence of prisons and jails; it makes them a social fact, part of the fabric of social existence for traumatized women.

This fact cannot be extricated from that fact that very little stage-two or -three trauma work is being done with women with histories of incarceration and drug addiction upon their release into the community. There are certain agencies and individuals that are doing this work, but there is a dearth of trauma-oriented community-based providers, particularly doing one-on-one psychotherapy in combination with medication or other modalities. Markoff estimates that serious trauma treatment takes approximately "three to five years."

Alisha thought that what she needed to recover was a one-on-one therapist in the community "where I can just vent. Just go and go hard. This is what happened to me . . . this is how I feel, you know what I'm saying." She lacked access to even a way of figuring out how she can get a therapist, however, as well as to the resources to pay for one. She was given a trauma-informed lens with which to inwardly peer at her own life, but there was no change in the facts of her past or in her prospects, especially since incarceration is a blight on her chances for work or housing. As linguistic anthropologist E. Summerson Carr has observed in her work on the language used in community substance use treatment programs, this orientation toward the inner self—which she posits is both cultural and political—leads counselors in these programs to "enervate clients' institutional critiques and discourage social commentary."[23]

Women in prison learn through programming that they are damaged, and possibly that it is not their fault. But the treatment they receive locates the problem within their soul and deep inner being. Inmates are told to re-narrativize the story; as Markoff suggests, "Helping women to craft a different story, which then increases their sense of choice and control, is really the bottom line." Yet the conditions of containment and confinement prevent the effective re-narrativization of the stories of these women's lives. What is the effect of empowering inmates psychologically while not addressing the structural violence in their lives, while not articulating and redressing the problem of how communities and social policies have abandoned many of these women before and after incarceration?

. . .

What imbrication of medical and sociocultural logics supports the rise of trauma rhetoric in prison as a means of dealing with traumatized, incarcerated women like Alisha, Shari, and Serenity? The prison, rather than recognizing that trauma is often a collective, complex, and historical experience of a group, selectively utilizes the embodied, individualized and present-oriented approach to trauma that addresses superficial symptoms and behaviors. This approach appeals to the prisons because they must "manage" these women (their suffering as well as their bad behavior) until their release, so containing the physiological and psychological imprints of trauma on these women is advantageous to the work of the prison. → perpetuating cycle

While few women feel healed by prison programming upon their release into the community, the prison creates an image that it is engaged in a paradigm of care attending to the unique nature of gendered suffering. Interestingly, women in prison are truly eager to find words and ways to manage their ongoing symptoms and distress. They are genuinely desirous of healing and participate actively in new ways to conceptualize themselves, their suffering, and their relationship to others. And they do acknowledge feeling safe in prisons and jails—not because they are truly safe spaces, but rather because the outside world is such a violent and chaotic place for poor women who use drugs.

The prison's endeavor cannot reckon with what is actually at stake for women because to do so would be to articulate the prison's own complicity in perpetuating traumatic experiences behind its steel doors, barbed wire, and prison bars. Alisha didn't blame the jail for her own problems and poor decisions. She just didn't want be there anymore.

She was sick of her life being on hold while others tried to diagnose or cure her. Instead, she tried to persuade the powers-that-be at the jail that she should only complete six weeks of the anger management class for her parole eligibility because her sister's breast cancer had come back. Even though this request was denied, she remained cheerful, hoping upon her release to "surround myself with people, in whatever field that actually cares about my well-being."

5

Where Medicine Is Contraband

There was a shake-up in the women's unit in the local Boston jail. The night before, several female inmates had been caught smoking crack. As a result, the entire women's unit was administered urine toxicology testing. Those who tested positive would be sent to solitary confinement (known as "the hole"). Refusal to take the test was seen as an admission of guilt.

Even within the supposedly contained safe spaces of the prison and the jail, so-called illicit drugs are everywhere. Getting substances into these spaces is difficult yet feasible. In Massachusetts, much of what has been labeled contraband is increasingly comprised of medications within the community. Of particular concern to jails and prison authorities is the FDA-approved medication known as buprenorphine-naloxone (Suboxone) which is prescribed for opioid use disorder. In the Massachusetts prison system in 2012, this form of medication-assisted treatment comprised approximately 12 percent of confiscated contraband.[1] Officials cite numerous ways in which this medication enters these facilities, including personal visits, stamps, even in prayer cards. Across the country, state prison and jail systems have struggled to control the steady flow of perceived contraband into the facilities; efforts have included the implementation of drug-sniffing dogs in Massachusetts and facilities banning kissing between visitors and inmates in New Hampshire.[2]

Mae, a twenty-three-year-old white woman from a small seaside town south of Boston, told me how she used buprenorphine-naloxone to get high in the state's only women's prison, MCI-Framingham. It was not her typical drug of choice on the outside. If she had an option, she explained, she would always pick heroin, since she found the taste of the dissolvable sublingual film strips "gross." But she admitted, "I mean, if I'm in jail, I was taking them just to get high." She explained the subtle physiological distinction: once her body was cleared of opioids after the forced process of physical detoxification, she would no longer be physically dependent, so taking buprenorphine might produce a mild feeling of euphoria. A quarter of a typical 8 mg pill could cost as much as $50 to $100 in prison, largely reflecting the limited supply (in contrast, one entire pill might cost $5 to $10 on the streets). It was hard for Mae to say no to the offer of a psychopharmaceutically enhanced escape, given the prison's production of boredom and a useless, often downtrodden, subjectivity: "Why not? You're sitting in jail, you know? I'm an addict, I like to get high, if it's offered."

Mae's mother, who also suffers from a heroin use disorder, was her source of drugs in prison, even sewing drugs into the hems of clothes to get them to Mae. Sometimes it would be oxycodone-acetaminophen (Percocet), sometimes buprenorphine-naloxone, depending on whatever was available. Mae recalls that her mother would send buprenorphine-naloxone strips in "those big orange manila, whatever; she would take the bottom off in the strips and put it in the glue and send it in. A lot of people like the pills because you can either shoot them or snort them, but they'll take the strips too if that's all you have."

Having access to drugs made Mae a popular and powerful figure in prison, but she shrugged it off. She told me that she would give drugs to her friends "for free" anyways, even though you had to purchase a needle off one of the women with insulin-dependent diabetes for $2 if you wanted to crush it and shoot it intravenously. Or you could crush it and simply snort it. For Mae, the imperative was to get rid of the drugs as fast as possible in order to decrease her chances of getting caught by the prison security officials known as IPS (Inner Perimeter Security). Many other inmates were happy to take them off her hands and share in the disjointed solidarity of getting high together inside. These women didn't mind going to solitary confinement if they got caught; one woman told me that at least she could get double food portions in the "hole" and not have to deal with the "catty bitches."

There are many kinds of substances that people use to achieve intoxication on the inside. Some are made "in-house," like pruno, a fermented homebrew made from sugar, ketchup packets, or canned fruit. Many were prescription drugs written for patients by doctors and nurse practitioners either within the jail or within the community, primarily pharmaceutical compounds to treat mental illness, depression, pain, and addiction. Even though prison doctors generally refuse to write for any medication containing opioids or that have mood-altering effects (they may not even be available on the institution's formulary), these medications somehow still manage to find their way into cells. Jails, which are institutions housing pretrial detainees or detainees with short sentences, tend to have higher volumes of illicit substances, as individuals move through the system more quickly and interact more with the outside world, but prisons still face the problem of drugs within their institutions.

This chapter examines how buprenorphine, an FDA-approved medication to treat opioid and heroin addiction, came to be labeled contraband in Massachusetts jails and prisons as well as around the country. How did a medical treatment become so taboo in the majority of American jails and prisons and get labeled as "contraband"? Why and how is this medication configured and imagined so differently by the incarcerated people who use them, by guards, and by prison drug treatment program administrators and staff?

. . .

Mae kept winding up incarcerated for crimes related to the hustle of obtaining money to fuel her ongoing heroin addiction (all for nonviolent cases like larceny under $250, receiving and supplying stolen property, breaking and entering, forging stolen checks). She had been sectioned to community treatment programs by her mother before, but when the thirty-day programs ended, and her drug use continued, she risked incarceration.

Nothing deterred her from heroin use. Mae had first learned how to inject heroin in a detox facility in South Boston after she went in for a bad habit: snorting Perc30s (a combination oxycodone-acetaminophen tablet containing 30 mg of oxycodone). She had been using approximately twenty to thirty pills a day and selling them in order to support her habit. At her first visit to the detox facility, she noticed that "everyone there shot heroin, and I was like, oh, maybe this is normal. They all looked like lovely, normal people." Someone at the detox showed her how to shoot up and within a week, Mae had moved fully into injecting heroin, doing it herself and for her boyfriend.

Prescription opioid pills had a particular allure for many young women I encountered. Historically, opioids were touted as particularly suitable treatments for essentially painful female physiological conditions like childbirth and menstruation. Addiction was an unintended but necessary consequence of treating pain; it was iatrogenesis itself: injury produced by standard medical treatment.

Mae explained why doing pills was morally superior to heroin: "Pills are fine, you can do as many pills as you want, but the minute you switch to heroin, you're a piece of shit." Others echoed this fine-grained moral distinction, claiming that "eating" pills was safer than shooting intravenously, given pharmaceutical standardization and ensured pharmaceutical purity (although this research was conducted before the peak of the presence of illicit fentanyl in heroin or other drugs). Pills lacked the symbolic moral degradation and the uncleanliness of the needle.

Historically, women as a group have been large consumers of pills and have been attractive target markets for pharmaceutical companies. Controlling women's emotional states with medication was always seen as a worthy pharmacological intervention; in recent history, recall "mother's little helper" (diazepam or Valium) and the widespread marketing of tranquilizers, barbiturates, and amphetamines to middle-class women.[3] Women as a group have and continue to be heavily prescribed opioid medications: one study found that women were more likely to have obtained opioids through a doctor's prescription than men and that women tended to report more functional impairment, higher levels of psychiatric symptoms, and an increased likelihood of using these medications to deal with negative affect.[4] A CDC analysis on prescription opioid use among women showed that deaths among women from opioid pain medication use had increased fivefold between 1999 and 2010; the report noted that women were a population of special concern for the development of opioid use disorder given their increased medical access.[5]

In many ways, women's increased access to these medications and subsequent risk for physiologic dependence and addiction was in part a byproduct of a medicalized sociocultural response to bodies in pain. It is nearly impossible to understand addiction without delving into painful worlds and bodies. Pain is deeply imbricated within our human experience, and it is a commonly cited reason for the initial turn to drug use; yet, as medical anthropologists and sociologists have observed, our responses to it have been dogged by moralizing and stigmatizing judgment.[6]

As often happens with many public health reports, there was no inquiry into why so many women like Mae were at risk of misusing or "abusing" opioid medications in order to get high. What made it so desirable to "get wrecked," wasted, completely black-out intoxicated? Why did so many women accidentally or intentionally edge into overdose and toward death while using these medicines, sometimes doing it again and again? What were the socioeconomic, political, existential, bodily and psychological reasons that women chose to use these medications to excess both inside and outside the prison? These reasons that women chose to use these medications to excess both inside and outside the prison were hard to incorporate in explanatory models and subsequent models of behavior change.

For Mae, even overdosing three times in one week was not enough for her to stop. The last time she left jail, she recalled, "When I got out of jail, not this past time but last time, I overdosed three times in one week. So, my mom, after the second time, started going to the hospital, because if I overdosed, [it] helps to be right there." It was their family version of harm reduction: to be as close as possible to the life-saving medication naloxone and medical facilities. She also overdosed repeatedly after leaving detox or short courses of treatment, since she would lose her tolerance in these facilities, a well-known phenomenon that actually increases risk of overdose and subsequent death.[7] Her brain was overwhelmed by the quantity of heroin she was used to using—half a bag (a relatively small amount in comparison to what she had been used to)—and she would overdose. As she told me, overdosing wasn't necessarily a bad feeling or a negative experience:

> One time in particular I remember, I literally thought I was going to die because I was so at peace, and I couldn't move, I could barely breathe that's how shallow my breathing was. And I was . . . the idea, I really thought I was overdosing that I was going to die, and the idea of dying didn't scare me at all at the time, because I was so relaxed, at peace. When I first started using, I know this sounds crazy, I really felt like I could take all my problems and really look at them and figure them out. I truly think I could, I knew what I had to do, I just didn't do it. But I felt like I could figure out all my problems.

It was also difficult to stop using because of her mother's own ongoing drug use in the family house that Mae still lived at. Mae recalls her mother using drugs throughout Mae's childhood: "I used to be left at crack houses and brought to bars at one in the morning; that was my life up until I was eight." Interestingly, perhaps because of the absence of racialized policing in their small, affluent white neighborhood on the South Shore suburbs, child protective services never became involved in Mae or her mother's lives. Decades later, her mother picked her up at the gates of the prison with a bag of heroin for her. Mae was necessary and useful to her mother, who would buy and supply the drugs, since Mae would hit her mother up (find and inject drugs into her veins); her mother found it too difficult to do it for herself.

Mae first started using drugs—snorting coke—when she was fourteen, after the trauma of finding out that one of her friends had died alone in his bedroom engaging in a choking game that was popular among teenagers at that time. When she was older, she enrolled in the army, where she told me that she was raped by a superior. When she reported it, her sergeant told her "it never happened" and she was dishonorably discharged immediately. Two weeks later, Mae relapsed into opioid use.

Mae was always an occasional drug dealer while she was incarcerated at the state women's prison or when she went to jail. She would also deal when she was on the outside—mostly in Perc30s—so dealing was nothing new to her. There was a significant number of women who sought relief from psychoactive substances and most of them knew each other in a loose extended network. For many, using drugs inside was just another fact of life. They used drugs outside the prison, often in spite of the potential deleterious consequences to their health or their well-being, and they used them inside just as readily.

Mae described an unspoken code of conduct between women who used drugs, illustrated by an experience while she was being held in the court lockup in Quincy, Massachusetts: "When I went to Quincy court in lockup, I made a couple of friends. Quincy court always has drugs. Always. Like this one girl she knew she was being released that day, and usually how it is, you're being released and you have drugs on you, you hand drugs back to people going back to jail, it's like the unwritten code of being an addict."

If she had a particularly large supply on her, she would deal by asking around, because it's difficult to know "who is going to get high in jail" since it's impossible to know everyone. Anyway, not everyone wants to use drugs even if offered. As she explained, one day she had a source of opioid pills: "And then the next day, the girl, one of the girls that was in lockup was going back to court, she's like I don't want these, I'm getting released today. I'll be sick for a couple hours [then be released and able to get drugs] . . . I'm like all right, I ended up selling those for sweatpants and other things too."

Some of this drug use and selling was made possible by the assistance of correctional officers (COs) who knew what was going on. As she told me, "One CO that I was kind of close with, all the girls were kind of close with him, he ended up getting fired. I was really upset about that, the last time I was there and got high, he said, you know, Mae, IPS is coming down to grab you tomorrow, so do what you want to do. I'm like, uh, well I leave tomorrow anyways, but thanks for the heads-up, so I could start flushing my system [by drinking water] the night before."[8] Numerous correctional officers in the state also faced charges of smuggling buprenorphine into the supposedly secure facilities.[9]

DRUG USE IN PRISON

Mae primarily dealt in and used opioids; oxycodone and heroin were her main drugs of choice. Part of why this might be the case relates to the forced detoxification and subsequent symptoms of opioid withdrawal. As described in a previous chapter, the symptoms of opioid withdrawal are extremely unpleasant, but women told me that the mental anguish was actually worse than simply "kicking it" (especially with methadone, a common medication for opioid use disorder treatment, since its long half-life means that it takes days to weeks to be eliminated from the body, thus having a particularly prolonged withdrawal syndrome).

Even if incarcerated women might lose physical cravings for opioids after a period of a week or so after detoxing in the prison's Health Services Unit at MCI-Framingham, the desire to locate and use substances to relieve emotional and physical distress—often a habit built up over many years—doesn't disappear so easily. As addiction psychiatrist Edward Khantzian has written, "A significant reason for the compulsion to use drugs is that individuals remember that the drugs provide control over and relief from intolerable emotional distress."[10] In addition to such emotional pain, there is the stress of being isolated from one's friends and community, overwhelmed with fear and anxiety, and physically locked into a small cell. Furthermore, many women suffer from a wide variety of embodied ailments related to their conditions of confinement, from insomnia to black eyes to upset stomachs. Their symptoms in these spaces are heightened, lacking the distractions or ways to self-soothe they had at home. Their requests for medications for anxiety and sleep are often routinely denied, so turning to substances is just another way some women endure their sentences.

For those in opioid withdrawal, taking buprenorphine-naloxone made sense, as it is approved as a medication to treat the painful symptoms of withdrawal. Many people buy buprenorphine on the street in order to avoid painful dopesickness. But how did it arrive? Like many other illicit substances, the medications would sometimes arrive in the mail, from visits, and sometimes, although rarely, even from prison guards. While buprenorphine is available in several formulations, including a sublingual dissolvable film strip or tablet, the strips often came into these facilities because of their widespread availability as well as their characteristics (thin and easier to hide).

Maria, a young Hispanic woman who was about to be released from the prison when I met her, told me that "word gets out" that someone has stuff and many people go "halves," or you "split it four ways," since it would be too expensive to purchase a whole one for yourself. Women might also wait until drugs arrive in a visit. For example, one of her incarcerated friends would be visiting with a loved one who brought some drugs in and "pretend to be eating a candy, and just eat it [a bag of drugs] . . . and then she'd go and vomit it up. But there was a couple times when they would call a code [prison in lockdown, so no one can transport between spaces] and she couldn't get out of the visiting room quick enough. . . . Then she'd be drinking all this poop medication [in order to defecate out the drugs]. That was one of my good friends, she actually passed away twelve days after she left."

Most women would engage in these transactions by exchanging valuable objects available for purchase in the prison's canteen, such as Reeboks or a nice sweatshirt or cosmetics, as a form of payment, since there was no actual cash in the prison. As Maria told me, women would trade these items for drugs: "People will die for canteen, especially if they're sober." What she meant was that these commodities—like sweatpants or makeup or candy—had even more salience and importance as cherished objects if women were not using drugs. They cared more about themselves, including the small pleasures they could take in their appearance, their diet, their own cells.

In prisons, sharing drugs could be many things, including manifestations of resistance, indifference, and boredom produced by structural violence.[11] As Meghan told me:

> I used Suboxone a couple of times, which is, um, on the street, it wouldn't do anything to me but after you've been clean for so long . . . I got jammed up [high]. And I did coke one time when I went to court, a girl was coming in off the street and she had some on her so we were doing it in the courthouse. And I got sent to the hole, I still had some. It was crazy, I would never recommend doing cocaine in prison. Cocaine isn't even like my drug of choice. I was just, like, . . . dumb, bored, basically. . . . Because you feel like

it's worth it. Whatever, I'm in jail. What are you going to do, you know? And a lot of times people get used to going to the hole.

When Meghan was in the so-called "hole," she would look out the tiny window there. Every day, her friends would wave at her from a tree in the yard that looked into the hole. It was an affirmation of solidarity and community. Meghan languished there twice for two-week periods because she was caught using even though she had used many times more. For Meghan, she felt she could survive two weeks of "anything"; for others, the idea of solitary confinement was intolerable.

Philosopher Lisa Guenther has written about solitary confinement using the philosophical orientation of phenomenology, more specifically the works of Emmanuel Levinas and Maurice Merleau-Ponty, to reflect on what about "the hole" is so disturbing. She argues that "solitary confinement works by turning prisoners' constitutive relationality against themselves, turning their own capacities to feel, perceive, and relate to others in a meaningful world into instruments of their own undoing."[12] In other words, solitary confinement, and jails and prisons more generally, create conditions for the possibility of self-destruction by denying the necessary sociality intrinsic to being human.

· · ·

While some saw using buprenorphine as a means of getting high, escaping the punishments, boredom and structures of affliction, others saw their illicit use as a form of self-medication and palliation of uncomfortable physiologic symptoms. Many buy it on the street—a process known by law enforcement entities such as the Drug Enforcement Agency as "diversion"—in order to self-medicate the symptoms of withdrawal. Large national surveys have found that most people who use it without a prescription by a physician or purchase it on the street or from a friend are self-treating withdrawal symptoms, trying to reduce heroin use, or treat cravings.[13] Stacie, a forty-year-old white woman from a rural part of the state, explained why she used buprenorphine-naloxone in jail. As she told me: "Quitting opiates is the hardest thing to do. It's impossible to be on nothing. People keep saying, I don't feel right, and they relapse, relapse, relapse." She had been arrested for violating probation and she arrived in full opioid withdrawal at the sheriff's station where another inmate gave her a dissolvable strip.

In a way, it was a gift from a stranger, an offer of psychopharmaceutical solidarity to care for a fellow inmate in distress. "I did Suboxone the last two months' at the sheriff's station and it wasn't coming up on drug screens in 2005," she told me. "It totally saved me. It helped me, helped me turn myself around." She thought that smuggling the medication into the prison could only help women with opioid habits inside: "I know that Suboxone is the answer for a lot of people in there." In her post-incarceration life, she received this medication regularly from her primary care physician and subsequently did not inject heroin for over five years. Maria seconded this idea: "I really want to get on Suboxone. It gives me energy; I feel less pain. I've had a lot of head trauma."

In fact, buprenorphine-naloxone, along with methadone, is listed as one of the World Health Organizations essential medications. In evidence-based trials, it has been shown to decrease illicit drug use, decrease rates of transmission of infectious disease such as HIV and Hepatitis C, and help engage people in medical care and systems of ongoing support. Treatment with buprenorphine has shown to decrease the risk of overdose and death dramatically.[14] In fact, several studies in prison and jail settings have shown that providing this medication to incarcerated people with opioid use disorder leads to decreased overdose deaths upon release. One study in England showed a 75 percent reduction in all-cause deaths with provision of these medications and 85 percent reduction in overdose mortality in the month after release.[15] So why would accessing or using such a medication be perceived as a criminal, or morally reprehensible, act?

Sharing medications, drugs, and paraphernalia between individuals as a form of care is an extremely common worldwide phenomenon, as anthropologists who have studied drug use have documented; on the street, such sharing is often a form of expression of solidarity, love, and care within a social unit.[16] It is common for people who use drugs to engage in practices of harm reduction that make engaging in risky behaviors seem somewhat safer. Mae used to do this when she would use heroin in a bathroom and call her boyfriend Matt. As he told me, she would call him and say, "Hey, I might not make it back. Can you stay on the phone with me just in case I die? That's great, I just want to hear my girlfriend die on the phone. That's the worst call. Random people do it to me too. Dude, I think I'm going to overdose, can you stay on the phone with me?" Drug use, in this way, is relational, knitting people together in both physiologic risk and reward. In carceral spaces, there is an even stronger shared sociality to the pain of physical withdrawal as well as the emotional distress of being separated from their community and loved ones.

Yet not everyone who has a substance use disorder uses when in prison or jail. In fact, for many, it might be the most significant "clean" time (or time not using substances) that they are able to acquire. Brittany, who was incarcerated for being her town's "Percocet dealer," told me that there was no way she would use inside, mainly because the price of a quarter of a buprenorphine-naloxone tablet was $70: "This is the longest I've ever been in jail, this is the longest I've ever been clean. . . . I mean, you could use in here if you wanted to, and I've turned it down . . . just because it's not worth it to me, it's really not. Plus, to be honest with you, it's Suboxone that mostly comes in here, and I don't even like Suboxone when I'm dopesick, never mind to get high off it. . . . It's ridiculous; you have to go to the hole. Then you have to pay for dirty urine. . . . My mom would find out, and she already doesn't want me coming back home." In addition to going to solitary confinement, women would lose other privileges such as visits, phone, and canteen. Maria wondered, "Is it really worth it, for one little high, is it really worth all that money and all that loss? Yeah, for some people it is."

. . .

While prison health care staff generally do not prescribe buprenorphine-naloxone or methadone, with some exceptions made for pregnant women, there are many other medications that they provide that flow into the prison's underground economy. Additional psychoactive substances that are often traded or sold in the prisons and jails include gabapentin (Neurontin), benzodiazepines such as alprazolam (Xanax) and clonazepam (Klonipin), chlordiazepoxide (Librium) or lorazepam (Ativan), and even anti-epileptic or anti-depression agents such as topiramate (Topomax) and bupropion (Wellbutrin). Maria told me how it works: "As soon as you get out of the med line, spit them back out, and people buy [Wellbutrin], they say it's like cheap coke." Others women even quickly vomit pills they are given by nurses and then put them up for re-sale. The prison calls this diverted movement "medication mismanagement," and it is "grounds for a disciplinary report if an inmate engages in the unauthorized possession, accumulation or misuse of prescribed medication."[17] Disciplinary reports could include going to solitary confinement.

Carceral healthcare is a heterogeneous and uneven space and accessing these psychoactive substances required a complex negotiation between providers and patients. It seems, perhaps paradoxically, that some patients lack access to essential medications, while others face overmedication. Some critics have argued that psychoactive medications are overprescribed in prisons and jails as one of several means to quell potential disruption or bad behavior. For example, in her research on women in prison in Massachusetts, the anthropologist Susan Sered noted that 56 percent of women inmates reported being treated with psychotropic medications compared to 12 percent of men; she writes that "these drugs often function to restrict autonomy in much the same way as shackles and solitary confinement."[18]

On the other hand, some providers are also disincentivized to give out any medications at all, let alone sedating or "abusable" medications. One psychiatric provider told me that he never prescribed quetiapine, an antitypical antipsychotic, because he didn't want "[the prisoner] to sleep through her sentence." Additionally, in settings with privatized prison health care contracts, costs are kept low by denying patients access to nonessential or expensive or nonformulary medications as well as discouraging expensive medical visits off-site at hospitals, clinics, or emergency rooms.[19]

Many people found these medications and their effects desirable, particularly those that had sedative qualities (both benzodiazepines and opioids, along with several antipsychotic medications). These substances promised to soothe psychological distress and discomfort in the harsh physical environment of the prison and the difficult social relationships caused by living in tight quarters. Alexis, a young Greek American woman from the New Bedford region of Massachusetts, told me that she first got introduced to benzodiazepines in prison when she told the prison doctor that she took them on the outside. She wanted them to control her anxiety, which she felt was the inciting affect leading to her drug problems, citing that "I'm a walking frigging heart attack waiting to happen." But what ended up happening was she "left [the prison] with a fucking bad habit because I kept buying them off other girls." She used to trade her desirable canteen items (sweatpants, candy, or coffee) for other women's medications. But the pills could only do so much to palliate her incarcerated experience: "This is a pretty horrifying place to wake up in. Regardless of how many Klonipins they feed you, it's horrifying."

WHERE MEDICINE IS CONTRABAND

In stark opposition to the ethnographic observation that sharing medication can be an act of community or care, and in contrast to a clinician's vantage point, in which medications are a means to palliate symptoms of withdrawal or cravings, the prison is focused on rooting out what they perceive as "contraband" medications such as buprenorphine-naloxone and punishing individuals for having it or using it.

In MCI-Framingham, possession of illicit drugs is one of several categories of inmate offenses. According to the inmate handbook, a Category 1 offense, the most severe type, includes the "introduction, distribution or transfer of any narcotic, controlled substance, illegal drug, unauthorized drug or drug paraphernalia." The less severe Category 2 offense is for using. There are even punishments for simply thinking about committing a drug crime. Drugs present a perpetual problem for prison management. In the spring of 2013, the Massachusetts Department of Correction ordered a policy change that reflected the perceived magnitude of the problem: they introduced drug-sniffing dogs into the visitors' waiting rooms at all the prison facilities. They argued that visitors—so-called "mules"—along with the mail, were the two main sources of drugs inside the prisons.

The letter to incarcerated individuals in the DOC facilities from the then commissioner, Luis Spencer, announcing the policy change, read: "The use of drugs many times is a root cause of criminal activity and continued drug use while incarcerated severely impacts your reentry efforts to return to the community better able to cope with the stressors of everyday life. . . . While we realize that visits are an extremely important part of your lives during your incarceration, the Department will not allow your reentry and treatment efforts to be derailed by illicit activities."[20]

The Massachusetts Department of Correction began communicating when they would detect or locate drugs with the public via Facebook, Twitter, and YouTube videos. It was part of a coordinated attempt to project an image of security and effective policing around drugs (they would post photos of said contraband with the hashtags #drugsmuggling #greatjob).

In this way, medicines such as buprenorphine-naloxone in prison morphed into "contraband" to security staff; some medications become what Mary Douglas has called "matter out of place," imbued with potential danger.[21] As the Facebook posts illustrate, security staff actively police this medication (figure 5). The mere presence of these unpermitted substances, simply put, disrupts the order of things. The stated reason for such intense scrutiny is that it could cause fighting, with possible physical harm brought to incarcerated women or the guards. Yet, anecdotally, in jail settings such as Franklin County House of Correction in

FIGURE 5. Massachusetts Department of Correction public Facebook post displaying various kinds of seized contraband, including buprenorphine-naloxone (Suboxone) films and other medications such as the antidepressant fluoxetine and a medication used for neuropathic pain (gabapentin).

Massachusetts, where jail-based buprenorphine treatment programs exist, incidents and reports of bad behavior have actually gone down since the programs started.

Yet there is another layer to having drugs in these settings. The presence of illicit substances suggested that inmates could theoretically achieve a level of intoxication, oblivion, relief, or escape from their punishments and the stated rehabilitation that they were supposedly receiving in prison, which then would reflect the failure of the prison and its staff to maintain order, to establish an abstinence environment, to properly enact punishments, and to deprive inmates of their liberty. Paired with a photo of heroin seized as contraband (figure 6), the Department of Correction wrote on its Facebook page, "Many of the women incarcerated at MCI Framingham have serious substance abuse issues and they would pay or do nearly anything to feed their addictions. It is our duty to keep them safe and aid them in recovery." Much like the physicians and social workers of earlier decades, prison officials adopted a patronizing attitude toward women: protecting immoral or depraved women from themselves and their incorrigible desires to use drugs. Ironically, the very thing they have been so actively policing—the medication buprenorphine-naloxone—was the very thing approved and intended to treat withdrawal and prevent drug cravings. If administered to treat opioid use disorder in theses settings, it could also potentially

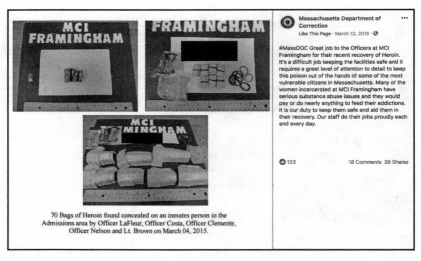

70 Bags of Heroin found concealed on an inmates person in the
Admissions area by Officer LaFleur, Officer Costa, Officer Clemente,
Officer Nelson and Lt. Brown on March 04, 2015.

FIGURE 6. Massachusetts Department of Correction public Facebook post demonstrating a heroin seizure and the correctional system approach toward drug use.

protect against overdose and death from more harmful opioids such as heroin or fentanyl.

Alexis and others were also critical of the prison staff for policing, punishing, and profiting off drug use in the prisons. The inmates believed that the prison literally profited because they would seize the inmates' personal funds (sent by family members and friends or earned in prison labor) as punishment. Brittany explained that they fined her $140 for the first urine test that showed positive for illicit drugs ("dirty urine"), in addition to being sent to solitary confinement for two weeks. If IPS guards handcuffed an inmate, everyone knew why. The fine for a second urine test that showed illicit substances was doubled. The prison treasurer would take the money out of the inmate's account, freezing her ability to buy canteen items like food, shampoo, or clothing. This greatly impacted women's abilities to tolerate the vagaries of prison life.

Testing was performed either upon suspicion that a woman was using or evidence of intoxication such as physical injury or having substances in her cell. The women in the Correctional Recovery Academy were subject to mandatory times of urine testing, including within twenty-four hours on enrollment, twice during the program, once during week of graduation, and also at the discretion of administrators. In addition to this group, there was also a "Suspect List" that was present at all the state correctional institutions comprised of "up to 10% of this institution's population" of "those inmates who pose the greatest risk to abuse drugs or alcohol."[22] Those individuals were tested monthly, to leave the list only after three consecutive months of negative drug tests.

The Department of Correction explains in its protocols that inmates can either plead guilty or take a confirmatory quantitative blood test from an outside laboratory using the gold standard of gas chromatography/mass spectrometry: "If the confirmatory test supports the positive initial screening result(s), the inmate may be held responsible for restitution regarding the cost of the confirmatory test(s)."[23] The inmate does not have to pay if the confirmatory test is negative. Only the guilty must pay. Included in the list of illicit substances are the medications methadone and buprenorphine as well as other medications such as benzodiazepines, barbiturates, amphetamines, and oxycodone.

Contraband, according to the Department of Correction, "increases prison violence, facilitates escapes, compromises staff and inmate safety, and negatively impacts reentry efforts. The existence of contraband also shatters the public's perception of security." The word *contraband*, from the Spanish word *contrabando*, meaning "smuggling," is defined as "any illegal or prohibited traffic"; in times of war, it can be "anything forbidden to be supplied by neutrals to belligerents in time of war."[24] This does in fact represent a new kind of war: the downtrodden versus their captors, a war against prohibition and failing War on Drugs policies. As Michel Foucault has written, "The art of punishing . . . must rest on a whole technology of representation."[25] The Massachusetts Department of Correction actively crafts this "technology of representation" using traditional media outlets, social media, and other sources of communication to the public. Achieving a "law and order" public perception is critical in their work of punishment; in many ways, it is everything. The presence of so-called illicit drugs, including medicines that they see as being "abused" or used to get high, critically damages public perceptions that the prison is a safe, secure environment where staff engage in rehabilitation of individuals with substance use disorders resulting in abstinence and success. It reveals the fragile philosophical tenets of the criminal justice system and suggests that the prison fails to produce reformed citizens.

Women are understandably confused by the disconnect they perceive in the way drug use is handled. In their prison-based drug treatment classes, they learn that addiction is a relapsing, remitting disease, a chronic disease like diabetes, but on the other hand, they are punished, sent to solitary confinement, and fined for ongoing drug use. In jail and prison, they are not allowed to access the evidence-based medications that community physicians and other experts even in their drug treatment classes tell them are critical components to a holistic treatment of substance use disorders. In fact, being caught using drugs in prison represents profit for the prison while they continue to be deprived of medicines that would treat and quell their cravings.

Furthermore, their ongoing non-recovery in the community, including multiple returns to jail and prison for technical violations of probation and parole (sometimes from urine drug screens that are positive for substances), in many ways ensures the continued existence of the prisons and the economic security of the employees of these institutions that are failing to provide inmates with the treatment they need and deserve. Instead of working with individuals who are struggling and keeping them in their homes and communities, people with histories of incarceration, who are caught in the nets of lengthy community supervision programs, are instead sent back to prison and denied life-saving medication, which at best is a repetition of an ineffective cycle and at worst is a practice that actually places them at increased harm, with greater susceptibility to overdose and death upon release.[26]

A LUCRATIVE MARKET

While some medications to treat opioid use disorder in prisons and jails were labeled contraband, others were being promoted and marketed as essential to these carceral spaces, including jails, prisons, probation, parole, and drug courts. Many other detailed accounts have examined the often nefarious role of pharmaceutical companies in promoting, ignoring, and falsifying information about opioid products they produce, beginning with FDA approval of extended-release oxycodone (OxyContin) in 80 mg and 160 mg tablets in the 1990s by Purdue Pharmaceuticals for the treatment of chronic non-cancer pain.[27] Purdue and other pain pharmaceutical companies engaged in aggressive marketing campaigns to primary care doctors, psychiatrists, surgeons, dentists, and pain specialists to garner sales of up to $3 billion of OxyContin in 2010; the commercial success of the pill was the product of marketing efforts unprecedented in the history of pain pharmaceuticals as well alignment with cultural shifts in the treatment and management of pain that were heavily sponsored by these companies themselves, leading to opioids being the number one most prescribed class of medications in the United States in 2011.[28]

Yet few have examined others in the increasingly big business of addiction treatment. Examining the case of one pharmaceutical company, Alkermes Pharmaceuticals, and its medication known as intramuscular naltrexone (IM-naltrexone, or Vivitrol) reveals the complexities of divergent and deeply rooted American orientations toward substance use disorders. This is an emergent space that I call "the prison-pharmaceutical nexus," and it demonstrates one attempt to profit off addiction and untreated social distress in prisons using biomedical technology and innovative drug delivery mechanisms.[29]

Historically, pharmaceutical companies have had an unsavory relationship with prisons, treating them as spaces of experimentation where the captivity of humans readily provides possible test subjects. As historian Nancy Campbell has shown in her disturbing research on the federal addiction research facility in Lexington, Kentucky, federal addiction researchers "were in the business of re-addicting prisoner patients for the sake of science. . . . This determination provided information used by pharmaceutical companies seeking to bring drugs to market."[30] Commercial research was also performed in such spaces. Between 1962 and 1966, at least thirty-three pharmaceutical companies were active in the testing of 153 pharmaceutical and cosmetic products on prisoners in the infamous Holmesburg prison experiments in Pennsylvania.[31]

The medication that would become marketed heavily to jails and prisons for opioid use disorder was first synthesized in 1963 by a chemist at Endo Pharmaceuticals, which was later acquired by DuPont in 1969. Naltrexone was a compound that belonged to a class of medications called opioid antagonists. It worked by binding to opioid receptors in the body and competing with other agents (like heroin, or fentanyl) that might want to bind to that same receptor. The theory of efficacy was that these medications would block the sense of pleasure or the reinforcing effects of substances such as alcohol or opioids. The website (vivitrol.com) proclaims it is not "a narcotic; pleasure producing; addictive; or associated with abuse."

The first major pharmaceutical life for naltrexone was as a medication called Trexan, which was approved in 1984 by the FDA for the maintenance of "the opioid free-state in detoxified formerly opioid-dependent individuals." This compound was felt to have dubious market potential at that time, thus the Special Action Office for Drug Abuse Prevention formed by President Nixon and the newly formed National Institute on Drug Abuse (NIDA) were critical in encouraging DuPont to bring the drug to market, promising the pharmaceutical company a special "orphan drug" status with seven years of exclusivity rights protecting its patent against any possible generic competition during that time. Secretary of HHS Margaret Heckler noted that this medicine strengthened "the recovering addicts' will power."[32] Unfortunately, Trexan was not well-received or understood and thus not prescribed widely by clinicians. This was not helped by the presence of an FDA black box warning about hepatotoxicity: there were concerns that many patients who might be candidates for the medication also had liver compromise from hepatitis.

DuPont continued to study the medication and noticed that there was some decreased alcohol consumption in animal models as well as decreased alcohol cravings in human trials when administered as a treatment for patients along with psychosocial interventions. Therefore, DuPont submitted a new indication for the drug in 1994 for alcohol use disorder to the FDA and the drug was rebranded and marketed as ReVia. Naltrexone was approved for alcohol use disorder after some evidence suggested that it decreased cravings in the setting of comprehensive psychosocial treatment (though there were some concerns that it was no better than a placebo without these additional interventions).[33] ReVia additionally had very limited success in this market and remained widely unknown or unrecognized by physicians and patients.[34]

In 2003, the pharmaceutical company Alkermes had recently received approval for a new delivery form, an antipsychotic known as risperidone. It was re-engineered in a long-acting depot injectable formulation, which allowed drug delivery of a medicine every two weeks via injection rather than daily as a pill. The company wondered if naltrexone was amenable to such a formulation, as the addiction pharmaceutical market appeared to be growing. They worked to gain FDA approval for a long-acting injectable form of extended-release naltrexone branded Vivitrol in 2006 for alcohol dependence and in 2008 for the treatment of opioid use disorders.

IM-naltrexone was marketed as a medication for opioid and alcohol treatment that did not replace one drug with another, a common misperception attached to opioid agonist medications buprenorphine and methadone. Many groups, such as Alcoholics Anonymous and Narcotics Anonymous, promoted the idea of being free of "dependency" on chemicals or other drugs, including medications such as buprenorphine or methadone. There was also concern among many potential patients about experiencing physical withdrawal from treatments such as buprenorphine or methadone if abruptly stopped and not tapered slowly off under medical guidance.

Nora Volkow, the head of the National Institute on Drug Abuse, praised the drug upon its approval, noting that the biochemical formulation was what would make the drug useful and worth the $1,000 per shot price tag: "As a depot formulation, dosed monthly, vivitrol obviates the daily need for patients to motivate themselves to stick to a treatment regimen. . . . NIDA is continuing to support research on Vivitrol's effectiveness in this country, including a focus on criminal justice-involved populations transitioning back to the community."[35]

From the pharmaceutical and marketing perspective, this formulation had the potential to solve the problem of patients who were deemed unable, unwilling, or simply too irresponsible to take their own medications for substance use problems. In addition, it was not a controlled substance like methadone or buprenorphine.

Volkow's words presaged Alkermes's rapid expansion and marketing of their medication into drug treatment centers, hospitals, and prisons and jails. While browsing the literature available for women in the state prison, the only medication information I found available was a Vivitrol pamphlet titled "Seeking Treatment Options for Opioid Dependence?" produced by the drug company in the resource classroom. I later discovered that the medication had penetrated a very rural and isolated tribal Native American jail in South Dakota: there was a refrigerator full of free sample injections, even though the medication was not affordable or widely available in the community that the jail served.

I spoke later to the local Alkermes sales representative about the company's involvement in local jails and prisons as we sat together in the waiting room of the OBOT clinic in Boston. He told me that the company was involved in a pilot program with a local county House of Correction where inmates who volunteered would receive the injection five days prior to release and the County sheriff's office would set up follow-up appointments with a drug treatment provider on the outside to receive monthly injections. The County jail was interested in several outcomes: rates of follow-up visits, clean urines, and most importantly, decreased recidivism.

When I asked about recidivism, the rep told me, "Are they coming back? The only good thing we can say so far is it has nothing to do with drugs or alcohol. . . . One of them was a woman and she slept at her boyfriend's house, and I guess that broke the rules of probation, so she ended up back."

The rep explained that the program was based on the supplying of free medications to the jail: "We're supplying the first injection at the county jails. That's a pilot program. I think what they're going to look at, if it does save them money, then it would behoove them." So, was there such a thing as a "free" injection? The medications were donated to these facilities with the expectation that jails might become bulk purchasers of the medication and that people who started on the medication might receive many more months or years of the follow-up injections in the community at the expense of government insurance programs.

As part of their bottom line, the pharmaceutical company needed to convince the government at local, state, and federal levels that starting naltrexone just before release could potentially decrease future criminal justice involvement. They had employees who specialized in navigating state/government affairs as well as the jail system. Alkermes, in their investor portfolio, explained it was a complicated policy environment in which there were numerous ways to profit: "Two epidemics are burdening state and local government: Opioid-related crime and overdoses devastating communities, impacting public health, public safety and child welfare" and "mass incarceration straining public safety resources." Getting the medicine out there and profitable was "a study in complexity" because of the "major public health crisis," "marginalized patients" and "complex access and reimbursement."[36]

Evidence of the efficacy of IM-naltrexone is mixed, and the medical and addiction community believes it might work for a small subset of people. The medication was approved in a placebo-controlled trial based in Russia (where methadone and buprenorphine were and remain illegal, unlike in the United States, where these opioid agonist medications are recommended as first-line therapy).[37] It is not as well studied as methadone or buprenorphine and is not on the World Health Organization list of essential medications. Indeed, a patient would need monthly shots for the duration of expected treatment, possibly for her lifetime. Each injection costs $1,386 to insurance companies, while the generic oral tablet equivalent costs approximately $4 per pill. Alkermes was hoping that the price of forced adherence was worth it, since the medical treatment of opioid use disorder has always been beguiled by the problem of volition. The company sought to appeal to criminal justice cultural orientations toward "abstinence," albeit with a twist—medication-assisted—and they marketed themselves as "abstinence."

Prisons and carceral systems represent a vast potential market for the treatment of drug addiction, and pharmaceutical companies are predictably plying their trade in a place where access to other essential medications for addiction treatment are seen as contraband. Yet there was a significant concern among many addiction experts that taking a dose of IM-naltrexone in jail, or prison, and not taking the next injection upon release in the community, could actually increase risk of overdose and death in the case of resuming opioid use.[38] This is because the individual would have lost tolerance to opioids, and using even just once could be deadly because of the loss of physiological tolerance induced by taking the injectable medication.

The danger with the prison-pharmaceutical liaison is the way in which treatment becomes tied to the social fact of incarceration or even more insidiously, through interactions with the widening net of surveillance and punishment systems such as drug courts. What is even more dangerous is that it accepts the premise that carceral spaces should be sites for the treatment of drug addiction. Across the country, judges in drug courts are ordering defendants to take these injections in prisons or jail prior to release, at the expense of offering buprenorphine or methadone that have established successful short- and long-term outcomes, as well as published outcomes showing decreased crime and improvements in recidivism.[39] Is this enmeshment of pharmaceuticals, prisons, and drug treatment the inevitable outcome of pharmaceutical logics adapted to social policies of incarcerating the poor and the sick?

THE CRIMINALIZATION OF MEDICATION

The questions of where, in what setting, and by what means opioids are taken into the body, are all critical to the apparent legitimacy of these psychopharmaceutical substances. One afternoon, I suggested to Kiara, a fifty-year-old black woman who was getting ready to leave prison, that it might be useful for her to enroll in a buprenorphine clinic upon her release in order to try to stave off a potential relapse to heroin use. 'Won't I get, you know, messed up?" she whispered to me in a husky voice. She was worried that she would feel high since she hasn't been using any drugs in the prison. She wasn't necessarily wrong: she might very well feel mildly euphoric, just as an opioid-naive person taking oxycodone for the first time after a wisdom tooth extraction might feel sedated or altered. The truth is that if I had administered the medication to her in a clinic, she might feel the same way, even in a sterile medical context where staff would monitor her physiological responses to a highly regulated and legal medication.

The consumption of pharmaceuticals—licit opioids as well as other psychoactive medications like tramadol or benzodiazepines or even sleep aids like zolpidem (Ambien)—has become a regular fact of life for most Americans of all walks of life. It is no different for women in prison, who experiment with these substances for a variety of existential, ethical, embodied, and psychological reasons. But it is only certain women's habits of consumption that are policed or marked as excessive, pathological, or criminal. Many women take oxycodone, some even to great excess, but only some go to prison.

This question of where, and in what setting, is critical. If a woman takes buprenorphine-naloxone medication prescribed to her in the hospital, she is safe from the threat of incarceration. But if she buys the same pill on the street, she risks arrest. Is she a patient protected by the legitimacy of a doctor-patient relationship, or is she willfully breaking the law, purchasing a medication prescribed to another to stave off withdrawal symptoms or cravings?

Careful ethnographic inquiry demonstrates how consumption of substances is not necessarily amenable to rational actor theories of economics or precise behavioral psychology. Rather, to sit with an inmate who wants to get high in prison because she simply doesn't care about the consequences and wants to escape the drudgery of incarceration is most telling. "I don't mind going to the hole," one woman told me, "At least it's quiet in there. You get double portions of meals." For her, the consequences are worth five minutes of pleasure or dissociation from her troubling circumstances.

It is in this space of psychological distress, of wildly swinging affects between utter despair and fleeting hope, where licit and illicit substances alike become like magic, transfigured into concrete means of temporarily lifting the weight of the world. There is ample distress in carceral spaces of unexceptionally ordinary life—when a woman feels tired and sore, for example, because she didn't sleep through the night with back pain on the too-hard or too-soft jail-issued mattresses, or it is freezing cold in the prison because of poor physical infrastructure—that forms the real physical context for drug use and "abuse" or "misuse."

In fact, the poor and rich alike are knit together in parallel cultural logics of accumulation and medicalization of distress. The playing field appears to be both leveled and yet distinctly worse for the poor, who end up criminalized, while there are often no or little consequences for people who sell, trade, and consume a variety of medications for pleasure or other purposes. The distinctions for those doing the consuming between licit/illicit and use/misuse/abuse therefore feel arbitrary, inconsistent, and morally fraught. Women who use heroin and other drugs will take substances procured from a variety of people and places. Medical students freely trade amphetamines, empathogens like mushrooms, and anti-anxiolytics with each other in order to achieve optimal embodied effects. Yet these different people and spaces have different social acceptability, surveillance, and subsequent policing practices as well as a variety of embodied effects that are culturally contingent upon place, individual expectations, relationships, value, and power systems.

Many of the women I met in prison were actually incarcerated on violations of the Controlled Substances Act for the possession of drugs or medications that were not technically prescribed for them. Mary, a forty-five-year-old white woman from Cambridge, was incarcerated for six months in the state women's prison for possession of a Class E controlled substance, a medication called gabapentin (Neurontin): "They're saying it was johnnies [Neurontin]. That's just what I pled out to. I had Xanax but it was in my mouth and I ate the evidence. . . . So, I got six months for it. Six months for something I didn't really do. But you know, I'm guilty of something. Just not what they're saying I'm guilty of." As Mary's case illustrates, the War on Drugs has rapidly expanded to ensnare people caught with a wide variety of medications, in this case, an anti-seizure medication, gabapentin, found on her person or in her possession. Markus Dubber, a law professor at University of Toronto, has argued that possession has replaced vagrancy as a tool to incapacitate "millions of dangerous undesirables for offenses with no human victim whatsoever."[40]

Mary lives in an era of strict pharmaco-surveillance where what some people have in their mouths or in their pockets matters, so she still felt guilty of inappropriate consumption. This is a socially mediated subjectivity that is compounded by structural vulnerability, leading to incarceration and even more debilitating consequences from such a life event. Her possession of so-called illicit drugs casts her and other poor women like her into the prison system and exposes them to subsequent stigma, degradation, and distress that being incarcerated almost by definition entails. Mary struggled with stigma and the shame of having been incarcerated upon her release. While she was eager to find a job as a nursing assistant using the resume she wrote in prison, she was unable to make it to appointments she made and felt discouraged by her criminal record. She ended up staying at her mother's house to avoid homelessness, and her mother was evicted from her elderly housing project for letting Mary stay with her. Mary decamped to the streets, where she got high on diverted methadone that she had bought from a friend. She overdosed on methadone and benzodiazepines twice and cycled in and out of psychiatric units and treatment programs over a period of several months.

Mary's case illustrates how simple possession of pharmaceuticals not prescribed for oneself can cast poor women into the prison system, further amplifying already downtrodden subjectivities and a sense of social unbelonging. Prisons and jails would much rather focus on "anger management" or "criminal thinking" cognitive-behavioral courses that aim to improve individual behavior and thinking rather than medications to treat substance use disorders. As sociologist Scott Vrecko has argued, these interventions "are used to produce better citizens, rather than to cure biological diseases—as 'civilizing technologies.'"[41] Incarcerated women with addiction are failed citizens; if they relapse or die upon release from prison, it is a tragedy, but ultimately it is seen as their own decisions to use harmful substances.

This narrow focus on individualized, embodied suffering does not reveal the upstream sources of such social suffering, including political and corporate processes such as the privatization of prison economies and additional extended community forms of poverty management whose surveillance, management, punishment, and rehabilitation schemas have taken the poor as a class for systematic social intervention and experimentation. These are spaces and institutions in which medicine has a complex, fraught texture. As physician-anthropologist Carolyn Sufrin has argued recently, medicine within such carceral institutions has the ability to transform what it means to care.[42] Yet the holistic effects on individuals remain overwhelmingly harmful, increasing the risk of harm and premature death. Recent data demonstrates the embodied risks produced by a policy of detoxing patients in the criminal justice system via an abstinence-based approach. There is a vastly disproportionate risk of death upon release: recent Massachusetts state data illustrated that the opioid-related overdose death rate was 120 times higher for people released from Massachusetts prisons and jails than for the rest of the population (see figure 7).[43]

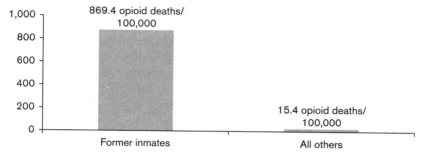

FIGURE 7. Increased risk of opioid overdose death for persons leaving prison or jail (Massachusetts Department of Public Health, An Assessment of Fatal and Nonfatal Opioid Overdoses in Massachusetts [2011–2015], p. 55).

In addition, the risk of death inside prisons and jails is also significant: there are ongoing increasing numbers of jail suicides in Massachusetts, particularly among people who were physically detoxing or had just recently completed the process.[44] These individuals are isolated, possibly kept on suicide watch, and provided a small arsenal of so-called "comfort" medications for symptomatic relief. Yet, the extreme physical distress, combined with the isolation and lack of care, can contribute to these fatal outcomes. It is psychic pain along this continuum—worsened by physical processes of detoxification that have short- and long-term neurobiological effects—compounded by despair, isolation, and harsh living conditions, that form "perfect storm" conditions for acts of distress such as suicide attempts. As anthropologist Lisa Stevenson observed in her work on suicide among the Inuit, suicides can be seen as refusal to "cooperate in survival," a complex tragic response to historical and cultural injustices as well as the bureaucratic indifference to their lives.[45] Might this be the case as well in jail and prison suicides?

In examining the phenomenon of criminalized consumption, this critical distinction between what comprises a "medicine" and what is "contraband" results in disjointed and at-times contradictory practice patterns between carceral medical, security, and community apparatuses. In fact, it epitomizes the long-standing, entrenched American debate over whether opioid use disorders represent a disease process or a criminal act, and as historians of drug policy have noted, the pendulum swings back and forth with expected consequences, while the rate of American drug use has remained roughly stable. Yet, can there be a third way, a path that recognizes the complexity of why someone uses and becomes dependent on opioids? Is there a path of recognizing humanity, a way of identifying the root causes of despair, isolation and unhappiness, compounded by access to substances that temporarily can alleviate these pains?

The philosophy of harm reduction offers a possible third way. Instead of forcing people to stop substances or lecturing them to have more willpower, harm reduction accepts that many people use drugs. It furthermore posits that people can use these substances in a more or less risky or harmful way (for example, snorting cocaine is safer than injecting cocaine, as it minimizes injection-related risks such as HIV, Hepatitis C, bloodborne infections or abscesses). In fact, trying to get people to stop using drugs, to attain abstinence, actually harms many people. Abstinence may be an eventual goal for some and may be the safest of all possible options, but our strong social insistence on stopping—while everyone else drinks, gets wrecked, and consumes all varieties of pills and other substances—in many ways also can damage people irreparably. Individuals often become caught in cycles of self-blame and shame and are held accountable for their perceived moral failures when, in fact, the structures that perpetuate and allow for these cycles are not critically examined. Such blame and shame cycles often are a reason cited for ongoing destructive use.

Harm reduction philosophy allows one person to recognize the common humanity of a suffering other and to extend help toward "any positive change" (made famous by Dan Bigg, a harm reduction pioneer from Chicago) to someone else seeking it. Harm reduction recognizes that drug use occurs, that many of the traditional licit/illicit distinctions are arbitrary and fraught, and that we could minimize harms that individuals face as they use drugs made even more dangerous by being driven to the black market. Instead of using pills (oxycodone, with an assured pharmaceutical purity), people are purchasing "fake" oxycodone and alprazolam contaminated with or containing fentanyl, increasing their risk of death. In Canada, the so-called street/black market was so dangerous when studied that researchers and physicians implemented IV diacetylmorphine (heroin) clinics that prevented people with heroin use disorders from dying by providing a safe supply of pharmaceutically manufactured heroin produced and regulated by the Canadian government.[46] While not a panacea, many of the worst harms and premature deaths of the most structurally vulnerable can be prevented.

It is tragic that our country links opioid use disorders and the American opioid crisis with incarceration as a social response. Other countries, like Portugal, have decriminalized drug use and have unlinked these social structures to positive societal results.[47] The tragedy is that incarceration has real, often permanently disfiguring, consequences for women with substance use disorders. Their lives prior to incarceration are already marked by structural violence and trauma and then additionally imprinted with the carceral footprint of despair. And it is poor women who use drugs, often disproportionately black or Hispanic— who are most often exposed to the threats of policing and violence, racism, sexism, and trauma—who bear the burden of punitive and puritanical American policies of mandatory detoxification in these spaces, with subsequent physical withdrawal that leaves them physiologically laid bare to the immense risks of preventable overdoses and premature deaths upon release.

6

Recovery Is My Job Now

I tried to get all kinds of different jobs. "You're not exactly what we're looking for." You have to fall back on what you know. For me, that was hustle, whichever way I had to do it. [Selling] pharmaceuticals, like Klonopins. I had to change with the times [shift to pills].

—Linda

"Works well in a high-pressure environment. Self-motivated and assertive. Enjoys working with people." These are some of the character and personality traits that Serenity has listed on the résumé that she is writing in jail; she is particularly proud that she has typed it up herself on one of the jail's three PC computers. This is only one part of her overall recovery and reentry plan: the rest of her agenda items include going back to school to become a registered nurse, actually following through with contesting the denial of her Supplemental Security Income application (SSI) and getting her own housing. She admittedly has a sparse work history, with no work in the formal labor market in the last ten years since she moved to Boston. She lists her previous work experience as "broad experience as licensed nursing assistant with certification in CPR." She also lists her experience working at a coffee shop in New Hampshire. Makes dough, handles the fryer.

Her résumé—like all résumés—tells a certain story about her life that has blotted out the gaps, the holes, the long stretches of emotional turmoil and interpersonal angst. In her case, the résumé skips over the time that she lost her job because she started using too many drugs and was unable to get up in the morning to go to work or the time when her personal house-cleaning business languished as she became increasingly dependent on heroin and spent all her waking hours scheming to get more. It glosses over the twenty times that she has been in and out of prison and jail, but then again, any potential employers will find that out soon enough. Her Criminal Offender Record Information (CORI) is "a mile long," according to her, although she admits that she has not actually seen it recently.

It is certainly not a lie that Serenity works well in a high-pressure environment. The streets of downtown Boston are a hard place to gain respect, to gain a reputation for being tough, to keep one's physical and psychic integrity intact. The ancient cobblestone streets are charming, perhaps even quaint in their unevenness, but they are also full of danger and uncertainty as she generates income between the hours of three and six in the morning via her steadier form of work. Sex always sells. When she doesn't want to resort to sex work—which she increasingly doesn't as she gets older and wearier—she buys drugs in a small bulk quantity and flips them in order to have enough for her own use. She is industrious in her penury, and as long as she can live from fix to fix, she makes do.

Serenity is not alone in her industrious poverty. She belongs to a wider class that sociologist Herbert Gans has called "the excluded poor" and "the blamed poor" and that historian Michael Katz called the "undeserving poor."[1] Through this lens, poor people are felt by others to be responsible for their penury; they are able bodied and could and should work; therefore, their poverty is a product of their own making. Nor is she alone in experiencing the insistent societal emphasis for her to get a job even though the job market has largely prohibited her entry except into its lowest, most undesirable rungs. The risks of employing anyone with a felony record, especially in a nursing home or a hospital like where Serenity aspires to work, are just too high.

Serenity knows this all too well, even though she can glibly speak of her career goals and work ambitions to any concerned drug treatment administrator or program staff in the jail. When she is released straight from the Boston Municipal Court on New Chardon Street and takes in the humid air of the Boston summer, finding work is one of the last things on her mind. She also does not report to probation. This breech of the rules immediately sets her up for returning to jail if she gets stopped by a police officer. She does not enact the plan that she has labored over in jail to go to a drug treatment program, to look for housing, or to start a tedious—possibly even fruitless—job search. Instead, she goes to her best friend's apartment, smokes crack with him, and then heads out to find heroin to come down off the frenetic crack high.

PUTTING WOMEN TO WORK

I was struck by the importance of the theme of working—or not working—among women leaving prison when I attended a meeting with several men from a local advocacy organization, Ex-Prisoners Organizing for Community Advancement (EPOCA), based out of Worcester, Massachusetts. They were in the early stages of a campaign addressing the collateral sanctions at the Registry of Motor Vehicles (RMV), which included a $500 driver's license reinstatement fee for anyone who had been convicted of a drug-related felony. This seemed to represent another collateral consequence of incarceration. In this group's opinion, it was an unfair and stigmatizing barrier to getting work, since having a driver's license was critical to getting to and from a job.

It dawned on me as we were talking about the campaign that this didn't seem to be a big issue for women leaving prison as much as it seemed to be for men leaving prison. I knew from working with many of the women that they didn't have their licenses either, so why didn't they seem as concerned about getting them back, about the implications for getting a job? I realized there was a distinctly gendered dimension to life after prison, to this question of labor. Why did the prisons and jails place so much of an emphasis on it for incarcerated women when it seemed sometimes far down the list of women's priorities upon release?

Within the sociological and policy literature on employment after incarceration, there is an epistemological orientation that affirms that work is a generally positive and stabilizing force in people's lives—in other words, work provides a necessary sense of daily rhythm and life structure. Criminologists emphasize the benefits of what they call a strong labor force attachment leading to less "antisocial" behaviors; this argument suggests also that decent jobs with some level of stability and prestige can reduce recidivism.[2] A report on women, incarceration, and work sponsored by the Women's Prison Association posited that "employment can be an integral part of a self-sufficient and independent life."[3]

Yet getting a job after incarceration was extremely difficult, and the mark of a criminal record in combination with structural racism created significant barriers to finding jobs. Racism also makes finding a job doubly difficult. Sociologist Devah Pager, in a groundbreaking study, sent white and black men out with the same résumé with and without a felony conviction for drug possession, and found that job offers were more frequently given to white men both with and without records than

African American men without a criminal record (the group that did the worst was African American men with the mark of a criminal record).[4] Unfortunately, there is not enough research involving women's prospects. However, one study published by an Arizona research group noted that in a poll of hypothetical employers looking at the same résumé, employers would have called back 57 percent of the men as opposed to 30 percent of the women.[5]

Questions of work and labor are central to philosophical notions of the good life and the good society. The Universal Declaration of Human Rights includes work in Article 23: "Everyone has the right to work, to free choice of employment, to just and favorable conditions of work and to protection against unemployment."[6] Work is intimately related to achieving a dignified life, one marked by one's contributions and ability to provide support for oneself and one's family. Work affords us a sense of identity and a way to move forward and proceed confidently in the world—what psychologists call "self-efficacy"—that is, the perception of one's own ability to face challenges and succeed in goals. Work can also serve for many as a stabilizing anchor to ensure that individuals feel a sense of purpose and belonging with a community of others.

Those who cannot or do not work tend to face stigma and pejorative moral judgments. To not work is to violate part of the human contract, to not participate in bettering the life of the community. Thus, one strong and commonly held sentiment toward people that use drugs who do not work is that they are weak-willed, lazy, and do not work by choice even though they could or should. This cultural orientation believes that drug users (and the poor more generally) profit from the rest of the laboring public's tax-dollars and productivity by relying on various government assistance programs. Sociologist Loïc Wacquant posits that we punish the poor with incarceration "if they prove too recalcitrant and disruptive" and are not successfully "steer[ed] . . . toward deregulated employment through moral re-training and material suasion."[7]

Furthermore, work serves as a strongly moralizing trope in American culture (take the vitriol among the seemingly endless welfare and work debates). Where we work and what we do shape our core identities, our sense of ourselves and self-esteem, and even our ways of being in the world. If we work, we are valuable. If we do not work, we are lazy and necessarily dependent on others who work for support and survival. Dependence, in our dominant cultural paradigm, is antithetical to the

American way of life, as Linda Gordon and Nancy Fraser have argued about our attitudes toward welfare and women who do not or cannot work.[8]

Work, therefore, was not surprisingly seen as critical to the reformation of deviant criminals. The iconic Eastern State Penitentiary in Philadelphia was founded two centuries ago on the Quaker and Progressive ideologies that prayer and work would lead to salvation and rebirth for the criminals contained within; while incarcerated, men would work for hours in isolation and total silence consistent with the philosophy of reform. Gustave de Beaumont and Alexis de Tocqueville, in their tour of the early American carceral landscape, recommended this model for prisons in France; as social historian Caleb Smith wrote, "The important thing, for them, was that solitude should be mitigated by labor. . . 'labor, by comforting them, makes them love the only means, which when again free, will enable them to gain honestly their livelihood.'"[9]

The notion of formal work for incarcerated women upon release is a relatively newer phenomenon. Historically, women were funneled into domestic chores and duties as the realization of their gendered destinies.

At MCI-Framingham in the 1930s, the administrators promoted a uniquely gendered prison work rehabilitation scheme, including classes on homemaking and gardening as well as an optional yet controversial day-labor indenture program, where incarcerated women were allowed to work as maids or cooks in the homes of middle-class community families off-site from the prison. The progressive superintendent of MCI-Framingham, Miriam Van Waters, came under fire for allowing the incarcerated women to actually earn money by this work. The superintendent argued that she wanted women to be able to be financially independent from men; she pointed out the inequities, including that men could get paid for prison labor but women could not. If women worked conditionally in the community, they were still paid only $3 to men's $8.

Later on, in the 1980s and 1990s, women were allowed to labor at prison-based industries; at MCI-Framingham, for decades there was a flag-making industry. The state-run prison labor industry (slogan: "Working on the Inside; Succeeding on the Outside") still exists in the form of MassCorr Correctional Industries, netting $10.8 million in revenue in 2005. A division of the Massachusetts Department of Correction, the stated aim of the prison labor program is to instill work discipline and contribute to decreased recidivism.

Preparing women to work was a central and important piece of programming in both the jail and the prison where I conducted my fieldwork. I found that the Suffolk House of Correction focused intently on the employment angle for incarcerated women in hopes of decreasing recidivism. They had recently received a grant in partnership with Northeastern University to start a career center in the jail. I spoke with one of the staff members at the women's jail programming department about the difficulty of employment prospects. She told me she wanted to make going to résumé class or the career center as routine and normative as it was to attend classes on parenting, domestic violence, and GED. She felt that it was generally unrealistic to expect that women would be stable enough to work upon their release, but that even if the career center made five women at least partially employable, then it would make the program worthwhile. The jail also hosted a mock job fair in which employers from the "outside" came in and women pretended to apply for jobs at their companies.

In the prison, the MCI-Framingham New Horizons Center (the reentry resource room for the prison), a poster on the wall exhorted inmates to "Dress for Success." It showed a cartoon of a black woman wearing a DOC prison jumpsuit looking at a mirror image of herself and seeing the same woman smiling back at her from the mirror wearing a red dress with a snazzy belt. Another sign in the room read, "Success in an interview": the pie chart underneath read "45 percent packaging, 35 percent responsiveness, 10 percent experience, 10 percent miscellaneous." Unfortunately for incarcerated women, the packaging is the permanent branding of incarceration.

WOMEN'S WORK READINESS IN JAIL

In my interviews, I discovered that having a stable or full-time job in the formal economy was usually absent from the life histories of incarcerated women. Most of the women that I met in prison and jail had life histories of seasonal, part-time, or "off-the-books" jobs. Most of them had not worked formally in the past five years or more. When I asked them what they had wanted to be when they grew up, they said they had had regular aspirations for careers with purpose and meaning, including doctors, nurses, veterinarians, and lawyers or advocates for children in difficult circumstances like their own. Not surprisingly, none of them had achieved these professions; only approximately half of them had acquired GEDs or high school diplomas.

The jobs that they had actually been able to land were more typical of the sub-proletariat or working class "pink collar" industry: hairdressers, medical assistants, billing, sales, receptionists, housecleaning, and nannying (only a few of them had significant career histories before they fell into drug use and subsequent unemployment—Lydia as a pharmacy technician; Diane as a unionized construction worker; Susie as a billing assistant; Serenity and Mary as certified nursing assistants).

The jobs they hoped to do in the future were largely defined by life experiences they had had more recently: most of them wanted to become certified alcohol and drug counselors. They saw it as a field in which their existential lived experiences might actually be seen as a job asset, not as a detriment. Many also aspired to rejoin or newly train in jobs in the medical field. Some hoped to become a phlebotomist, since they could manage to hit scraggly, shrunken veins on themselves and others across a variety of bodily terrains.

Many of the women turned away from a labor market that systematically excluded and disempowered them. Project Place, an organization in the South End neighborhood of Boston, seemed to grasp this dilemma. The organization has a long-established history of working with incarcerated populations, specifically around employment and housing. They run a well-regarded program called CREW (Community ReEntry for Women) that has won numerous awards and accolades for its reentry work with the Suffolk House of Correction. For example, the CREW project was named a 2012 "Bright Idea" by the Ash Center for Democratic Governance and Innovation based at the John F. Kennedy School of Government at Harvard. Boston's longest-serving mayor, Thomas Menino, who served five terms, said that Project Place literally cleaned up the human detritus of Boston with its work: "Of all the programs we do in this City, Project Place is my favorite because it really does make a difference. It helps clean up the city. It also helps clean up people's lives."

The CREW team is based at Project Place in the South End, but it also sends staff members into the jail to run classes on employment and job readiness. I met Polly Hanson, the program director of CREW, at the modern, spacious Project Place building in the South End.

The program, Hanson told me, began in 2007 with a Department of Education grant focused on job readiness for women. In the beginning, they had to adapt the program to the realities of women's lives: "[We] learned pretty quickly that we had to back things up a couple steps to get women prepared to even think about the process of looking for work, so, really addressing self-confidence and just self-conception, and frankly even a belief that work is possible." The class then started with four weeks of these life skills concepts and then four weeks of job readiness; this morphed into six weeks of life skills and then two weeks of job training.

Throughout the class, CREW instructors hoped to help women deal with the complexities of their lives and life after prison by teaching them coping skills and how to make good decisions. They also encouraged women to come to the Project Place office in the South End upon release to take advantage of "wrap-around services." Project Place hoped that they could provide women with ongoing case management, employment opportunities, and housing help, among other things that women might need. They hoped to serve as a "one-stop shop" for women leaving prison.

Hanson noted that the CREW program had to bring the women down "out of the clouds" and back to the realities of their lives, trying to reconcile what women wanted to do for employment in a perfect world with the kinds of jobs they might actually be able to realistically get: "Everybody wants to very much go into caretaking roles and definitely the medical profession. And it is very challenging, especially for women who have CORIs, and especially if they are specifically related to intravenous drug use. . . . You can't be a phlebotomist. It's not going to happen, you know." The women face dismal job prospects: "How can it be something that's not working at Dunkin' Donuts that feels very dead-end and then you hit your limit and it's like, well, it's easier to just not work." Or possibly, I wondered, they could make more money selling drugs outside a Dunkin' Donuts, like Brittany did, than working for the Dunkin' Donuts.

Hanson put forward the sociological argument that work is a stabilizing structure and provides an orientation to people's lives. She knew that getting a job was low on the list of priorities for women leaving prison, but she argued that it was just as good as any other place to intervene (whereas competing agencies might focus on providing housing or mental health/medical care). Amid these competing rationalities toward well-being after leaving prison, Hanson tried to emphasize that getting a job could be good even in the context of life stressors: If you get a job, then you don't have to spend as much time at that sober house that you hate, with all its rules and regulations and restrictions! But she also understood, as she put it, that, psychodynamically speaking, it's a complicated situation for women who use drugs and have been incarcerated. She explained:

> People [are] taking opiates to . . . disconnect. . . . It's antithetical to being like, I'm going to dive in, get up at seven, and I'm going to go be in the world. Because I'm removing myself from the world [by doing drugs] and so there's so many things that come up that are about removing, but then that removal breeds depression, isolation, and then it becomes this cycle. But if you try to clear up the haze, and you try to connect or stay present, you are overwhelmed by all the packed-down trauma and pain that everybody's been avoiding the whole time.

So it is precisely not being a part of the world that many women who use heroin seek to achieve. The focus on employment and reentry, therefore, is much more complicated than simply preparing a résumé.

The issue of trauma kept bubbling up to the point of detracting from their main goal of talking about employment readiness. Hanson elaborated the difficulty that trauma poses for their program: "A huge part of the curriculum is trying to develop a new identity or patterns that might be related to the histories with trauma. I have actually encouraged us to do a little less delving into [that], because I think it's too destabilizing and I think it takes away from building the skills to cope, so I'm actually trying to do more identifying red flags and building coping skills toolbox kind of thing, because they're all too aware of their trauma in so many ways, and it's uncontained."

The concrete changes they made after Hanson's suggestion to do less "delving into" included eliminating the week on parenting, which involved a deep dive into how they were parented and how they themselves parent. Too much "stuff" kept coming up. Hanson conceded that "[trauma is] coming out every pore of so many of the women that containing it is more than a full-time job and it's very hard for them." Was it ideal for a job treatment readiness class to unleash the significant traumas that were ubiquitous in the lives of incarcerated women?

Hanson noted that of the women who took part in CREW, 33 percent were able to get some kind of job upon release, based on their internal data. Unlike their male counterparts, most of the women did not take up the Project Place offer to work part-time there and train in the food service or facilities maintenance enterprises.

The post-prison lives of women were often marked by anxiety and full-time day-to-day chaos. Serenity actually was in the first graduating cohort of CREW in 2007 and had taken the class several times since then during various stints in jail. She liked CREW and thought that it "breaks you down to build you up" and was hard work ("You have like forty pages of homework a night"). She said she had "learned a lot about myself taking CREW," but she never went to Project Place after getting out of jail.

PROFITING OFF THE INEVITABILITY OF NON-RECOVERY

Serenity was arguably more valuable to the new economies of rehabilitation and treatment in her lack of recovery than in any future employment she might ever attain. As a woman with a chronic condition such as opioid use disorder, she cycled in and out of increasingly for-profit, privatized drug-treatment schemes, prisons, and spaces of health care. Within these systems, she was a source of income to neoliberal regimes that profited from the inevitability of relapse, the fact that she would "keep coming back" (to adopt a phrase they say in AA). She constantly moved within overlapping and fragmentary nodes of care and punishment in ways that generated profit while contributing to an increasingly downtrodden subjectivity.

Serenity received conflicting information from her doctors and program administrators. She didn't know what to prioritize when she left jail. Maybe she should have just focused on taking care of her HIV, since she had become resistant to many of the drug regimens over the years: "That's what they say to me. Take care of yourself. Recovery's your job [now]." Work was far from her mind.

. . .

After Serenity and I first talked in the Lemuel Shattack Hospital outpatient buprenorphine treatment clinic (OBOT), I wondered if we'd ever met before. Something about her looked familiar—maybe the sparkling green-gray eyes, the quirky jangle of her jewelry, a piercing dry commentary on street life—and then I remembered that we had met before, about three years earlier, in the Boston jail. At the time, I had been going there with a social worker from the Shattuck Hospital to set people up with primary care, mental health care, and addiction services if they were uninsured.

In the three years since we had last seen each other, Serenity's life had gone much the same as the previous seven, largely marked by an abject and cyclical movement between prisons and jails, hospitals, shelters, and the streets. Serenity, in accordance with our society's attitudes toward self-care and the fervent belief that one can make decisions to leave this "lifestyle," was plagued by feelings of guilt and misery.

The past several years were full of tragedies, accidents, and bad luck. Serenity had been incarcerated ten times in the past ten years—for larceny, possession, and prostitution—all nonviolent crimes arguably related to her social dispossession. She was homeless, preferring the routinely precarious danger of a life on the streets than the unbending rules and meddling supervision of a shelter system, a sober house, or a drug treatment program.

At this time, she was in an inpatient three-month drug treatment program, nearing her graduation. This was the longest time in her thirteen-year drug-using career that she ever stayed at a program. She had been at this program before but was kicked out when they were taken shopping for sundries at a pharmacy and Serenity was caught shoplifting. After that, the police ran warrant checks on everyone in the program, and apparently half the participants got arrested as a result, so the program director wasn't keen on letting Serenity back in this time. But surprisingly, he did.

We were making plans to take her to the court to deal with at least one outstanding warrant she had. One was for selling drugs in a school zone; the other was for "common nightwalking." At a meeting of advocates to reform the drug laws, someone once quipped, "All of Boston is a school zone." A recent, albeit minor, win for criminal justice reform occurred in Massachusetts when they decreased the size of the school zone from 300 feet to 150 feet.

Serenity was pretty sure that the charges would be dismissed, but she still had an outstanding bench warrant to show up in court. There are generally two responses to having outstanding warrants: run or turn oneself in. Most people run. They often manage to run for quite a while; their risk for getting picked up by the police depends on where they go and stay—if they are homeless, for example—or if they continue to engage in behaviors like shoplifting to support their drug habits. It's critical to pick the right time to present oneself to court; if you're in treatment, there's a chance that the judge might be more lenient on you.

We were hoping that since Serenity was in a three-month program, they would be lenient on her. But we had to admit the possibility that she might have to go to jail. I was planning on driving her to court. We hoped to bring a letter from the director of the outpatient addiction clinic as well as a letter from the director of her treatment program, along with her urine drug screens that showed no illicit substances. We picked a day to go. When I called Serenity at the treatment program's phone number that day, she said we couldn't go since she didn't have approval to leave the program or a letter from the director yet. So we waited.

In the meantime, Serenity graduated the program. This was the first time she had ever graduated anything. She technically graduated when they found her a bed at another residential treatment program, even though she had failed before at that house. When they find you another bed, you just feel lucky that you're not getting discharged back to the streets. Even if it's a program you've failed at before, maybe this time the treatment will stick.

But Serenity didn't last more than six hours at her new program. Her boyfriend, Oscar, came to find her and they picked up again, using heroin. She headed back to the streets. It was hard for her to turn her back on her friends, who had given her clean jeans or loaned her money when she needed it. Sometimes, it's the little acts of kindness between people facing immense poverty that make it possible to locate a will to live. It was impossible to avoid "people, places and things" as they say in AA.

After a month of no contact, Serenity once again called the Outpatient Buprenorphine Opioid Clinic. She reported that she was in a detox facility near Boston Medical Center. We made plans to bring her to the clinic, try to start getting things in order for her. These detox programs are an increasingly short process, down to three to five days. Most detox facilities don't have the staff or the resources to help people find somewhere to go after the detox. There are fewer and fewer long-term drug treatment beds, even relatively short thirty-day ones. And what is the financial incentive for detox facilities to actually help cure you of addiction in the long term when they can bill MassHealth (Medicaid) multiple times a year for your stays if you fail to get better?

During the detox program, Serenity was handed a list of phone numbers and expected to make phone calls to treatment programs to see if they had space for her. After all, that's a vital part of treatment, taking some responsibility for your addiction and participating in your treatment plan. What that means, though, is getting yourself on a lot of wait lists, learning to call the programs in the afternoons, when other people have left and groups are less likely to be going on. When Serenity was calling, there was an estimated thirty-two hundred people on waiting lists for residential treatment programs.

Instead, we made a plan that I would pick up Serenity at 10 a.m. on the morning of the last day of the program and bring her to the OBOT clinic. When I arrived at the detox, I made my way between a dumpster and a long length of fence to an unmarked door that is the entrance to either the detox or a homeless shelter. I was buzzed in through this door. The lady at the front desk looked up with disinterest. When I say that I am Serenity's ride, she says, "I can neither confirm nor deny that she is here or that she left."

Months later, Serenity showed up at the clinic. She told me she had left at 8 a.m., knowing that I was coming at 10. "I had big plans," she said simply. It wasn't anything personal. Many people use the detoxes as a way to moderate or diminish their tolerance. They are safe havens when you run out of money or drugs and also the energy and where-withal to acquire money or drugs. Many people go right back out intending to use again. Those who don't necessarily plan on that course of action have to then figure out how and where they're going to "detox from the detox," since they sometimes administer methadone to help you feel better, which lingers in your system. Even for women and men who do find a place to go in a Transitional Stabilization Services (TSS) or a Clinical Stabilization Services (CSS) program, the urge to leave and use is strong because they still feel physically ill, sometimes partly from the methadone administered there.

We were all relieved that Serenity was okay when she showed up at the OBOT clinic the next time. In the intervening six weeks of being missing in action, her phone number minutes ran out, and her medications, including her HIV medication, had been stolen in a shelter. That's just a well-known peril of shelter life, since medications may be the most valuable possessions you own.

Sometimes she would show up to the clinic on a Friday afternoon. She told me she might fill her prescription for her medication (if the clinic agrees to let her back in) for a $3.50 co-pay, or even get the co-pay waived at certain pharmacies where they know you. Then she would have a week's worth of these tablets, so approximately fourteen tablets, that she could sell to people who were getting dopesick and didn't want to go through withdrawal. She could sell them on the street for $10 a pill; $150 can get a lot of heroin.

She even sometimes would take her medication intermittently and use heroin as well, although she claimed that she was often "dumb" about it, using heroin too soon after she had taken the medication and thus couldn't feel anything. This is because the medication buprenor-phine blocks heroin's action at the brain receptor; it sits on the receptor more tightly than heroin, and the heroin floats around, unable to bind, producing no physical effects. She told me that she hates herself for it:

"It's pointless, I know, because I'm taking Suboxone. I'm good, and then somebody's in my face, loading a needle, "Oh, you want half of this?" Yeah, okay, you can't feel a fucking thing. All you're doing is giving yourself a dirty urine, so when you get picked up you really fuck yourself. How smart can you be?"

Serenity tried to sign herself up for a six-month program at a residential treatment facility in Quincy. To get in, you need fourteen days of "clean" time. Serenity couldn't even get to those fourteen days without using a substance that would show up on a toxicology screen. She attributed this primarily to her homelessness: "That's our biggest problem now, being homeless, being around drugs." We tried to plan to find a date when she could turn herself in to see the judge. We practiced a story for the judge about why it had taken her so long to turn herself in. And she knew that she had to produce a urine drug test without illicit substances for the probation officer. This drug test result is necessary, but not sufficient, for avoiding jail.

One thing that kept Serenity going was the memory of her children and the potential, albeit slim, to be back in their lives at some time in the future. Like most other women who use drugs, Serenity prized her relationship with her children and her memories of mothering them. She hadn't seen her children in ten years, but she was so proud of them, especially the oldest one, Megan, who was now a mother of two children. "When I look at her, I know I didn't make junk," Serenity beamed, thinking about Megan. Serenity accredits part of Megan's strength and morality to the way that she raised her. When Megan told Serenity, "Mom, I love you, but you're making bad choices and I can't have you in my life," Serenity took it as evidence that she did right by this daughter in some way. "I had a hand in that," she explained.

Megan and Serenity had a loving yet tortured relationship. When Megan was fifteen, she confronted Serenity in their small apartment, insisting that if her mother didn't shoot her up, she was going to go find someone else to do it. In despair, Serenity agreed. It was part of being a good mother, to do it safely, to clean the area with rubbing alcohol, to make sure that you were in a vein. She was afraid that her daughter "wouldn't know you could always put more in." If someone else did it, she might overdose, or "give her too much and take advantage of her." Megan and Serenity used together for a year. Serenity figures that "children learn what they live."

One day, they were in western Massachusetts and they were arrested for shoplifting and found with a bag of heroin. Serenity and her boyfriend had moved to Massachusetts to be closer to their dealer. Serenity's mother bailed her out, but her boyfriend's mother had refused to bail him out. Later, Serenity learned that his mother had coerced him into signing over guardianship of the kids. Serenity was furious: "I couldn't stand to look at him. I tried for a couple of months but I couldn't even look at him. I hated him, I felt like he gave my life away."

It's common for people dealing with addiction to say they are trying to "stuff my emotions." Serenity and her boyfriend had a $500-a-day habit between the two of them. Disgusted by the sight of the father of her children who had signed away her life, Serenity engaged in a series of self-destructive thoughts and behaviors, including trying to overdose on heroin many times. By her own account, it was twelve or thirteen times. She also knowingly had unprotected sex with someone who was HIV-positive, hoping she would die. She likes to say, "Joke's on me! Guess it don't work that way."

JAIL (AGAIN) AND COURT

The next time I saw Serenity she had been incarcerated for forty days. Word on the street was that she was locked up. It turned out that she was, that she had been arrested on the previous bench warrant for a hand-to-hand in a school zone that we had tried to have cleared up. She imagined that someone called the cops when she was walking through a park in Chinatown near South Station. She had just emerged from an alley where people go to sleep and get high when she was picked up by a "couple of young rookies."

So it was back again to "the only detox I really know": jail. She received some chlordiazepoxide (Librium) while she detoxed in jail "only because I told them I drank" in order to feel a little bit less uncomfortable. She told me she had actually secretly wished to get locked up to just get hold of her heroin habit: "Every time I sit on the church steps getting high, praying to God, just send me to jail. . . . And the thing is, I can't go see [my social worker], but two weeks later, I always end up in jail."

In jail again, she was happy to see me when she saw who had called her out of her cell. She was always happy to see me when she wasn't using and she always avoided me when she was. Serenity was getting ready for her court date. She expected that she would not get a chance at bail because she had too many "defaults"—that is, she would be released from jail contingent upon her promise to show up for her court date, but she never would. Serenity hoped to bring this case to trial, not wanting to plea out, but she worried about her lawyer not being very good.

She was otherwise feeling well, noting, "I haven't missed any of my [HIV] medication in the forty days that I've been here." She was glad that she was not on the street, as her boyfriend, Oscar, had tried to kill her, vowing to her that he didn't care if he went back to prison. Here inside she was comfortable. The staff, the case workers, the guards, they all knew her.

She hoped that at her court date in a couple days she would be sent back to jail until she went to trial. The reason was simple: "I don't use when I'm here." She could very well access illicit drugs, but she didn't. She felt safe and calm in jail and received her HIV medications regularly. There was a rhythm to being in jail that she lacked out on the street: "Breakfast between 7 and 7:20, locked back up quarter of eight. Come out, take a shower. Locked back in at 11. 12:20 come out, eat, locked back up till 1. Out till 2:30. Then we lock in for another hour, come out at 3:30. Eat at 4:30. Locked up till 7:30. Locked up at 9:30."

Serenity was worried about being released into the streets of Boston. She told me: "I was just talking to my Unit Officer. I did the three months [in a drug treatment program]. I graduate. I get out, to what? To go nowhere. And three months is not going to fix me. Six months is not going to fix me. It's not! And that's the reality of my world. I want to go somewhere that's for like a year, eighteen months. That's what I want."

And perhaps not surprisingly, she was released from court directly into the streets of Boston, where she had no supports. Getting a job was even less on her mind than getting her medication. She sought out heroin, a consistent decision to "get wrecked" after forty days, without any substances in her system. As she recounted, "I hated myself, I hated looking in the mirror, and heroin numbed that pain, heroin kept me pain-free, desensitized."

At times, she reflected on when she used to be a functional drug user when she was in New Hampshire. She dabbled on the weekends (snorting lines of cocaine, or smoking marijuana), but it never interfered with her ability to work cleaning houses or work at the nursing home. She wished she could get back to that time—with her "job, home, [and] sanity."

MARY'S JOB SEARCH AFTER PRISON

In contrast to Serenity, Mary was someone who adamantly claimed that she wanted to work when she left prison. We met several months before she was released from MCI-Framingham. She was eager to get a job, she told me, and she had taken the reentry class offered at Framingham prior to her release. According to the Department of Correction, the Reentry and Employment Readiness Workshop tries to prepare individuals for the reality of imminent release:

> The 10-day Reentry and Employment Readiness Workshop meets for 2.5 hours per day and is offered to inmates who have a defined release date. During the Reentry and Employment Readiness Workshop, reentry planners facilitate curriculum designed to assist inmates in the development of the necessary skills that are needed for successful transition back into the community. The focus of the workshop is employment readiness to include resume building, cover letter, job application, mock interviews and how to maintain employment. The workshop also includes social support, housing plans, financial awareness and budgeting, educational referrals, criminal impact and attainable goal setting. Every inmate who attends the workshop will receive an Employment Readiness Release Portfolio. This release document can include identification, resume, cover letter, practice job applications, WOTC forms, Federal bonding, MassCor work verification, transcripts, certificates, and licenses. Once the inmate has completed the workshop the portfolio is stored within the institution and distributed on the day of release.

When I spoke to Mary two days after she was released, she told me that she was released with no plan and no formal address to be discharged to. Apparently, she had fallen through the cracks in the prison computer release system and no one had been assigned to help with an individual discharge plan. She told me that they had lined up one potential drug treatment program for her—a therapeutic community in East Boston. She had been there before and found its humiliating techniques unbearable: "I'm not opposed to most therapeutic communities, but this one they make you wear signs and a dunce hat and stuff like that. Seriously, I would rather be on the street than go to this ridiculous program. Of course, that was the one with availability."

Instead, she went back to her mother's apartment in Somerville. She wanted me to help her look for a job by typing up the résumé that she handwrote in the employment readiness class at the prison. She lamented that the reentry class was far too short: "You need more than just one week [of the program] before you leave."

She was hoping to find work as a home health aide or a nursing assistant. She told me about her previous work and educational history: She had dropped out of high school (but soon thereafter obtained a GED) and had worked as a camp counselor, a nanny and at Dunkin' Donuts and Bruegger's Bagels. She also had started doing a nursing certificate but floundered with ongoing dabbles in drug use. She had always wanted to be a nurse because "I think I'm empathic and good with people. Not everybody's fit for every job."

Mary had kept all the papers from her reentry class in a yellow folder with a quote from Martin Luther King Jr. pasted onto the front: "If you can't fly, then run, if you can't run, then walk, if you can't walk, then crawl, but whatever you do you have to keep moving forward." She handed me a folder full of papers, including upcoming court dates for custody of her children, a soft-core pornographic letter that another inmate had written to a boyfriend and formal paperwork proving that she had been discharged from the prison.

One of the papers in her stuffed yellow folder was entitled "Interview Etiquette" and spelled out the soft skills necessary for presenting oneself. Were they arguably futile attempts at altering one's habitus? The papers spelled out exactly what not to wear: tight or low-cut clothes, objectionable hats or shirts. Don't chew gum or smoke or eat. It coached job seekers to use the person's first name at least once in the conversation— "Thank you, Bill."

The folder also contained examples of cover letters and résumés and information on how to do a budget and obtain a credit report. Mary had also filled out a worksheet entitled "My Skills." Under Skill 1 ("motivational skills"), she wrote "settle disagreements, relate well to others, persuade and guide, sell ideas/promote." Under Skill 2 ("interpersonal skills"), she wrote "helpful, empathedic [sic], positive attitude." Within the area marked Skill 3 ("leadership skills"), she wrote, "manage self, identify problems and solutions, accept responsibility, adapt to new situations." I felt both proud and saddened reading her list of self-reported skills. How could this list ever manifest as a formal job that allowed her to have an adequate income and a quality life?

Mary had been incarcerated at least five times for charges ranging from possession of controlled substances (gabapentin, Class E substance) to assaulting a police officer, a situation that she remembers as resisting arrest while intoxicated at a music festival. This technically gave the chunky, middle-aged white mother a charge of a violent felony. This conviction, in and of itself, would largely prohibit her from ever joining the caring profession that she found so appealing. She tried to practice writing out how she would deal with the question of her felonies: "Yes I've been convicted of a felony. I've had a difficult period in my life where I've made poor choices. I've learned from it and have worked to change."

In the reentry program, she also was tasked with anticipating what are called her main "speed bumps." The first one was already filled out: "I have a record," it reads. She filled it out optimistically: "I can look for CORI friendly jobs. I can use the incentives to help me. After 10 years I can get my record sealed." Her second "speed bump" she listed as "staying sober." Tools she listed to overcome it: "go to meetings, hang around sober friends that have good recovery."

Would her goal of sobriety after release from prison ever be achieved, I wondered? When I talked with Mary at her mother's apartment in senior public housing in Somerville, a small town north of Cambridge, she was excited to get a job. She had been released a week before and actually made contact with me thinking—a common mistake—that I was a doctor. I got a text message from her two days after she was released from MCI-Framingham "Dr. Sui. Need help with something. My boyfriend n I had an accident n I need plan B. it costs $50 so I would need a dr. to prescribe it, so I can pay for the prescription w/ my insurance card that way I would be able to acquire the medication. Don't know if u r able to assist. Let me know please."

I encouraged her to go the local public hospital's emergency room, where she obtained Plan B with her insurance card. She was in the meantime squatting illegally in her mother's apartment; they had snuck her in by having her carry a bunch of boxes in front of her face while passing before the apartment building's security camera. Her mother was already being evicted because Mary had stayed there several months earlier while on "the [home monitoring] bracelet." No one who was not on the lease was technically allowed to stay in senior public housing, and Mary used her mother's address for her probation, so the apartment complex found out.

Mary was pursuing a number of potential jobs leads. She heard that a gym in Porter Square was "looking for employees desperately" and that a telemarketing group in Porter Square called Integral Resources hired people with records. She even reached out to Integral Resources. I thought she had scheduled an interview, but she never had. She told me she had a new outfit from T. J. Maxx, so she would be "dressed appropriately." I met up with her boyfriend, who was homeless living in Harvard Square, and gave him the résumé and cover letters that I had typed up for her. She had never worked in telemarketing before. Her résumé listed several jobs as a nursing assistant at facilities that no longer existed. The people she listed as her supervisors could no longer be contacted. She wanted me to highlight skills she had acquired in her capacity as a nursing assistant: "Answering phones, people skills, reliability, dependability . . . plus positive attitude that is contagious n makes for a pleasant work place."

I knew that she could run a business. She had sold drugs for three years in a low-level operation near Cambridge using her contacts and her boyfriend's up-front money. She was able to answer phones, reliably supply drugs, and use her people skills to get and maintain customers. This was all consistent with her positive attitude and upbeat work ethic. She also had escorted for an upscale company in Boston, with a different boyfriend. After a while, "He was a deadbeat and I had to always get the money [for heroin by escorting]."

When I talked to her several weeks later about how her job search was going, she told me she never went to any of the potential places of employment. She had instead been getting "wrecked," as she confessed to me later. She did not make it to the doctors' appointments she had made and was now sleeping on the street, since her mother had been evicted. She was using heroin and, intermittently, buying buprenorphine-naloxone on the street, in an attempt to "try to break the habit." She had in the meantime since we last talked acquired a "wicked bad habit." She was also convinced she was pregnant and wanted a maintenance medication therapy for her heroin addiction such as buprenorphine (proven very safe and efficacious during pregnancy). Additionally, she hoped to enter an inpatient drug treatment program, mostly because she didn't want to be street homeless anymore. She had also missed a critical court date for her son's DCF status/custody.

Mary was the most job-oriented of all the women I met who were leaving prison. I admired her for her sheer determination in this regard, but ultimately, she was too burdened with the task of survival to carry out the job search. I tried in vain to set her up with an appointment with the director of the OBOT clinic—not necessarily to get on the medication per se, but just to have someone to talk to who understood her situation and was willing to brainstorm ideas with her. Numerous times I encouraged her to go in even though she didn't have an appointment. She sent me a message after one futile attempt: "Kim, I didn't go the appointment. Sorry it took me so long to get back u I guess as u probably know a person who is an addict can get caught up. I really dont want to be this way anymore. Prison for me is the wanted or unwanted boundaries placed in your head not necessarily where your feet are. So, addiction is much like a prison of its own. Living in unacceptable conditions or what should be."

What struck me about Mary was the way in which she wholeheartedly embraced the logic of recovery and the importance of a job to that recovery, but her social situation was dominated by her relative inability to make decisions that could extricate her from the morass of her unhappy life. Was she an active agent of her own self-destruction, refusing to get better?

Work was no means to salvation for Mary. In fact, she was systematically excluded from participating in it. Her job search was rather a reminder of her existential failures and the low social value that women with her life experiences held in our social compact. Working was therefore poorly regarded as a space for generating positive emotions, experiences and meanings; drug use, on the other hand, held out the promise of providing positive, albeit transient emotional and embodied experiences. As Mary told me, after taking several methadone pills that Scott had acquired on the street just days after her release, "Drugs are very seductive, once you dance with it, once you have it, it feels too good to just stop, not caring that it's not good for you."

WHAT WORKS?

Women like Serenity and Mary lack the social, educational, or cultural capital to leave lives largely defined by poverty and poor health. Their relationships, their abilities to take care of themselves and others and the many kinds of contributions they bring forth just being in the world are sorely undervalued and underweighted in a society where having money, privilege, secure housing, and good health, comprising the ability to live a life of modest material comforts, is hard fought and increasingly hard won. Policies such as guaranteed minimum income in countries such as Switzerland or Finland could greatly benefit formerly incarcerated women like them, keeping them off the streets and away from risky forms of generating income.

Women like Serenity move through worlds in which for-profit and profitable not-for-profit institutions dominate and shape the course of their lives. Women with long-standing opioid addictions are not just forms of profit for these industries; they are also the straw-women of the War on Drugs who absorb a collective hostility and resentment, fulfilling some deeply rooted American desire to punish those seen as dangerous or deviant. Women are punished and criminalized for their sickness, their inability to not get well. Our notions of recovery and relapse in drug addiction as chronic open up women's lives for infinite points of state, for-profit, and nongovernmental surveillance, regulation, and intervention.

Yet not all the women I met experienced the devaluation and disempowerment of alienation from the labor market and from being incarcerated. Mae, the twenty-two-year-old whose mother would sneak her drugs into the prison, returned from prison to her wealthy and white seaside community. She did not look for a job and she did not try to go back to school—there was simply no economic imperative. She had no idea what she wanted to do or be and was comfortable sleeping in the twin bed of her childhood home. She toyed with the idea of going back into retail but didn't like the idea of standing on her feet that long. While her parents pressured her to get food stamps to help the family out, she was not particularly economically pressed to get a job.

When I met up with her at a ritzy Panera Bread for lunch, she told me, "I'm really lazy about filling out paperwork, you know what I mean? I wish I didn't have to fill out job applications. I wish I could just go in." She had plenty of heroin: her mom would buy the bag, so she wouldn't get in trouble. Her mom needed her to shoot her up, so it "worked out."

Mae was much better off than many of the poor heroin users I met. She had a steady supply of drugs, a stable place to live, and the general support of her family. Her days were spent leisurely, and while she saw her heroin use as potentially problematic in the future, it was a manageable habit. She perceived herself as safe from the police, since she only had one dealer, and all her deals happened inside and not on the street, where the risk of police seeing a deal and arresting her was far greater.

While at the minimum-security prerelease facility for women, Mae did not work. That was not uncommon. Even though the prerelease was unlocked, and women were encouraged to get jobs and would be transported by the prerelease facility to and from these jobs, of the several hundred women there, only a handful were working. There was a widespread refutation of the idea that working was valuable, that labor was a means to salvation, as Max Weber had suggested.

Being locked out of the formal labor market did not mean that women were disinterested in working or the forms of meaning and potential benefits that working could confer. Brittany had discovered some dignity, albeit in the underworld, by seizing control of her town's oxycodone-acetaminophen market and becoming the top supplier and pill dealer in town. In her work as a drug dealer, she had the freedom to organize her own activities, to charge her own prices, to make her own "plays." She had reliable customers and people relied on her. It was empowering to be even a lower-mid-level drug dealer in a world dominated by men.

After she was released from prison, Brittany's father eventually managed to get her a job in the shipping and packing division of the company where he had worked for the past thirty years. It was important for her to "just get a job and have a safe place to live; those are the two main things that I need to be focusing on." She was worried, though, because shipping and packing seemed boring and tedious, and the money she would earn would be a trigger for her. Any amount over $100 would be a trigger for buying dope, and in her enterprising mind, she would immediately try to flip it—to get her drugs "for free."

Boredom is the foresworn enemy of recovering heroin users. One of the greatest risks of relapse to heroin is boredom, as all addicts are told repeatedly in drug treatment programs. They are often asked, "What are you going to do to keep yourself busy?" It is a serious question—this question of busyness.

People with heroin addictions—when they are actively "feeding" a habit—are some of the most industrious people around. They work hard, because if they don't work hard, they will suffer physical consequences like painful withdrawal symptoms. The constantly looming threat of withdrawal forces people into activity. Recovery or sobriety, on the other hand, can be plagued by boredom. Narcotics Anonymous warns that addicts in recovery have to be vigilant against boredom. In one of the NA texts, it reads: "After the hell of our addiction and the roller-coaster craziness of early recovery, the stable life may have some appeal—for a while. But, eventually, we realize we want something more. Sooner or later, we become turned off to the creeping monotony and boredom in our lives."[10] This boredom, according to a pervasive and pejorative cultural logic, is mostly one's own fault. It is one's moral obligation to keep busy. To fail to do so is un-American.

This denial of values so cherished by American capitalist ideologies is a maddening refutation of dominant middle-class morality. Poor people who refuse to be a redundant, cheap, and expedient labor force are punished with new forms of banishment and racialized second-class citizenship. Poor women who seize control of their lives by becoming drug dealers mirror the cultural logic of capitalism, as other ethnographers have investigated in their front-line work with drug dealers.[11] They are punished for being caught participating in attempts at making labor meaningful according to the dominant capitalist ethos, for trying to derive value and self-efficacy in one's work.

While the prisons and jails try to highlight the work they do to help women get back to work after incarceration, in fact, only a very small percentage of the state correctional budget is spent on reentry programs as well as other proven evidence-based solutions to getting women out of poverty and out of the prison system. In fact, in Massachusetts, a three-thousand-person waiting list for participation in the Boston Prison Education Project, a college-level education program, effectively shuts people out for years. The overall Department of Correction budget for FY2018 was over $600 million, with only $250,000 earmarked for "reentry programs."[12] Such programs can make little headway against the vested interests of prison lobbying programs and correctional officer unions. Not surprisingly, these unions often lobbied against treatment programs.

Treatment receives an ever-smaller sliver of the overall Department of Correction budget. In other states, like New York, they believe that giving women access to higher education—to college degrees—keeps them from coming back to prison. Women on the Rise Telling HerStory (WORTH), an advocacy organization led by formerly incarcerated women based out of New York City, stresses that educational opportunities helped lift them out of poverty. In this way, many women were able to find self-actualization and economic empowerment and dignity in concrete new and meaningful ways, rather than remaining mired in joblessness and economic precarity upon release.

As it currently stands, women who use heroin and end up in the criminal justice system, ultimately are punished by the mark of a criminal record—a modern day scarlet letter. They are denied any entry into forms of work they find meaningful and then blamed for their lack of a work ethic, prudence, and self-discipline. And as they have done with trauma work, the prisons and jails put aside the fact that being incarcerated is in and of itself the single largest impediment to well-being for the future life prospects of these women. Their post-incarceration lives are marred in so many often permanent and deeply painful ways: their children might be taken away and put into foster care, they might be unable to find housing or employment, or they could face serious disruptions in close relationships and social supports. The interrupted life that incarceration represents, with its collateral and oftentimes permanent and stigmatizing consequences, means that meaningful work for women remains even farther out of reach.

7

Life and Death after Jail

Life exists only in bursts and in exchange with death.
—Achille Mbembe (2003:15)

Shooting intravenous drugs means you might die at any moment. Every time you load a needle, try to find a vein that isn't collapsed or shrunken into itself, draw the plunger back, check for blood, and release the drugs that you've acquired on the street into your vein, there is that risk that you might die in ten minutes, one hour, one day, one week. The drugs might be bad, either too strong or cut with some strange substance you didn't expect to be there. They could contain rat poison, or embalming fluid, or fentanyl. There is a risk that your needle, or simply your skin, or the water you used to cook drugs, carries some bacteria that finds easy passage to the valves of your heart, where it can lodge and grow into a ball of bacteria, and then move into other organs, like your lungs and your brain. The needle can be iconic for danger, but what you do in order to get drugs can be equally dangerous.

For Lydia, what started as an innocuous-appearing cut in her armpit ended up as a case of necrotizing fasciitis, the worst physical malady she had ever experienced related to her drug use. But even before her illness, Lydia had existed in a kind of nether zone, a death-in-life. She had been incarcerated many times for drug use, and social institutions like the prison and the hospital often unwittingly expose some people like her to injury and death along the moral fault lines of our society while protecting others. The so-called "mad, bad, and sick" are the ones who are exposed to death's reach. They include the friendless, the surly, the unpleasant, the badly behaved, and the ones whose anxious presence can come across as unbearable.

Lydia had already died many deaths. She had endured the "civil death" wrought by being in prison, the soul-destroying experience of incarceration and solitary confinement. And the institutions in which she and many others cycled—including hospitals, jails, prisons, detox programs, thirty-day treatments—often overlay death as a foreboding possibility in the lives of women who use heroin. Maybe Lydia was already dead—dead to communities and passersby who drove past where she was sleeping at night under a bridge. Maybe she had become dead to her family, who disowned their lesbian daughter, the one who became a dopefiend and stole their television to exchange it for drugs. Maybe she had become politically dead, erased from the voting rolls while incarcerated, no one's constituent. Maybe her story had fallen on deaf ears in her community, people who felt nothing but fear seeing her on the street at night.

Lydia had certainly been left for dead before. She had also left others for dead, afraid of the police finding her in a house with an unconscious heroin user if she called 911, because she was deathly afraid of being hauled off to jail herself. It is "worse than death," she says, to be wracked by sweats, shakes, and the runs of dopesickness in a ten-by-ten cell with five other equally sick women undergoing the unnecessary throes of forced withdrawl. No one said it would be pleasant. Living close to death means living close to the vomit, diarrhea, and mucus of bodies in violent revolt.

NECROTIZING FASCIITIS

It started with what seemed like an abscess in her armpit and some kind of associated rash. These kinds of symptoms are not atypical in the life of a heroin user. Usually they can be ignored, until they can't. Until it gets too painful, too large, too red, too swollen, too hot. Until she feels a little bit too sick and feverish for the dope to take the edge off. "You don't look so good," people said to her. "You should go to the hospital." When prayers and shrugging it off yielded no resolution, she finally went. She told me: "I was in full-blown feeling bad. And as the pain got worse, the more drugs I did to get rid of the pain, the more delusional I became, the more crazed I became. By the time I got here, this whole [right] side, this was all swelled up."

The doctor who examined her right armpit wrote in the chart, "Deroofed, draining (grayish fluid) abscess of the right axilla with swelling erythema warmth and induration noted inferolaterally extending down the right flank and to the right side of the back, extreme tenderness to palpation without evidence of subcutaneous emphysema, (+) urticarial rash bilateral lower extremities with excoriations noted b/l." He was concerned about a serious, life-threatening problem. In summary, "There is concern for necrotizing fasciitis and plans for the OR [operating room] are made emergently."

Rushing Lydia to the operating room for an infection might seem a bit extreme, but necrotizing fasciitis is a soft tissue infection that can lead to destruction of bodily tissues, septic shock, organ failure, and death within several days.[1] If suspected, it represents an immediate surgical emergency. Infections like Lydia's enter the body through the skin via certain ports of entry—in this case, most likely a needle that Lydia's friend had used to try to drain the abscess or even from syringes she had used days to weeks earlier—but it was nearly impossible to tell exactly.

In this condition, after bacteria from the skin gets inside the body, it tracks along the fascia that keeps the muscles contained in certain arrangements, thriving in an environment with relatively low oxygen. It could then lead to rapid multi-organ system failure and death; mortality rates, even with the proper therapy, are high. The treatment for necrotizing fasciitis is an old and crude but efficient solution: cut the infection and the dead tissues out (debridement) and administer broad-spectrum antibiotics. Every twenty-four hours the wound is checked for more necrotic tissue. In Lydia's case, she went to the operating room seven times for debridement. Finally, she underwent a split-thickness skin graft from her right thigh to cover her affected side. The surgeons at the academic tertiary care hospital had needed to remove part of her *latissimus dorsi*, a muscle in the upper side of the back, since it had been badly infected and subsequently damaged by the infection (figure 8).

Lydia was discharged after spending forty days in the hospital. At one point during her hospitalization, she had commissioned her friend Juan to bring her up some heroin since her doctors were not giving her enough pain medication: "All I wanted was to be comfortable," she said. She told the hospital that she was returning to an address that was a room that she had been renting in Chelsea for $200 a month, where she was allowed to sleep on the floor in the bedroom where Juan and his girlfriend slept. The hospital set her up with Visiting Nurse Services who would take care of her wound and her skin graft. No one asked if her place was safe, if her roommates were using drugs and if she would have difficulty abstaining from heroin upon her release from the hospital. She was counseled to stop using heroin and given verbal encouragement.

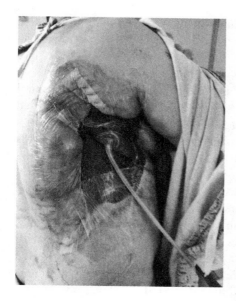

FIGURE 8. Photo of Lydia in the hospital recovering from her surgeries, taken by author, used with Lydia's permission.

I spoke to Lydia on the phone the day she was discharged from the hospital. She said she wasn't deemed sick enough to go to a rehab facility or another hospital. It would also have been difficult to find her a rehab bed given her history of substance use. Rehabs—not immune to social stigma—were reluctant to take people with complicated social histories and didn't want to take anyone who could cause trouble or whose homelessness could turn into a stay of uncertain duration.

I asked her what her plan was in terms of drug use. She told me flatly, "There's no plan." She said that she had always thought she would go to a rehab facility and that she would "take care of that [drug treatment] from rehab." She hated this particular hospital even though they saved her life: "This hospital has done so much shit to me."

Lydia's reaction to her hospitalization makes clear the ambivalence that patients, particularly people who use drugs, feel about these spaces of supposed care. For her, the hospital represented a space of containment and confinement—imposing judgments and controlling her movements and her visitors in keeping with stigmatizing assessments based on her appearance and her chart. The hospital staff did not like it when she strapped her WoundVac (surgical internal system of drainage) to her IV pole and went outside to smoke. It defied the hospital's order of things. Even though this hospital had saved her life, she felt the sting of perceived mistreatment more strongly than gratitude for the saving of her life. She fixated on the unkind nurses, not the particularly skilled phlebotomist that we once encountered together when I was visiting her. The world was generally antagonistic toward her and she had learned to respond in kind.

Rehab beds were few and far between, and staying in the hospital one more night would be costly.[2] Instead, her discharge plan included follow-up with a primary care doctor (she did not have one) and surgical follow-up a week after her discharge. Yet, even though Lydia was discharged from the hospital, she was far from well. Even though staying in the hospital one more night in order to chart a more successful discharge plan could possibly have kept her from returning to the hospital, the logics of efficiency superseded all other possible logics of care.

I worried about the seeming inevitability of her return to drug use, since it was not addressed by her surgery team in her discharge plan. Also no one thought to give her naloxone (Narcan), a medication used to reverse opioid overdoses. Lydia and I discussed her trying buprenorphine-naloxone therapy. She told me, "I'm kind of relying on the Suboxone to keep me sober." In my mind, I calculated the number of weeks it generally takes people to get into a buprenorphine clinic or find a primary care doctor wiling to prescribe it. The wait list was at least four weeks, at minimum. Of course, she could buy it on the street if she so desired, although she would have to pay the street's mark-up rate. But why would she buy one pill on the street for $10 when she could have the stronger high of heroin for the same price?

Many might view the necrotizing fasciitis as an embodiment of Lydia's deviant moral behavior, one of the terrible outcomes of years of "wicked" bad habits like shooting heroin and cocaine together, or shooting anything intravenously, or using any drugs for euphoria. It has eaten up her body and taken away her precarious good health. It has left her more disabled than ever before, even more vulnerable to the vagaries of street life—getting robbed, attacked, beaten up. She is left in disrepair in both body and mind. Her new body disgusts her and anyone who sees it, a monstrous body that makes us aware of how human we all are; it scares us.[3]

Lydia saw her new body as broken and raw. It did not function well. She grappled with what anthropologists Gay Becker and Sharon Kaufman have called "the unknowable future" and her prospects of an incomplete recovery of her former body and mind.[4] Like people who experience a debilitating stroke in Becker and Kaufman's work, she was made to feel responsible for any failure to physically and mentally recover, as well as for her failure to work and contribute to society with her compromised new body. Yet perhaps her damaged body was not the inevitable outcome of her choice to use intravenous heroin. Perhaps it was a culturally produced entity, the end-product of social disgust and repudiation—a literal turning away—from Lydia and people like her who use drugs.

PARKING LOT: A PRECARIOUS LIFE AFTER HOSPITALIZATION

One week after Lydia is discharged from the hospital, I find myself in a deserted parking lot in Chelsea, a small municipality just north of Boston, warily clutching an iced coffee (for Lydia), my own black coffee, and two bags of food that I had just picked up at a nearby Dunkin' Donuts. Chelsea is a vibrant community with many different immigrant cultures. It is also very poor, with 23 percent of the population living below the poverty level and 44 percent living two times below the poverty level. It is home to many immigrants from Spanish-speaking countries (62 percent Hispanic), refugees from all over the world, as well as a substantial community of heroin users.

Lydia directs me to meet her in a parking lot behind a three-story apartment building. Sitting next to a dumpster, I call her and she tells me she is on the toilet. I assume that means she is shooting up. I can't help but wonder if Lydia is setting me up to get jumped in the parking lot, but I dismiss that as overly paranoid. Finally, she emerges from a dark corner. We head to the back steps of a house where her friends are "passed out" inside.

A torrent of anxieties erupts. She speaks frenetically in a staccato-inflected Boston-Italian accent, a fast, nonstop whine. Her housing situation with Juan, her friend of ten years, is tenuous, and he has kicked her out today after they had an argument. She is indignant because she noticed that he had been stealing her stuff, specifically her Celtics cap, her body wash, and new packs of boxer shorts she had gotten at CVS. Nothing is safe from him. "I thought I could trust him!" she cries out in frustration.

The conversation is heavily one-sided. She is clutching at her pants that have no belt. They must be two sizes too large. She is wearing a large men's button-down shirt. Her monologue jumps from the ACE bandages that Juan stole to not getting enough prescription pain medication to the amount of weight she has gained since her hospitalization. Then it is on to her constant fear of withdrawal and her inability to get enough pain relief. She tells me that she asked her mother for some of her mother's Percocets, since her mother owed her $200, but her mother refused to give her any for her pain.

Jackie, the only girl she felt she ever really loved, is still more in love with the needle than she is with Lydia. Lydia called her up after her surgery even though they'd broken up at least two years ago. She pleaded with her for help: "I said to her, 'Listen, are you getting high real heavy?' I was like, 'because I need somebody to help me. Are you able to at least fucking help me put on my socks and shoes and maybe untwist my shirts and shit?' She was so fucking high." Now Lydia is gasping for breaths between tears like a toddler in a fit of rage and hurt: Lydia had tried, when she got out of jail two months ago, to get back together again with Jackie. She went and "partied with her and offered to take care of her drug habit and make sure she would never want for fucking nothing if she would stop [prostituting]." Lydia left Jackie's place in despair. "If I wasn't every fifteen minutes handing her dope, she fucking would do what she knew I didn't want her to do, pick up the phone and call a trick to make money."

No one is really around to take care of Lydia now after her brush with near death. Urban drug use can be a desolate, lonesome scene. Lydia takes care of herself as best as she can. Her mother has refused to take her back home, having many years ago ceased to offer her love and care in the face of Lydia's contagious and destructive drug habits. She was relying on "tough love" to keep her dangerous daughter at arm's length, but it forced Lydia into desperate and unhealthy situations.

Since she began staying at Juan's, largely caring for her wound by herself, Lydia had made one human connection that helped her hang on: a visiting nurse, Cecilia, who came to Jose's house once. She was gentle and taught Lydia how to take care of her wound, to paint the raw edges with sepia-brown iodine and wrap her bandage in a certain fashion. Lydia cried thinking about her kindness. The next nurse that came was negligent in her wrapping; she had a thick Caribbean accent, and Lydia could not understand her at all. The bandage was too loose and the wound wept painfully. I suspect there was some racism or xenophobia involved in Lydia's dislike of her care.

"I'm not going to try to kill myself," she says, sobbing, "But I fucking can't wait for this life to end. I've been through so much and seen so much that I don't need to see anymore." Eventually, I learn that the visiting nurse services were cut off because Lydia left Juan's place, which she had listed as her address. It was a precarious life to which Lydia clung that day in the parking lot.

Lydia was trying to take care of her wound as best she could. While she was at the hospital, she had taken things from her hospital room and given them to Juan to take home for her. "When I was in the hospital," she explained, "and I do it even when I'm not hospitalized, when I go to the doctors, I go through the drawers and I take what I want. Every time he came up, I gave him a bag full of stuff: powder, those tiny shampoos, gauze, tape, scissors, ACE bandages. He swore to me that he never touched anything; we'd go through it all when I got home. I get home and all those things he wanted are not in the bag, but he swears he didn't touch anything." She is furthermore upset because she had agreed to share the stuff with him; indignantly she remarks that she is "not a cheap piece of shit." Yet they argue over who can have the extra towel. "I can't have it? They were fucking in my room, I'm the one who fucking wanted this shit!"

One of the biggest sources of anxiety for Lydia is the fact that she might go back to jail, that she could always get picked up by the police: "The last place I want to be is jail. I don't want to go back. It's so boring, and I can't stand having fucking piss ants push me around and telling me when I got to go to bed, and the showers are horrible and the food sucks and if you don't have money you're fucked. And the girls are so immature, all they want to do is fight."

She is fairly certain there is a warrant out for her arrest issued by a judge in Chelsea for receiving stolen property (two packs of cigarettes). This is because she was hospitalized during the court date; for anyone who does not show up to his or her appointed court date, the judge automatically issues a bench warrant, allowing the police to arrest the individual in question at any time. I am secretly not convinced that the jail would be a worse place for her than her nomadic existence shooting heroin and trying to take care of a full-body surgical wound by herself. But Lydia insists that her freedom is worth all the existential and physical anguish she is currently enduring. She doubts she would be able to keep her wound clean in jail nor does she trust the jail staff to take care of her in her debilitated condition. On top of that, she would not be able to endure the constant attacks on her dignity and sense of self that being incarcerated incurs.

What Lydia wants to do, in an effort to feel safer, is to walk over to a community-based organization where she heard that they have free, public computers. She wants to print out photographs of her surgical wounds and bring them to the courthouse: "I feel so much safer even with the pictures of the injury in my pocket" (see figure 8). For people like Lydia, very poor people who live on and off the streets, the police are the biggest danger. They are bearers of harm and suffering, not safety. So just having the printed copies of the photographs on her person will make her feel safer from the police. All the police in the area know her, and she is at great risk for being stopped by the police if she is homeless, wandering around, and buying and selling drugs: "The stigma sticks. The cops—it doesn't even matter if I've been sober for months, and I had just relapsed that day, they all still treat me like it's never stopped. They have no clue that I ever had a real life."

When we pass through the doors of the community-based organization, we head to rows of gleaming new personal computers that are free to the public, intended primarily for people to look for jobs or housing. As we walk behind a row of computers, I see Lydia duck down quickly. She has found a $20 bill. She turns to me, "I would turn this in and I really would . . . but over the past three days the amount of money that I lost, that I borrowed . . ." She trails off. "You feel bad about that?"

I reassure her that I honestly don't feel bad about her keeping it. Lydia signs into Facebook to find pictures of her leg and torso that she had posted for her social network to see. I feel glad that we finally have a tangible goal. She has difficulty locating the photographs. One of them, of her leg where they took the skin graft, she sends from her phone to the Facebook website. She pecks out the caption underneath: "It's picking season!" She laughs to herself about her gutter humor, over the impending itch associated with the healing process.

Then she turns to me and asks, "What's Microsoft Word?" I am shocked, instantly realizing the vast digital and educational disparities between us. I tell her what people use Microsoft Word for. I am surprised that Facebook has helped her bridge into a world of computers and technology. I wonder if Facebook and cheap smartphones are ways that people lacking a traditional education link up in new social configurations to create virtual communities of people who use drugs. I see that at one point in the past Lydia had posted about having heroin on her page: in her words, "CHINA porcoilen [sic] white baby!"

When we are navigating around on the website, she shows me photos of Rita, her Puerto-Rican ex-wife. Lydia is disdainful of the way her weave looks now and claims that when they were together Rita's hair was a priority. She sees a message from her stepsister that says, "My mother died." Lydia starts to cry, because her stepsister had just yesterday asked her for money ("I'm hungry") and Lydia had wanted to send her $75, but instead spent it on drugs. She tries to avoid thinking about her stepsister; she is too ashamed: "I'm a fucking mess. I don't know how to face her right now, for the money and then this [her stepmother's death]. I just want to tell her that I hate myself right now." She has a mostly tortured and one-sided conversation about how she really should send her sister some money, but she feels that she doesn't even have enough for her own needs.

Finally, we manage to get the photos printed and leave. On the way back to the parking lot, we meet two separate men who greet Lydia effusively. Both of them are heroin users and part-time dealers. After we leave them, I convince Lydia to visit a primary care doctor at the local community health clinic where I volunteer occasionally. The clinic is in Chelsea, and over the past three years, I had been involved in an effort to create a focus within the student-faculty collaborative clinic on the health of formerly incarcerated people returning to the area. One unique aspect of the clinic was the provision of co-located primary care and psychiatric services. I thought that since it was in her neighborhood, she might actually show up.

She seems relieved that I will be there the night that I scheduled her two appointments (one with primary care and one with mental health), but she was hesitant. She wants to test out the doctor first, to see if they have rapport. I write down the appointment times that they have been able to make for her—three weeks from now (and that is an expedited visit). I will actually be seeing patients that night in my role as a fourth-year medical student, so I tell her that I will be there to take care of her. She seems particularly interested in getting on buprenorphine-naloxone to help quell her heroin use. I can only hope she will come.

THE HOUSE OF CORRECTION AND CIVIL DEATH

Lydia is living a sort of death-in-life existence marked by uncertainty about where she will go and what her life will be like. Even in the absence of identifiable ongoing disease—the surgeon felt that she was recovering nicely from her surgeries and hospitalization—she is not well. A staggering number of institutions have failed her, in an ongoing synergy with her own despair and self-harm.

Institutional logics have created a bewildering, jagged mosaic of experiences that culminate in an affect of despair. The institutions mark her as a bad person; they leave her with an upset stomach, headaches, and a deeply embodied mistrust of hospitals and social service agencies. Lydia also lives with the enduring stigma that is written into her patient medical record—she smokes, she exhibits opioid-seeking behavior, and she is an IV drug "abuser," as noted in her chart. Pejorative language such as "abuser" and "addict" actually change clinicians' behavior for the worse according to a study conducted by John Kelly of Massachusetts General Hospital. He found that among six hundred clinicians interviewed, the ones who read the word "abuser" in the chart were more inclined to act punitively toward the patient.[5]

What made Lydia feel most afraid and what kept her up at night was the prospect of being arrested. What she wanted most of all was a life free from prison and from the police that would bring her back there. It was a haunting possibility that she felt she could never really escape. She craved a life outside of carceral spaces, no matter how destitute or downtrodden. Having been incarcerated many times before—at least twenty times—she professed numerous times that she would rather die than go back to prison.

Prison scholar Caleb Smith argues that the prison's power is intimately related to being a death-giving institution; in fact, it is a juridical-civil institution precisely intended to enact a so-called "civil death."[6] His historical investigation into the early colonial Houses of Correction (precursor to modern jails) and prisons as a uniquely American product sheds light on the complex notion of civil death. Smith summarizes the Gothic concept as "a legal fiction indicating 'the status of the person who is being deprived of all civil rights.' In the United States, civil death statutes have dictated the felon may not vote or make contracts. He loses his property. In some states his wife becomes a widow, free to remarry without divorcing him. *Thus the incarcerated contact retains his 'natural life'—his heart beats on, he labors and he consumes—but he has lost the higher, more abstract, civil life that made him fully human in the eyes of the law*" (2009: 29; italics mine). Smith explains how in the early American Houses of Correction—with major design input from the Philadelphia-based physician Benjamin Rush—the concept of civil death was intrinsic to the enterprise of punishment. Civil death was necessary for the act of incarceration to do its work at reforming the bodies and souls of the deviant; only in the prison would the individual undergo resurrection and rebirth into the human community upon his release. Only through the process of civil death could individuals then be properly stripped of prior sin and immorality, then capable of being reformed by the prison, learning how to govern themselves upon release.

American prisons have a sordid history rooted in the dehumanization of poor people and people of color, in permutations of the convict-leasing system, chain gangs and slavery.[7] And although Lydia is not black, she suffers from a specific kind of civil and social death that takes gender and sexuality and class as key determinants. She is routinely incarcerated in the Suffolk House of Correction for being homeless, for being suspicious-looking, for dressing like a man. Lydia is not healed by the time she spends in prison; rather, she has been contaminated and harmed by it.

COURT: FACING THE THREAT OF CIVIL DEATH

I am not entirely surprised when I get a phone call from Lydia at 8 a.m. the next Monday. "Did you just call me?" she asks. No, I say, half-asleep. "Are we going to court today?" she asks me. Then she starts in on a litany of issues: "I don't even know where I am. I don't have any clothes. I'm wearing the same clothes." I head over to Chelsea. We agree to meet at the Dunkin' in front of the courthouse at 10 a.m. to give her enough time to get dressed. I am crossing the bridge into Chelsea from Boston when I get a phone call from Lydia: "I fell back asleep, after we talked." An hour later, she shows up, telling me she was late because she was taking a back-alley route in order to avoid a cop car that she had seen.

After going through the metal detectors, having to throw out our precious coffees, we head into the courthouse. It is mostly empty, unlike the bustling Boston Municipal Court. Most people are standing in line awaiting the court officers. Apparently the first person that needs to see Lydia is her probation officer. The probation officer is a dour-looking, middle-aged Hispanic lady with short-cropped hair. A flash of recognition lights up in her eyes as she sees Lydia. The woman calls Lydia over: "I'm going to detain you [in jail]. I asked for detention for you. Did you go to that program?" Lydia protests, mumbles about being in the hospital. The probation officer is angry and seems intent on sending Lydia to jail. She appears to have made up her mind as soon as she laid eyes on Lydia. I wonder if this is *bureaucratic indifference*, as anthropologist Michael Herzfeld has written about, but then I realize that this woman is displaying actual and very strong negative emotions, bordering on anger, combined with significant power.[8] I think it is more appropriately bureaucratic ill will, an attitude of bureaucrats on the frontlines of social agencies that can determine the fates of smaller peoples' lives. This woman has the power to send Lydia to prison right now.

First, though, there is the paperwork. Lydia gives all this information, stating her current address as her mother's house, which I know is a lie. I notice the probation officer misspells much of what Lydia says to her even when Lydia spells it out. The probation officer finally turns and acknowledges my presence: "What are these surgeries for? Who are you?" And to Lydia: "Is she authorized to speak on your behalf?" Yes, Lydia responds. I tell the probation officer I'm a Harvard medical student and that Lydia recently had necrotizing fasciitis, that she just had six or seven surgeries. We show her the pictures of Lydia's surgery. The probation officer doesn't really look at the photographs, even though Lydia was so insistent on the photographs as the ultimate proof of her suffering, her damaged body. "Fine," the probation officer says. "At least you're getting medical help," she waves toward me. "I'm going to go in there and say you need a date for a final surrender hearing."

So, it's not really a victory, except that Lydia doesn't have to go to jail immediately, that very same day. It seems like a punt, but to Lydia it is the best possible outcome. Lydia and I walk to the bathroom first before heading into the courtroom to wait to see the judge. Lydia starts to cry, dabbing at her eyes. It's a cry of frustration more than anything. I try to console her, "Hey, we got what we wanted right? You're not going to jail." "I can't go there, not with this!" she says, motioning to her bandaged right side. "That bitch! She was gonna send me to jail, you heard her."

Lydia and I head off into Courtroom 1. It is overly air-conditioned inside, but Lydia still keeps nodding off next to me, her head falling down and jerking back up. We spend so much time in the courtroom that I have to go feed the meter with some nickels. The judge finally calls Lydia's case and gives her a new court date and a pro-bono lawyer. Lydia asks for a warrant recall, and the lawyer moves her hand to signal, "meet me outside the courtroom," except she doesn't show up. We don't know where to stand in order to get a warrant recall, but as Lydia explains to me, if you don't have the piece of paper in your hand, sometimes the computer system doesn't register that the warrant has been recalled. This has happened to her before, apparently. She insists on having the physical piece of paper in order to feel protected from the police.

A thin young woman with white-blonde hair spots us as we wait in a line that we think might be for a warrant recall. "I've been looking for you," she says to Lydia. "I came to court for Chris, but I came too late. It already happened. He has nine months in Walpole" [MCI-Cedar Junction-Walpole, a maximum-security men's prison]. She waits to walk out with us. Lydia asks her if she heard about the two girls who were hacked up with machetes last night "by the Mexicans" in the square in Chelsea. "Little Tara?" the girl asks. "Oh Tara. Yeah, I know her. She cussed out my mother one time."

They start to talk about what those two women were doing robbing men. "You know how the girls are," Lydia says, "they go out, they rob their tricks." The young blonde woman chimes in, "And usually they get away with it too." Lydia, who is Italian American, goes on to talk about how many "wetbacks" (derogatory slang for Mexican Americans) she used to rob. She seems to think the "girls" got what they deserved: "They shouldn't have been doing what they were doing." The cool flatness with which they speak about a violent murder of two acquaintances is disturbing to me. Violence against women is mundane, a simple fact of life. I feel nauseated by the entire discussion.

When I say goodbye to Lydia, I think about what would have happened if I had not been there to vouch for her, to wield my social capital as a medical student at a local prestigious institution, to pull the powerful bureaucratic ill will of the probation officer more in Lydia's favor. I am certain that she would have been sent back to jail for the bench warrant that had been issued for her. The cycle of institutionalization would have continued. Lydia would have endured a painful detox from opioids in jail, and the cycle would have gone on, uninterrupted, business as usual.

THE PRISON AND RISK OF DEATH

What is important in this case is how Lydia's life after jail (and life after hospitalization) is dictated by her fear of ongoing criminal justice involvement and its long shadow, a form of civil death for a woman who dares to pass as a man, who sells drugs, who perceives of herself as an underdog and someone fighting for fellow underdogs. Her embeddedness in the carceral system makes extrication from its maws nearly impossible. The mere possibility of incarceration, with its attendant physical discomforts, poses a deep persistent threat to Lydia's days and nights. She goes nowhere without worrying about her route and how she will avoid a run-in with police.

In addition to this, she also faces tangible and very significant risks to her chances of achieving health and happiness upon walking out of the interlocking steel-plated doors of the jail. She had left jail three months earlier, after spending three months in the Suffolk House of Correction for something she adamantly insisted she did not do. When she bailed herself out after her next court date, she said goodbye to all her jail friends, wishing them well. She changed out of her jail clothes and back into her street clothes consisting of checkered boxers, jeans, and a blue collared shirt—the clothes she had been wearing when she was arrested. They were stale and wrinkled from sitting in property. Juan was waiting with some heroin. She could not wait to get high; the cravings were overwhelming. It was like every fiber of her body and breath yearned for heroin. Time to party, she told Juan.

Ingrid Binswanger, a physician at the University of Denver, conducted seminal research that showed that leaving prison is an extremely risky time period.[9] Rates of overdose within the first two weeks of release from prison are staggeringly high, both anecdotally and in Binswanger's study (they found that someone leaving prison has a relative risk of overdose death 129 times higher than someone from the general population). She and her colleagues' 2007 study examining rates of mortality among people living prison in Washington State showed that the adjusted relative risk of death from any cause among former inmates in the first two weeks out of prison was 12.7 percent higher than the that of the general population.

There was also evidence that a single episode of incarceration could be even worse for women than for men in terms of mortality. In a study published by sociologist Evelyn Patterson, she found that "during the first period, 1985–1987, male prisoners lost 13% more years of life than male non-prisoners, and female prisoners lost 76% more years of life than female non-prisoners."[10]

There are many possible physiologic as well as social reasons that people leaving prison face such a disproportionately high risk of death. One is loss of physiological tolerance—that is, relative abstinence from opioid use during prison means that if someone uses heroin again after a long period of nonuse, even a small amount could have deadly consequences. Using half a gram or one gram of heroin (which in this era could be cut with or entirely fentanyl, a much shorter-acting and more lethal opioid) can overwhelm the brain's opioid receptors, leading to the suppression of the brain's respiratory center, increasing risk of respiratory depression, overdose, anoxic brain injury or death. Thus, it is critical to advise and educate patients to engage in harm reduction techniques, including giving naloxone, advice to "go slow," or do a test shot (doing small amount, then taking more later after a period of time). In Lydia's mind, every time she was released, she wanted to get as close as possible to overdose without actually overdosing.

In recognition of this increased risk, the Boston Public Health Commission had sponsored an overdose prevention effort led by a Boston neighborhood coalition in the Suffolk House of Correction. The intervention was to train and certify volunteer male inmates in the drug treatment division of the jail to learn the signs of an overdose and reverse an overdose with intranasal naloxone. Upon their release from jail, people who had been trained could present the certificate and receive several doses of naloxone at the Boston Public Health Commission offices about half a mile away on Albany Street, although only a few of them walked the two blocks to actually pick up the medication upon their release. The curriculum instructed the teacher to explain why incarcerated people were at such a high risk of overdose. The teacher there bemoaned in his lecture that four of the men in the previous group in the class had died upon release and how this happened repeatedly.

Some women's decision to pick up heroin immediately upon release was often made weeks or days before actually even getting out. Incarcerated women told me they felt torn: they want to stop using, but they also intensely mourn their loss of freedom and they go back to drugs as an expression of that freedom to choose. They feel that time in jail or prison is a massive interruption in their lives. They often feel compelled to make up for lost time, to blaze more brightly and strongly than before.

As public health practitioners and clinicians, we counsel them to do test shots: do a little bit, then do more later. Yet this is precisely what they do not want to do. Their greatly elevated risk of overdose upon release, then, are directly related to the fact of having been incarcerated. Incarcerated women who use drugs upon their release, as Lydia told me, wanted to use because they craved more intensity. They wanted to feel and experience a rush of being alive, of being free, unshackled from their involuntarily confinement (and usually abstinence) in carceral spaces.

In Lydia's case, what she craved perhaps most was freedom, to be able to exert autonomy over her body and what she did and not do with her time, even if she knew her behavior was unhealthy. Once she left jail, she started using immediately: "I didn't have a habit, but throughout my partying I got robbed." She was back in her stomping grounds (Revere and Chelsea) but "I got robbed in Revere when I was getting high. I got robbed for $3,000 that week [first week out of jail]. I got robbed almost everywhere, almost all the places I went partying, but that's because I was being overly generous. People saw that I had money and drugs and I was being overly generous. Nobody needed to rob me. But I got overly high and they would take advantage of that fact." Lydia was doing her favorite: speedballs (injections of heroin and cocaine). She had nowhere to go and would stay with different people in exchange for drugs. As she would proposition them, "Let me stay the night, then I'll get you high all night long."

Yet she felt vulnerable to the predations of not-so-friendly acquaintances who took her drugs and money. Why did she keep doing it? Why couldn't she stop? And like other women I met, she felt that getting arrested and having to go to prison was a long and irritating interruption in her life. Serenity felt the same. It was, therefore, her "mission" to finish where she had left off. She recounted that "every time I go to jail, I feel like they interrupted what I was doing and I'm not ready to stop yet, so I still have that mission to complete. And so that's why I go out [to the streets to use] a lot."

Longitudinal social science studies similarly suggest that being incarcerated is a factor in long-term poor health outcomes. Sociologists Susan Sered and Maureen Norton-Hawk conducted an archival study of 839 women released from MCI-Framingham in 1995.[11] Of those women, they found that at least 97 of the women had died within fifteen years of release from prison; the median age was forty-four, the primary cause of death included alcohol, HIV/AIDS, drug overdoses and pneumonia. Forty-four years, almost half of the life expectancy of a woman in the United States (eighty-one years). The life spans of the women in the study were more equivalent to the life expectancy of a woman in war-wracked Sierra Leone or the Democratic Republic of Congo than one in a well-off city boasting many resources and one of the country's top health care institutions.

A TOWNIE AND A GUINEA

I first met Lydia when she was in the Boston jail serving a three-month sentence. She was in a bad mood because she had just had to say goodbye to her girlfriend, who had been released earlier in the day. She was also fixated on not having showered in the past several days and was worried about smelling bad. She had no time to shower because her girlfriend was leaving and they wanted to spend a quiet hour together in the yard before she left. She also felt self-conscious because she was not wearing a bra, since one of the other "girls" was supposed to wash it but hadn't finished it yet.

At first glance, Lydia, who goes by the name Leo when she is in prison, appears very much like a man. She is short and usually wears her now graying hair shaved close to her scalp. She is also overweight, a fact that she bemoans, as it tends to indicate to her a soft and aging body that is slowing down. Meeting Lydia for the first time, I was struck by her thick black eyebrows and facial hair above her top lip, her gender-nonconforming body. She exuded an aura of toughness, pugnacity even. It surprised me that Lydia always had girlfriends, until I realized that what she probably had to offer was a lot—that is, her street-smarts and the desire and ability to provide a sense of safety to a woman. She wanted to and was generally able to fulfill many of the roles of a desirable street partner, usually performed by male figures—procuring drugs, taking on the legal and physical risks associated with getting drugs, and so on. When she and I were walking the streets of Chelsea, where Lydia roams using and selling drugs, she told me to "walk on the inside of the sidewalk, and she would walk on the outside, closer to the cars, so no one would think I was working [prostituting]." But interestingly, she identified as a woman, a lesbian, and simply as gender nonconforming. This was a long-standing conflicted identity that stemmed from her fraught relationship with her Catholic mother.

Lydia reminisced about growing up in Charlestown in the 1960s and the 1970s. It was a different time back then, when the Mafia ran Boston. The city was rife with racial anger and violence over busing. Charlestown in particular was an iconic neighborhood of white violence, the mob, working-class first- and second-generation Irish and Italian families.

Lydia's family was one of five Italian families in an all-Irish block, and her father was a bank robber who went to jail when she was only three years old. She remembers growing up when the so-called "Code of Silence" of gangs was rigidly enforced and she was forced to fight often, as detailed in Michael MacDonald's memoir of growing up in the similar neighborhood of South Boston (Southie).[12] Lydia fondly remembers having done an errand for Whitey Bulger, the notorious Boston mobster who ran an Irish gang all over Boston with his Winter Hill gang based in Somerville. She was ten when she had to do an errand for Whitey: "And I did a little job for him. I was supposed to get rid of a car for him. Yeah, I wasn't such a good kid. I was a troublemaker, but I had a good heart. I was always for the underdog, probably because I felt that way."

Lydia experimented with drugs but, in fact, had done nothing "serious" or "hard" like heroin until she turned thirty-five. Prior to that, she had held down many jobs, including a long stint for Teamsters as a pharmacy assistant. At thirty-five, she met and fell in love with a young woman named Rita, who was eighteen years old but lied and told Lydia that she was twenty-one. They got married at Rita's insistence. Meanwhile, Lydia's brother had a stroke and Lydia was struggling to take care of him at home. Rita was physically abusive, so Lydia left her and then was homeless, living under bridges. When she was incarcerated for being homeless (for trespassing) she was locked up, and there she met Jackie.

Jackie was the one who introduced her to heroin. They actually met in jail as "cellies" (cell mates). Lydia recounts how they got together as a couple: "Just when I got comfortable with Jackie being my cellie, she moved out. I was so fucking offended. I guess her and this other girl had been trying to be cellmates for a while and it finally came through. . . . I was on [floor] nine and she was on ten. When she was on ten, I heard somebody say to me something about my girlfriend, and I said, 'Who's my girlfriend?' And they said Jackie. So, we got to know each other a lot through letters before they moved me upstairs [to ten]."

Their relationship began in an extremely old-fashioned way, with letters. Being in the antiquated jail led to many relationships via other nontraditional means. Sometimes women would stare across the yard at the men at the other part of the jail. In a wonderfully creative twist, they could take the water out of the toilets in their cells and talk back and forth to their boyfriends through the antiquated pipes.

Jackie and Lydia got released from jail a week apart. After they got out of prison, Jackie went straight back to shooting heroin and would "pass out immediately." Lydia tried it, first by sniffing it for three days or so, but was jealous that Jackie was getting "instantaneously wrecked." Lydia first learned how to shoot up in her foot, because she learned from Jackie, who had already used up all her other veins: "I would shoot up in my foot because that's where she was shooting up. I remember back then if I didn't shoot up in my arm, then that meant I wasn't a fricking addict or a junkie."

It was difficult for Lydia to use too much heroin herself because she was always "babysitting" Jackie, whom she was afraid was going to always overdose and die "because she popped a lot of benzos and did a lot of dope," which increased her risk of death. For many years, Lydia felt that taking care of Jackie was her life's mission. Jackie's use was frantic and manic at times; she would shoot up as often as ten times a day, driven by the haunting and traumatic memory of mother's death by heroin overdose. Jackie had been using with her mother at the time her mother overdosed and died, but she was "too wrecked" to notice that her mother had not just "nodded out" but actually stopped breathing and died. Several hours later, she came to her senses and discovered her mother's lifeless body next to her. Lydia thought maybe she could save Jackie, and caring for her gave her a strong sense of purpose. Yet Lydia could never get at the core of Jackie's suffering and her hellbent desire for oblivion. She could not save her from her demons and could not help her stop.

POST-INCARCERATION PRIMARY CARE CLINIC: MEDICINE AS RISK REDUCTION?

Even after she had left Jackie, Lydia still couldn't combat her physical dependence on heroin. She had been to a now-defunct community-based drug treatment program for three months, but she relapsed at drug-filled halfway houses upon completion of that program. There were too many young, beautiful women who had drugs and attached themselves to her. I had hopes that she might be able to find some respite in the post-incarceration clinic that I worked at that was based in her neighborhood. Physicians have argued that there is a public health role for medicine in ameliorating the harms of incarceration.[13]

The night that she is supposed to come in for her appointment at the clinic, I call her. She says she is planning on coming in. She tells me her habit has worsened to approximately two grams of heroin a day (one gram more a day than usual because of the pain from her wound) because she was cut off the prescription pain opioid medication refills in the meantime. She is afraid that her side might have become reinfected.

I encourage her to come in to the clinic and assure her that we can help her. I am secretly worried, though, that we can't help her. What can we do? Suggest she go into detox or go back to the hospital where she was discharged so cavalierly back to the streets to be homeless and begin heroin use again?

I notify the team at the clinic that she is coming because she is sending me text messages at every step of the way as she tries to get to the clinic. She is ten minutes late, then twenty minutes late. The teams of students able to see patients are in short supply, and I am holding out with my first-year medical student to wait for Lydia. She keeps sending me text messages: she is on the bus. She is coming from Revere, where she has been staying at Jackie's house, using. Now she's at the place where she is keeping all her belongings. She is waiting for another bus. Finally, she shows up, thirty-five minutes late.

In the meantime, I have been trying to teach the medical student about necrotizing fasciitis. I am also interested in teaching him the social medicine aspects of caring for a patient like Lydia. How can we get her to a clinic? What do we expect to do for her here and what does she expect us to do for her? How can we have an encounter where everyone feels accomplished? How can we address the upstream causes of her poor health—like her homelessness and ongoing heroin addiction— from an outpatient community clinic visit?

"You didn't have to come in tonight," I say to Lydia when I see her, congratulating her for even showing up. A lot has happened in the few weeks since I last saw her. She was staying at a friend's house—a fellow heroin user—and a couple of them left to get food. When they came back, their friend had overdosed and died.

Lydia is a wreck. She holds a baseball cap in her hands and twists it around, her eyes sparkling with tears about to spill out onto her cheeks. I try to calm her down, reassure her. We bring Lydia to meet the psychiatric team. The psychiatric resident suggests that Lydia needs to go to a detox and then a program; she should take an ambulance to the main emergency room tonight. She agrees, but hesitates, "I want to go in. But I didn't know tonight. I left my wallet and stuff at this lady's house that I'm staying at. I want to have my stuff." So we agree that she will come in the next morning at 9:00 after picking up her things. She promises to come back.

Then, in a separate room, we help with her wound. My first impression of her healing skin graft is the raw skin of an uncooked turkey. I am very careful as we view and clean the area. In fact, it does not actually seem to be infected.

I make sure to ask her several times if she is comfortable with the way we wrapped her wound back up. These skills are rarely, if at all, taught in medical school. I knew from the past that she had been doing it herself a particular way, and that the nurses had done it in some ways that made her feel dissatisfied or upset later on. She said we had done a good job. I wonder if I am perhaps overly attentive to the suffering of people who use drugs, aware of how they have experienced so much painful needling at the hands of health care workers. But I feel like such extra care and attention is critical.

The attending physician who is supervising our team wants to get labs (blood work) for diabetes, cholesterol, HIV, Hepatitis C viral loads, and to check immunization status. Lydia pleads with her, no, can't we do that another time? My veins are shot. I argue that we should try to come to a middle ground: Can't we do it another time? Didn't we get a lot done with the most pressing issue of the night? We triaged what was important to Lydia and just established a human connection based on respect and dignity. We agreed to do bloodwork at another visit. How can we work on the big issues of social and structural violence in her life if she does not show up because she thinks we don't respect her?

The next morning, Lydia does not show up at the clinic as promised. She texts me a month later that she wants to go into treatment: "Ooh im just now able to get into the house I had to leave the last time I textd u so she [Jackie] could make $$ [prostituting] so we wouldnt be sick my body was just so achy but im just now able to shower&get ready2go the only thing thats ok about it is im only a bus ride & a few block walk so once im on the bus it only takes me 15-20 to get there." An hour later, "within the hour, I'm almost ready to leave." Later, "I'm on the bus now im scared! Will they find me some place [to detox] cuz now im out on the street if not." I am afraid to reassure her because I don't know if I can trust in the medical system behind me: for the receptionist at the front desk to treat her with dignity, for the line at the psychiatric emergency room to not be out the door, for her to feel trust and compassion from the doctors and nurses, for the system to have a detox bed to which she can go. I try to reassure her as best I can.

At the time, in 2012, it was the standard of care to send patients to a detox program in order to get all of her substance use in order. In many places around the country, this is still the norm. Yet, in some parts of the country today, it would be feasible and reasonable to initiate her onto low-threshold buprenorphine-naloxone on the very same day and visit. We should have given her this medication, written by physicians who have completed an eight-hour opioid treatment training course and can prescribe for clients who see them in the outpatient office. She could have filled the prescription and then taken it the next morning when she was in mild to moderate withdrawal. The buprenorphine would have quelled her cravings and quieted her use, and we could have checked back in with her about adjusting the dose in the next several days or within a week.

As a future physician and an anthropologist, I wanted to believe that the clinic could be a force for good. Yet could it actually be a means of addressing the structural violence in Lydia's life? She left, and she did not return for a while. But finally she did. We were there for her, regardless of when she returned, and we were compassionate, and she seemed to remember that. I wondered how the clinic could have possibly addressed Lydia's anxiety and despair. Perhaps most difficult of all was to address Lydia's enmeshment in the carceral system that posed such a barrier to her ongoing well-being. Did our community-clinic have the capability to protect her from this? If we didn't, could we envision programs that could?

In other countries such as Switzerland, the Netherlands, Denmark, Belgium, Germany, and even Canada, they have heroin assisted treatment (HAT) programs. In such clinics, patients receive injections two to three times a day of pharmaceutical-grade heroin or diacetylmorphine in regulated, medically supervised sites. These studies have shown significant improvements in quality of life, lower crime and overdose incidence, and greater treatment retention and social engagement.[14] Could Lydia and other American heroin users like her have benefited from such a program that would provide them with a daily dose of the substance that they had become dependent on, protecting them from crime, hustling, and the vagaries of dopesickness and incarceration?

I learned later that Lydia did in fact make it to the community clinic's urgent care center, and she was sent by ambulance to the emergency room at the main hospital. She stayed two weeks in the psychiatric inpatient unit, detoxed with the community-based standard of care, and was eventually set up to go to the Barbara McInnis House, a well-regarded health care and social service provider for medically complicated and homeless individuals. I imagined that things might be looking up.

ILLICIT DRUG USE AND GOVERNANCE OF THE SICK AND POOR

Working closely with Lydia—and others similarly marked by our state institutions as the most deviant, aberrant, or morally suspect—I wondered how and why anyone would care about her. I came to believe that Lydia's suffering and illness was part of a scheme of governing life itself—or biopolitics—in which she had been simultaneously assisted by the state carceral apparatus and yet left for dead.

Philosopher Michel Foucault defines *biopolitics* as "the endeavor, begun in the eighteenth century, to rationalize the problems presented to governmental practice by the phenomena characteristic of a group of living beings constituted as a population: health, sanitation, birthrate, longevity, race."[15] The population itself became constituted as an object that could be known, studied (quantified by various measures), and intervened upon as a form of governance. According to this theory, the new right of modern power was the "power to 'make' live and 'let' die."[16] Significantly, however, it did not supplant the traditional power to "take life or let live" (as governments or rulers usually could just execute citizens at will) but, rather, combined with it in complex and historically variable ways. Medicine and its increasingly effective therapeutic armamentaria, in combination with the flourishing of biological sciences and the science of population and disease identification and mapping, including public health, were critical to enabling this shift to modern power.

From a biopolitical perspective, the question remains about whose bodies are the sites of positive forms of intervention/optimization, and whose bodies are the sites of negative intervention or simply abandonment; it seems that not everyone is at risk for the same sorts of interventions in the name of health. Why is the terrain of biopolitical schemes such an uneven one, where women like Lydia seem condemned to a life of suffering and despair? Are those who are "let die" the individuals who cannot or do not "exercise biological prudence, for their own sake, that of their families, that of their own lineage, and that of their nation as a whole"?[17] Or are they those who are marked as dangerous, morally unsound, or biologically risky for the population as a whole?

The bodies of women who use drugs have historically been seen as sites for social intervention in the name of the good of the social body, as is evident from ongoing efforts by a nonprofit organization sponsored by a right-wing billionaire to offer voluntary sterilizations to women with drug problems in exchange for $300. Also, recently the state of California was found to have coerced sterilizations of over 140 women with low health literacy and multiple structural inequalities while under the authority of the California prison system.[18] There have long been state-sanctioned gender violence and interventions directed toward controlling the reproductive functions of women, especially women of color, who disproportionately face increased policing and criminalization of poverty, reproduction, and substance use, as Dorothy Roberts and others have argued.[19]

How do people like Lydia—those marked by our state institutions as the most deviant, the most aberrant, or the most morally suspect—come under regimes of knowledge and discipline? What is the value of the lives of the poorest of the poor? How, and in what ways, is their suffering and illness part of a scheme of governance of life itself?

Foucault did not elaborate on what axes of social inequality would become the grounds for intervention on the population or who would decide, carry out, or make policies based on such data. What were the factors that determined who would be subject to interventions to optimize the length or quality of their lives, on the one hand, and who, instead, would be subject to interventions to keep them at bay or to neutralize or minimize the potential dangers or costs they imposed on everyone else? In his discussion of racism, however, he did note that racism gives the state the moral justification to "foster life" or "disallow to the point of death."[20] Foucault elaborates that when he speaks of death and killing, "I obviously do not mean simply murder as such, but also every form of indirect murder: the fact of exposing someone to death, increasing the risk of death for some people, or, quite simply, political death, expulsion, rejection, and so on."[21]

This new concern with population that states began to have allowed for finer distinctions; interventions by the state would occur not only on those who were thought to be more useful in terms of labor, but on all bodies to greater or lesser degrees. Foucault traces this change specifically when he charts how the needs of the "sick poor," which had previously been relegated to the charitable associations, became a central concern of the State itself. The poor, the disabled, the elderly, the sick, and the infirm had previously been relegated to the domain of religious charity; in a biopolitical framework, they were now critical to a scheme of governance and poverty management; as he wrote, to make "poverty useful by fixing it to the apparatus of production."[22]

While poor people in this schema could not in and of themselves be profitable, attending to their poverty could perhaps be made useful by binding it up with an emerging capitalist system; the contemporary prison system has become indicted as a system profiting off the inevitable incarceration of the poor.[23] The poor and the sick were now seen as sources of potential contagion, danger, and moral contamination—in other words, they posed "internal dangers" as Foucault observed—to the rest of the population.[24] These could and should be contained. Incarceration was one way to contain and manage the social ills of the entire society more generally as well as potentially contribute to economies built around such institutions.

Lydia's story illustrates some of the specificities and messiness, and the fault lines along which our American society decides whose lives matters and why, as well as the consequences and complexities of living various forms of political, social, and civil deaths after hospitalization and jail. In Lydia's case, her alternating casual and despairing attitudes toward living and dying were intensely shaped by the despair she felt upon being released from the hospital's surgical service back to a rooming house full of fellow heroin users. If I had not been involved, it is doubtful that Lydia would have made any primary care appointments or attended one at all; in fact, at the primary care appointment where I was seeing her, she told the attending physician that she would not have come—would not have managed to come—if not for me.

The hospital where Lydia had spent several months as an inpatient could be congratulated for providing excellent clinical care: they had saved her life by accurately diagnosing the early warning signs of necrotizing fasciitis and giving her the appropriate and necessary treatment. During her stay in the surgical intensive care unit, they performed all the necessary measures to keep her alive. Was it the hospital's fault that Lydia lied, that she said she had a home? Was it their fault that she rapidly became homeless again and resumed drug use?

Lydia's experiences after discharge from the hospital demonstrate the failure of our health care system to treat the so-called "social determinants of health." Lydia's tenuous housing and her ongoing polysubstance use put her at high risk of not doing well. Yet these problems are somehow more difficult to address than the antibiotic selection and her wound care instructions, which seem more practical and pressing. The other problems are relegated to "social work" or a realm outside of medicine. Yet these are the problems that keep her sick and prevent her from getting well.

Perhaps this is why Lydia was sent home to the streets to take care of herself, in the context of modern hospital payment schemes that could not factor her distress or risk into their calculus of deservingness and worth. She subsequently endured a ceaseless, manic anxiety over her precarious social situation. This anxiety and despair about her circumstances were directly brought about and shaped by institutional processes and outcomes related to her hospitalization and her previous incarcerations. She once told me, "I'd give anything to have my boring little neat life back."

Having been incarcerated also greatly shaped Lydia's subjectivity and her sense of being in the world. When she first got out, she felt compelled to "party" in order to acknowledge and seize her newfound freedom, to exert her personal agency in a world in which she is generally assumed to be powerless. Being incarcerated had given her time to think about her life and her decisions, but it had also taken her temporarily out of the game of life. As she put it, "In jail, I kept contemplating whether I was going to go back [to drug dealing and robbing drug dealers], and you want to know what's crazy? . . . I'm still breaking the law [by doing drugs]! I'm like, well at least I ain't breaking the law by stealing out of stores, and robbing, and I don't rob your average fucking person."

Leaving Suffolk House of Correction without treatment for opioid use disorder certainly put Lydia at increased risk of overdose and death. If she had been locked up at Riker's Island in New York, which has been providing treatment with medication for opioid use disorder for over thirty years, she could have accessed either methadone or buprenorphine during her incarceration, and would be provided with a seven-day prescription of buprenorphine if she left ("walking meds"). Such low-barrier access to medications can be a critical difference between life and death; it is a practice that simply recognizes the tumultuous and chaotic circumstances surrounding leaving jail and prison.

Furthermore, Lydia could not turn to her family to provide her shelter from her dangerous life on the streets. Her immediate and extended families were rife with their own substance use issues and trauma that are all too common in low-income families. Lydia's biological father was a convicted bank robber, and when they hung out together, "I picked up his bad habit of becoming institutionalized," going in and out of jail. One of the cousins that she was particularly close with, in what was thought to be a paranoid psychotic break, had raped and killed his own mother. One of her girlfriends had been murdered in 1995, and Lydia still felt traumatized from that incident. Her sister had become addicted to heroin as well, and her mother misused prescription opioids and benzodiazepines in order to self-treat her own anxiety and sleep problems. Her tight-knit Italian family was breaking apart at its heavily worn seams; they had reached the limits of caring for themselves and their ability to extend care to Lydia. Her mother would not let her come back home even after her hospital stay, encouraging her to go to another hospital or a rehab program. Anywhere but home.

Lydia had reached the limits of care in a familial social network that had once cherished her and was now repulsed by her. It is the same contradictions that we see in her relationship to the state, in the carceral embrace that is also a shackle; it contains and punishes the poor but keeps them close. Lydia's immediate social world and her larger place in the world as a citizen were in arrears; she endured a social death as well as a civil death, both of which were sources of ongoing sorrow and despair. Her multiple transgressive identities in combination with oppressive social structures were what mired her in this state of affairs.

Sociologist Beth Richie argues that women like Lydia are particularly unprotected from the state; in fact, many times they are actually seriously harmed, hurt or even killed by the state services and institutions that claim to be protecting them. Although mainly focused on the violence against poor black women in communities of concentrated disadvantage, Richie uses the term "prison nation" to outline why the reliance on the formal criminal justice system and associated bureaucracies of control and surveillance have made women more vulnerable to ongoing violence and hardship instead of protecting or serving them.[25] Writing from a black feminist perspective, she points out that women who appear deviant often become embroiled in carceral social services and institutions because of the "prison nation" apparatus, including probation, parole, home supervision, welfare, child protective services, or other forms of frequent state interaction and subsequent policing.

As a result of her life being dominated and determined by her involvement in our "prison nation," Lydia's treatment at the hands of the state, the health care system, and even her community of family and friends, was harsh, and she consequently limped along in death-in-life. While her life was marked often by despair and hopelessness, I believed the most tragic part was the internalized symbolic violence of her situation: she sincerely believed that this suffering was ultimately her own fault, a by-product of her diseased brain just doing what it always did: "A big part of me is like, 'stay sober, stay sober.' I want to get my life back. I worked all my life, and just in this little seven years . . . I don't know how I'm getting my life back. Want to, want to, want to, but want to get high."

8

Conclusion

Breaking "Wicked Bad Habits"

It's hard to think about getting better from anything in prison or jail, let alone a condition as physically and psychologically entrenched as heroin addiction. I recalled one of my fieldnotes from the jail which illustrated some of the tensions involved in jail-based treatment.

RECOVERY CLASS (FIELDNOTE)

> *It is Wednesday at 3:30 and time for Recovery Class in the Suffolk House of Correction. It is graduation day, the last class of an eight-week-long session. Today the group learns they are getting certificates, but they don't seem particularly enthused. Jamie, a petite, middle-aged white mental health counselor at the jail, is running the group. Jamie is working hard to figure out what the group likes; she wants their feedback. She is anxious, like a teenager seeking acceptance from the popular crowd.*
>
> *Today she tells the class that they are going to do vision boards, gesturing to large stacks of magazines she has brought in for the exercise. Only four women are present today, since some other students are in the hole [solitary confinement] or have missed too many classes. Jamie begins with an explanation of the vision board: "Yes, a collage, what you want your future to be like. What you see, what's important, where you're going. Because you can't go there if you don't see it right?" The class is silent. Brandy, a young African American girl with dreads, pulls out a picture of Jack Daniels in a magazine. The coordinator tells her: "You know what? I'm going to build a picture and put that over all the good stuff because that's what happens right?" Silence again.*

Jamie continues, reading off a piece of paper: "A vision board is about much more than just writing down goals, dreams, and aspirations and cutting out pictures. So, when you're creating a vision board, think about what really works for you and begin to see clearly and build the perfect you. . . . If you can't see it, you can't imagine it, you can't reach it, it can be as big or as little, it's all up to you guys, what's important to you, where you're going."

Nataly, a middle-aged Hispanic woman, immediately refuses to participate. "I don't feel like doing this," she states flatly.

Jamie talks to them about self-affirmation, like "saying positive things to yourself in the mirror," while the women discuss if they would date bi-sexual men or not. Some crack jokes as they leaf through the magazines. About one outfit, one woman proclaims, "I would definitely have mental health called on me if I wear that."

I think about how much of a disconnect there is between the coordinator and the students. I pity the coordinator and the way that the women largely ignore her attempts to engage them in recovery talk.

Jamie asks one woman named Kathy who is incarcerated for heroin-related petty theft, "What do you think this has to do with recovery?"

Kathy replies, "I don't know."

Jamie: Do you look to the future?

Kathy: No.

Jamie: Thinking about right now? So, when you're clean, or you're trying to get clean, you start to look at the future. And it can be overwhelming, and being on the outside, so if you start to think about what it is you want and what you need to get it, it gives you a chance to start to think that there's more to it than just using."

Brandy: I need four pieces of tape.

The women coo over makeup, hairstyles, dogs, and cars. Sometimes brief moments of their life flash into view.

Jamie: What would you do when you get dressed up?

Brandy: I go out and drink.

Jamie: What are you going to get dressed up for now?

Brandy: I don't know, get dressed up and show off, show off my curves.

Jamie: What do you like to do besides drink?

Brandy: Fight.

Jamie: Okay, well that's not good, fighting.

Brandy: You should see me . . .

Jamie: Does fighting go with drinking or do you fight if you're not drinking?

Brandy: I can have a fight if I'm not drinking, if somebody pisses me off.

"Recovery"—whatever that means to people—seems so difficult, especially after jail, and the vision board exercise is almost painful to witness. How can doing this collage, looking at all the things you currently do not have, change the way your life will be on the outside? I keep thinking of all the structural barriers standing in the way of the happiness and well-being that all these women want and deserve. Structural barriers like racism, poverty, gender discrimination, segregation, lack of education and opportunity. I wonder about the futility of this exercise. It is exacerbated by Jamie's

inability to meaningfully relate to the lived experiences of the incarcerated women. It is the refusal of the jail to offer them medication treatment for addiction that could save their lives. It is the fact of incarceration that will make future employment near impossible. It is the violence of neglect, and it is the irony of this program that gives the appearance of effort but cannot actually provide safety, care, or any reassurance of future well-being.

. . .

I reflected on this seeming impossibility for women to get well after incarceration as I was in Boston preparing to give a talk. I had finished up my fieldwork research several months earlier but was in the process of completing and writing up my dissertation. I had reached out to Lydia to see how she was doing and she called me back that night. Usually her phone went straight to voicemail and I would leave long-winded messages imploring her to call me back or text me. The last I had heard from her she had gone into a treatment program.

Lydia wanted to tell me how good she was doing. She was doing so good, in fact, that her mother had let her come back home to stay for a while during Christmas and the holidays. She asked me if I had any paperwork showing that she had been in the hospital because she had a court date that she had failed to meet because she overslept. I told her I had papers showing she was in the hospital many months ago—were those what she wanted? She did, it turns out. I didn't know how it was going to prove that she was unable to go to the court date she had just missed the day before, but if she felt better about having discharge papers from several months ago, I was happy to bring them to her. She anxiously asked me when I could be at her mother's house.

We agreed on early the next morning, a Wednesday. I planned to go over to my office at Harvard, print the papers out, and then head to a nearby suburb where her mother lived. Lydia was pleased with this plan. Later that night, I received a text message from her with her mother's address. She also wrote a me lengthy note: "Kim, I wanna thank you so much for all that you've given me you've done wonders for me in the short time we've known each other & my heart is filled with so much thanks& appreciation you will never know how much &i love you for all you have done THANK YOU SO VERY MUCH HOPE YOU HAVE THE HAPPIEST OF HOLIDAYS SINCERELY LYDIA."

The next morning, after I dutifully printed out the paperwork that she wanted, I called her, ready to take two buses to Everett. She didn't pick up and she didn't answer my text messages. I had decided many months earlier—having gotten burned several times—as a general rule, to not go anywhere without confirmation of the plan on the actual day of a meeting. So, I waited for her to get back to me. I did not go out to Everett. I figured she had just overslept or that her phone had died. She tended to sleep badly at night and often slept late into the morning or even into the afternoon.

Several days later, I got a call from the clinic. Lydia had overdosed and died. Her mother found her on the bathroom floor the morning that I was supposed to head over there. After we had talked that last time, she had headed over to Chelsea, her old stomping ground, to see a friend. She must have scored some heroin and just did too much. Her mother and I talked, trying to make sense of the tragedy in its immediate aftermath: "But she was doing so good! That's why I let her come home." Unfortunately, being "clean" and "sober," in the conventional sense—having lost physiological tolerance—made her susceptible to overdose. She hadn't been taking buprenorphine-naloxone or methadone, two very safe medications that could have possibly prevented her death.

I was wracked with sadness over her death. I could only imagine the heartbreak, devastation, and trauma that people experienced who were present with loved ones when they died of overdose or discovered them dead. And sometimes that happened over and over again.

I thought very seriously about what we—the clinic, the doctors that cared for her, and even me personally—could have done to prevent this. In my mind I conducted a "morbidity and mortality review," which is what many hospital systems and medical teams do when someone dies of what is flagged as a possible systems-based error on the part of the health care institution or a team. The most egregious example is when someone dies on an operating table, and user error on the part of the surgeon or another team member could have contributed to it. The goal is to identify how to change the system in order to prevent an adverse outcome (i.e., do we need to provide more education about this, or do we need to change the hospital electronic medical record to prompt physicians to do this, or do we need to double check the medication order, etc.).

In Lydia's case, I thought that certainly we should have prescribed her naloxone so that she or others could use it to reverse overdoses. In my own clinical practice at MGH-Charlestown many years later, we would hand out naloxone kits to those at highest risk, and Lydia certainly would have qualified as such. But maybe we should have handed on a naloxone kit to her mother, as it would be technically impossible for Lydia to use it on herself during an actual overdose. Maybe we should have called her mom in for a group/family-based visit to make sure her mom knew how to administer the medication.

Maybe, I thought, we should have been more explicit not to use alone but rather to use with friends, in relative safety. To always use with a friend or a buddy. To have check-ins to make sure that people knew where she was, even if she was alone. I think about Lydia every time that I testify and teach about safer consumption sites (also known as overdose prevention sites, or safe injecting facilities). These facilities operate around the world explicitly to prevent fatal overdose deaths and to educate people on safer drug use techniques. These are spaces where people can bring a pre-obtained drug supply for personal use into a facility and use them within an ordained space. Not a single person has overdosed and died within them.

Over a hundred sites have been operating for several decades in other countries across Canada, Europe, and Australia. These sites are operated and staffed by volunteers, peers, or health care professionals who can administer supplemental oxygen, rescue breathing, and/or naloxone and activate emergency services to administer care in case of a potentially fatal overdose. In the era of fentanyl and the increasingly unsafe street drug supply, where a fentanyl or fentanyl analogue overdose could be fatal in the span of ten or fifteen minutes, this seemed like a commonsense and rational public policy option. Places such as Insite in Vancouver, British Columbia, furthermore, offer people the option to enter detox or treatment programs on the spot if they desire such on-site treatment. Using principles of harm reduction, or "meeting people where they're at," means acknowledging drug use and acting compassionately toward them. There are even women-only safe consumption sites because of high rates of sexual violence and harassment, as well as a variety of sites that offer safer smoking spaces for people who smoke methamphetamine or crack cocaine. In many ways, these places serve as a means to protect people from the harms of the outside world—including cold temperatures or exposure, police violence and arrest, or simply the stigmatizing glare of neighbors who don't want them to use on public benches or parks or in coffee shop bathrooms.

Besides advocating for supervised consumption spaces, I wondered what else we could do as primary care physicians to make the clinic a site for ameliorating the wounds of social injustice. I remember bringing Lydia to the post-incarceration clinic. How could we have made it better for her?

I think it is critical to envision new ways to provide care in which the physical brick-and-mortar clinic is not so central and the doctor, too, can be decentered. We should be employing people with histories of incarceration and drug use as community health workers to lead our efforts, as in the excellent Transitions Clinic Network model. Shifting to community health workers reminds us that seemingly simple interventions like "accompaniment," as popularized by the medical advocacy group Partners in Health, can and should be utilized at home.[1] We should be investing in people with histories of incarceration and substance use to go to college if they desire and harness the many kinds of experiences and expertise they already have in their lives. We should be supporting their families, their children, and their immediate social networks. We should be mobile, bringing care wherever it is needed—under bridges and into homes as Boston Healthcare for the Homeless does. We should be breaking down the walls of so-called "professionalism" and taking care of people when they are in the most danger. Our health care teams should be texting with patients if that is how it is easiest to communicate with people so that we can get them help, get them out of danger. What if Lydia had called or texted me as she was about to use that fatal shot?

Such new models that de-prioritize the space of the clinic and create alternative spaces for care and engagement are urgently needed. Primary care doctors currently just don't have the time to help Lydia navigate bus schedules and her anxieties in order to get to the clinic. If she missed her appointment by over half an hour, she simply would be rescheduled and not be seen in most clinics in this country. Every clinic should have some time allotted for walk-in hours or flexible scheduling. There are innumerable ways we can envision providing better care for people who use drugs and people leaving jail and prison.

SOCIAL JUSTICE AND HEALTH EQUITY IN THE UNITED STATES

As "global health" has become a buzzword, entering households and appealing to individuals previously untouched by medical anthropology or social medicine, it has become increasingly important for me to resist the call to explore the suffering of others on distant shores. I have always been interested in thinking critically about local injustices and inequality here in the United States, dating back to my education as an HIV/AIDS activist while an undergraduate at Columbia University in New York City. I learned about activism from people who used drugs, homeless individuals, former prisoners, and queer people who had mobilized for the sake of their lives during the 1980s HIV epidemic. Together we are part of a social compact, with shared futures and common histories. Our fates are bound together by fact of geography but also by common governance, institutional policies, and cultural orientations. I increasingly felt a tension between what was known as "global health" and the work that I did in health care among the disenfranchised and the precariously positioned in Boston.

Through the pursuit of this local work, I perceived that the study of the suffering of local people was eclipsed and often viewed as less interesting (much less fundable) than the suffering of a more exotic other, even though health disparities and stark inequalities existed right here at home. I was told many times throughout the early stages of my research to go abroad; that is what anthropologists do in the Margaret Mead tradition. We go to Papua New Guinea. I was told by many to go study people who use drugs in jails and prisons in Siberia because that was fundable; that was what we deemed appropriate and compelling ethnographic work. I declined.

But studying social suffering close to home is an enterprise just as complex—and arguably more difficult—as studying it abroad. It is messier to separate out the forces at play when they are things that we see so often that they become invisible. Thus, my project was partly motivated by a desire to speak against this imputed hierarchy of suffering that exists still in academia. I have endeavored to show that poor women in the prison system are complex, interesting, and morally worthy of study and advocacy. These women wanted to participate and were grateful to be heard and acknowledged, to have their stories used to teach others. They believed in the value of their lives and their stories. No one believed anyone would be interested enough in their stories to write a book on the subject.

This book is also about much more than just opioid use disorder and problematic substance use. In many ways, our society is bound up and obsessed with drugs. Philosopher Felix Guatarri suggests that we are all complicit in addictive and compulsive behaviors, and this is one of the cultural tendencies of late capitalist modernity; he says we are all connected to drugs in our "taste for disaster" and "a drive for the end of the world."[2] He points to watching television as a particularly pathological preoccupation but one that is hardly criminalized. The objects of our various fixations and desires are usually rather commonplace: food, sex, exercise, work, gambling, the internet, our phones. We actively seek out disconnection from an overwhelming world through the routine comfort of interacting regularly and predictably with things. What substances and objects do we all variously utilize as we seek to minimize pain and maximize positive feeling?

Prisons are also about a long-standing spiritual and cultural insecurity regarding punishment and fear. Within our moral order and cultural schemas, they exist to serve the anxieties of some in our society who fear others. They are institutions that not only represent profound racism and classism but also function as a means of social control within a political economy of blame and fear. And the people subjected to incarceration are those like Lydia who are subjected to anonymous deaths. Many groups of people are fighting back against the politics of fear and insecurity that perpetuate the existence of prisons and jails.

The groundswell for the decriminalization of substance use is happening now. As is the groundswell against the use of prisons and jails as a social solution for poverty, unemployment, drugs, and racism. Angela Davis and Gina Dent note that the incarceration of women worldwide is part of a long-standing practices of economic exploitation, colonialism, and fear of a unified feminist movement.[3] Intersectional movements are working to highlight how multiple axes of oppression converge to maintain social structures and ongoing inequality. The crisis we face is not opioids. The crisis we face is a war on people who use drugs and on our reliance on incarceration as a catch-all policy solution.

Organizers and activists both locally and federally are fighting against incarceration and the criminalization of drug use, demonstrating the dangerous linkages that result in an uneven social exposure to harm or death that incarceration poses. Groups like my organization, Harm Reduction Coalition, and many others stellar leaders such as Drug Policy Alliance, Homeboy Industries, Exponents, VOCAL-NY, EPOCA (Ex-Prisoners Organizing for Community Advancement), Families for Justice as Healing, Black and Pink, ACT-UP, Law Enforcement Against Prohibition, Critical Resistance, and many others are organizing their communities, changing legislation, and exposing how harmful policies directly affect people's lives and must and can be changed. People who use drugs are forming drug users' unions and are standing up against the macro-political forces that coalesce and seem to conspire against their livelihoods and life itself. There are also movements across the country resisting the building of jails and prisons and the use of community supervision programs, such as probation and parole, as well as against the dehumanizing practice of shackling incarcerated women when they are giving birth.

In California, there is strong community resistance to the turn to "gender-responsive" rhetoric used to build more prisons and jails for women. As Cynthia Chandler of Justice Now writes regarding California's Gender Responsive Strategies Commission's suggestion to build four thousand five hundred new prison beds for women who were deemed low risk: "This model is dangerous to incarcerated women because it embeds a mix of paternalism and imperialism, racism and classism—all promoting the idea that prisons can be safe, respectful, dignified places where we can do what's best for our 'downtrodden' sisters. The model includes no critique of prisons or the role prisons have played in dominating poor women and women of color."[4] Others are raising awareness of and protesting the anonymous deaths of loved ones held in federal and local immigration detention facilities including private for-profit prison groups.

Everyday people, too, are out changing the paradigms of caring for people who use drugs in their communities. Harry Leno, tattooed, pierced, and shaggily white haired, was one such man I met. He would head out in his beater car to Lowell and Lawrence, two North Shore suburbs, every Tuesday with packs of needles, ties, cookers, Band-Aids, and sharps disposal containers. Wearing a Veterans for Peace T-shirt, he handed out the supplies to people who used heroin, providing them with clean needles while taking back their dirty ones in the sharps containers. At the time of my research, he was accompanied by Stacy, an MPH student from Boston University who did the accounting. They called themselves "Love and Safety."

Lawrence and Lowell are struggling postindustrial mill towns with not enough jobs and serious economic difficulties. At the time, people told me that Lawrence is the closest thing to an open-air drug market near Boston; many people came from all around the eastern part of the state to buy heroin or pills in Lawrence. Lawrence felt like a ghost town when I went there with Harry. The tired dusty downtown had only a handful of open storefronts. We quickly found a rooming house—where people paid by the week for an individual room with a shared bathroom down the hall—and visited two of the people in the building to give them supplies and collect their sharps containers filled with used needles. People who use drugs want to use responsibly and dispose of their works responsibly. They don't want to contribute to litter in their rooms or on the streets.

Harry told me his strategy for finding people who use drugs was via the "seek-and-find" method. He went to them wherever they were living—under flatbed trucks, in "empties," or in rooming houses—or just found them walking around on the street. There was one McDonalds that many women who used drugs and sold sex would utilize, and Harry often met them in the parking lot.

"Love and Safety" never knew how many sterile syringes they would be able to give out. This was because they never had a constant supply of needles. They rarely had the much-requested bacitracin packets that users applied to try to prevent skin infections (the bacitracin was too expensive, but Harry and Stacy did give out alcohol wipes). Harry and Stacy handed out upwards of two thousand syringes a day, easily taking back sharps containers with the same quantity. But their supply was limited, and they constantly worried about not having enough for their regular clients. Their regulars would tell them new places to go—"You know, you guys should hit up Apple Street, there's a lot of people that need these"—but Harry was afraid to expand without knowing if he would have enough supplies to expand responsibly. They also didn't have nearly enough of the overdose medication, naloxone, which was most needed by people using drugs to prevent overdose fatalities among their friends.

Technically, giving out sterile syringes is no longer illegal in Massachusetts, although Harry had been hassled and arrested for "possession" (of drug paraphernalia) over the years since he began doing this work, which he started when the HIV/AIDS epidemic began to hit hard in the 1980s in poor neighborhoods of Boston such as Chelsea and Roxbury.

Harry lamented that no one else was "seeking and finding." What he meant was that few others were proactive or imaginative enough to envision or enact a paradigm shift one user and a time. People who use drugs are generally told to go to clinics, hospitals, pharmacies or drop-in centers to get sterile syringes, but Harry knew the large majority wouldn't do it, largely out of shame and fear of stigma. Many people would rather reuse a needle until it became extremely blunt.

Harry's supply was constantly limited, and he was a small unit of defense in an ongoing endless war on people who use drugs, who risked acquiring infections like Hepatitis C or HIV from sharing syringes because of policies and practices born of discrimination. Yet, somehow, he was not discouraged. Many of the women that I met in prison and jail knew Harry as the "old man with needles." They were grateful that he didn't judge them, and they credited their relative health and well-being to his kindness, his weekly commitments to them by just showing up, and his acknowledgment of their common humanity. He simply offered love and safety. How can one man's volunteer work be translated into evidence-based and sustainable community public health policy?

One source of indeterminacy is that changing the way we as a society envision and grapple with drug use means we have to become more comfortable with the social fact of drug use. Many people use psychoactive substances and generally can function well in their social roles as parents, workers, children. A small and visible minority develop problematic substance use. They and we need social policies that actually help and not harm. By accepting the social fact that people experiment and use drugs for a variety of reasons, understanding with compassion and curiosity why people might use substances—for pleasure, for relief of anxiety, for a feeling of being all right in the world—we can figure out how to minimize the harms and equip people to do so. We need to radically rethink our healthcare systems, recognize our own internal biases and fears, and legalize and regulate drugs to take them out of the shadows and off the streets. Expanding programs such as prescription heroin and hydromorphone (as they are doing in Canada) is one way to make opioid use safer than reckoning with an inconsistent, often fentanyl-laced (poisoned) street supply.

Many believe legalization and regulation of all drugs will change the landscape, as they have done in many countries such as Portugal. Prohibition has done innumerable harms, driving people away from using safer substances to tainted and unpredictable supplies of much stronger drugs produced and smuggled into the country to fuel the black market.[5] Legalization of marijuana has already begun to affect and alter landscapes of substance use: in many states across the country, as marijuana became more available in a licit market (either medicalization or full legalization), rates of opioid analgesic overdose deaths across those states decreased.[6] We don't know exactly why, but we might suspect: if people are self-medicating painful conditions, then marijuana is harm reduction; marijuana has never been reported to cause respiratory depression and death as opioids commonly do.

In all these efforts, we need to closely examine and de-link the political philosophies and systems that have made jails and prisons so central for drug treatment in this country. We also must consider what the unintended effects of our own well-intentioned responses to addiction might entail. As my mentor Arthur Kleinman has written, "Institutional practices make health and social problems more intractable and deepen both the sense and substance of misery."[7] How often do our policies inadvertently stigmatize, with policies like not offering hepatitis C treatment to people using drugs or making people exchange needles one for one instead of allowing them to take what they need? We are supposed to help and comfort, but instead often contribute to ongoing suffering, with our language, actions and policies.

Philosopher Glenn Loury reminds us that we all are complicit in a system of structural violence—what he calls "the moral problem we face . . . that we law-abiding, middle-class Americans are the beneficiaries of a system of suffering rooted in violence meted out at our request."[8] He urges us to all to think critically about our own positions as well as recognize the racist structures that support our lives (whether we want to or can see them or not) and question our own involvement in their continuation.

We in the medical profession and within the social sciences must seek to be more imaginative and critically engaged in little and big ways, in the clinic and beyond. We must partner with and learn from those most affected and do what we can to bring them to the table, lift their voices, compensate them for their time and expertise and involve them in research design and implementation. We must look at structural racism and institutional stigma in our own clinics and departments and hospital systems. We must speak out with whatever power and authority we have, whether simply as citizens or as professionals, working toward a world where doing justice does not involve prisons and treating addiction does not involve incarceration. One of the doctors I worked with when I visited Cook County Jail in Chicago called the jail a "factory of sorrows." I have written this book to raise our collective awareness about the institutional sources of sorrow and suffering in our midst, against these ongoing "factories of sorrows" that operate in every county, city, and town in our country.

People who shoot heroin intravenously refer to the process of using as "getting well." They use to avoid the physical symptoms of withdrawal and can get caught up. People who live for years with an opioid habit and physical dependency—what in Massachusetts is referred to as a "bad habit," or a "wicked bad habit"—no longer use in order to "get wrecked." It is often simply to prevent the pains of withdrawal. What I argue we need to do now is to examine how prisons and jails wreck the lives of people who have used drugs. What actually makes it difficult or impossible for them to recover their lives, their health, their children, their sense of dignity and normalcy after incarceration is *the fact of incarceration itself.* How can we help them "get well" from incarceration, from their destructive substance use? My prescription would be to keep them out of prison and jail in the first place, and if I could write it for all of them I would.

My work as the medical director of the Harm Reduction Coalition involves trying to write that prescription. We must not take the structures and institutions of power as a given. Instead, we must do more than we ever thought we could to reenvision and enact a different world. Can we reform our systems of healthcare and punishment to avoid such ongoing wreckage? Is transformative justice a way forward?

We all can try something new. You don't have to be a physician or a lawyer or a researcher or a social worker. It simply means calling to mind the actions of regular people like Harry, people who want to live in a different and more humane world. Does anyone want their local McDonalds bathroom to be the place where your neighbor's son died alone, without access to the care or compassion of someone who can administer him the opioid overdose reversal agent naloxone? I don't think we want to live in those towns, and yet every day without legally sanctioned supervised consumption sites we continue to do so.

There are other ways to get involved. Maybe it means having a meeting with the locally elected sheriff to ask about transparency and accountability regarding matters that affect the community, including treating people who use drugs with decency and asking for access to evidence-based medications like buprenorphine or methadone. Or maybe it means that we vote, or go to community meetings about new jails or decriminalization of sex work, or maybe donate to campaigns for less harmful district attorneys and prosecutors. Holding Harry's message of love and safety at heart, I hope that this book can be a starting point for conversations in our communities, advancing us together towards the goal of health justice for all.

Notes

1. INTRODUCTION

1. Hedegaard, Minino, and Warner (2018).
2. Raikhel and Garriott (2013: 8).
3. Kneeland and McDonald (1966: D6).
4. Courtwright (2004).
5. Substance Abuse and Mental Health Services Administration (2018a).
6. Markel (2011).
7. Sufrin (2017).
8. Rhodes (2004).
9. Waldman (2012: 225).
10. Sawyer (2018).
11. Wilson (1987). See also family physician Howard Stein's (1990) psychoanalytic interpretation of why we vilify drug users as objects of public policy.
12. Bobo and Thompson (2006); Alexander (2010).
13. Humphries (1999); Garriott (2011); American Civil Liberties Union (2013); Benson (2009); Brandt (2009); Tracy (2005).
14. Garriott (2011).
15. Coakley (2012); Valencia and Ellement (2013).
16. Estes (2012).
17. Comfort (2007).
18. Ferguson (2010); Harvey (2007); Maskovsky (2005); Fairbanks (2009); Wacquant (2009).
19. American Society of Addiction Medicine, "ASAM Addiction Terminology," quoted in Graham and Shultz (2003: 1601). Also interesting is the fact that the *Diagnostic and Statistical Manual* (DSM-IV), the standard diagnostic guidelines for psychiatrists, no longer has the clinical diagnosis of "addiction," preferring the less pejorative, though arguably less recognizable term, "substance use disorder."

20. Koob and Volkow (2010); Lajtha and Sershen (2010); Everitt and Robbins (2005); Leshner (1997).

21. Szalawitz (2016).

22. Courtwright (2001: 123).

23. Acker (2002); Musto (1999).

24. Garcia (2010).

25. Farmer et al. (2006); Bourgois and Schonberg (2009); Singer (2005); Singer (2008); Carr (2010); Garcia (2010); Fairbanks (2009).

26. Metzl and Hansen (2014).

27. The Pew Charitable Trusts (2018).

2. THE BEAUTY SHOP AND THE SEGREGATION UNIT

1. Smith (1959: 6–7).

2. Gilligan (1993: xvii).

3. Kajstura (2018).

4. Pellens and Terry (1928): 499.

5. Pellens and Terry (1928: 545).

6. Pellens and Terry (1928: 600).

7. Pellens and Terry (1928: 586).

8. Kolb's (1925) classification included five types: (1) Normal individuals accidentally or necessarily addicted in medical practice; (2) Carefree individuals devoted to pleasure seeking and new sensations; (3) Definite neuroses (4) Habitual criminals—always psychopathic and (5) Inebriates. See Kolb (1925).

9. Musto (1999: 158).

10. Acker (1997); Campbell, Olsen, and Walden (2008).

11. Campbell (2007: 58).

12. Clark (1961: 216).

13. Kandall (1999: 103)

14. Holiday and Dufty (1956: 130).

15. Anslinger and Tompkins (1953: 256).

16. See Cuskey, Moffett, and Clifford (1971). Also, this rate of relapse was not significantly higher than that of their male counterparts at Lexington. M. J Pescor (1941) suggested that about 30 percent of addicts at Lexington were abstinent after three years of release. Hunt and Odoroff (1962) found that more than 90 percent of addicts treated at Lexington who returned to New York relapsed.

17. According to Hunt and Odoroff (1962), before 1950, 10 percent of black addicts at Lexington were female and the figure doubled to 25 percent by 1955. Black women represented one-third of the female admissions to Lexington by 1965 and half of the admissions in 1967.

18. Dodge (2002: 29).

19. Rafter (1990: 26).

20. McDowell (1950: 101).

21. Freedman (1996: 128).

22. Smith (1959: 6).

23. Smith (1961: 20).

24. Foucault (1995: 172).

25. Smith (1959: 5).

26. Smith (1960: 5).

27. Freedman (1996: 190).

28. McDowell (1951: 7).

29. Spurr (1955).

30. Neiberg (2012), interview with author.

31. Van Waters (1957: 1).

32. Smith (1960: 2).

33. Warren (1953: 7).

34. Smith, (1960: 18).

35. Foucault (1995: 126). Foucault notes in the same work that the carceral system moved away from the spectacle of public torture to a hidden system exerting total control over not only the body but also the soul and the mind. Prison officials necessarily recruited the emergent psychological, social, medical, and legal professionals in their tasks of punishment, surveillance, and social control as occurred at Framingham. As Foucault wrote, "If it is still necessary for the law to reach and manipulate the body of the convict, it will be at a distance, in the proper way, according to strict rules, and with a much 'higher' aim. . . A whole army of technicians took over from the executioner, the immediate anatomist of pain: wardens, doctors, chaplains, psychiatrists, psychologists, educationalists" (1995: 11).

36. Smith (1963: 41).

37. Smith (1961: 20).

38. Neiberg and Clary (1962: 21).

39. American Bar Association and American Medical Association (1961).

40. As *The New York Times* reported, Dole and Nyswander started a demonstration project with four women addicts after their initial hesitation to experimentally treat women due to concerns that methadone would negatively affect hormonal cycles. Three years later, fifty women were included in their New York-based research group of 383 heroin addicts. See also: Todd (1975), Fraser (1997), Gearing (1971), Newman (1988).

41. A study by Janet Sansone (1980) found that in a study of 641 residents in the Odyssey House TC, retention rates for female addicts went from 37 percent at twelve weeks to 10 percent at forty-five weeks (as opposed to 53 percent for men to 34 percent, respectively). See also: Soler, Ponsor, and Abod (1976).

42. DeLeon and Beschner (1977).

43. Blake (1970: 1).

44. Kneeland (1973: 10).

45. Harvey (1970: 1).

46. The *Boston Globe* editorial page wrote about the "double standard for addicts," wherein "the so-called 'street user' is more likely to be rejected as a patient and referred to a public drug program. The wealthy addict is more likely to obtain protective treatment, perhaps by referral to a private rehabilitation facility where the addict's identity is a closely guarded secret." See *Boston Globe* Editorial Board (1980: 1).

47. *Boston Globe* Spotlight Team (1979): 17.

48. Dietz (1980: 1).
49. Chinlund and Lehr (1987: 1).
50. Coughlin (1987: 48).
51. The Superintendent Kathleen Dennehy said that the woman was punished for stealing bread because inmates "hoard bread and sugar to make hootch [prison alcohol]." See McNamara (1992a).
52. McNamara (1992b: 14).
53. O'Neill, Lehr, Butterfield, Tlumacki, and Rodriguez (1995: 1).

3. HEROIN IS MY COUNSELOR

1. Commonwealth of Massachusetts (2016).
2. See Freedman (1996) for a detailed description of women's prisons. I also spoke to the Massachusetts State Archivist Stephanie Dyson, who told me that women who drank or drugged had also been sent to the Bridgewater almshouse (1854) and the workhouse; in 1922, the women were sent to a special department at MCI-Framingham, the women's facility. The women would continue going to Framingham for the next eight decades for civil commitments. For the men, a new facility opened called the Massachusetts Alcohol and Substance Abuse Center (MASAC) for both criminally and civilly committed men in 1992—they were not technically sent to prison for addiction.
3. Depew and Esiobu et al. (2014).
4. Testa and West (2010).
5. Bourgois and Schonberg (2009).
6. Beletsky, Ryan, and Parmet (2018).
7. Massachusetts Women's Justice Network (2013).
8. Merrall et al. (2012); see also Binswanger et al. (2007).
9. Strang et al (2003).
10. Leukefeld and Tims (1988, 1993).
11. In 2010, I spent the summer in Cook County Jail in Chicago, one of the largest jails in the country. The jail had a standing inmate population of approximately ten thousand people, give or take a couple thousand, and over one hundred thousand people cycled in and out of that jail per year. That jail took a different approach to opioid addiction, at least taking into consideration the painful nature of detox. For inmates who came into the jail reporting that they had been on methadone maintenance for opioid addiction at community-based clinics, the jail would verify it with the caseworker at the clinic and would then "dose" the inmate the next day. Inmates would then be tapered off methadone (reported to have a worse detox than even heroin—it "gets in your bones and you can feel pain in your hair") over the course of approximately twenty-five days. Today, it would be evidence-based practice to continue patients on their medication throughout the duration of incarceration. See Nunn et al. (2009).
12. Krawczyk et al. (2017).
13. Substance Abuse and Mental Health Services Administration (2018); Saia et al. (2016).
14. Spectrum Health Services (2010).
15. Lansing (2012).

16. Yablonsky (1989); Yablonsky and Dederich (1965); De Leon (2000); White and Miller (2007).

17. Spectrum Health Services (2010).

18. Densen-Gerber (1973: 41).

19. James (1914: 67).

20. Feldman (2018).

21. Massachusetts Department of Public Health (2016: 28).

22. The woman who died was named Nicole Davis and she was twenty-four years old. She had no criminal history and was incarcerated at MCI-Framingham for a civil commitment to a thirty-day drug detoxification program. Her suicide was the sixth in one year in state prisons, and a seventh occurred days later at MCI-Walpole, another state prison facility. See *Boston Globe* Spotlight Team (2007).

23. Hser et al. (2001)

24. Bourdieu (2000: 221).

25. Hansen (2018).

4. DISCIPLINE, PUNISH, AND TREAT TRAUMA?

1. See Dennehy (2005); Bloom, Owen, and Covington (2003); Greenfield and Snell (1999); Elliott et al. (2005); Substance Abuse and Mental Health Services Administration (2011).

2. Western (2006); Western and Pettit (2005).

3. See Fullilove et al. (1993); Walsh et al. (2012); Ouimette et al. (2000); Kessler et al. (1995); Teplin, Abram, and McClelland (1996).

4. Baillargeon et al. 2009.

5. Ciechanowski and Katon (2012).

6. McHugo et al. (2005); Clark and Power (2005).

7. Morrisey et al. (2005).

8. John Geoghan was a priest who was symbolic of the Boston Roman Catholic sexual abuse scandal. He was accused of sexually abusing more than 130 children over his thirty years as a Boston-area priest. While he was incarcerated in protective custody at MCI-Shirley, one of the medium-security men's prisons in Massachusetts, his cellmate, who was serving a life sentence without the possibility of parole, murdered him. After this high-profile incident, the Department of Correction underwent many reviews of the prison system as it came under increased scrutiny see: *Boston Globe* Spotlight Team (2002), Farragher (2003).

9. Dennehy (2005: 4)

10. Dennehy (2005: 61).

11. Mack v. Suffolk County, 191 F.R.D. 16 (D.Mass.2000); Murphy and Rezendes (2002).

12. Stern et al. (2002); Tompkins (2004).

13. Latour and Farragher (2001: A01). Additionally, in September 2013, Mojica was arrested in a nine-month gang sweep operation called "Operation Dethrone II" in Chelsea, Massachusetts, conducted by the United States Attorney General and the Suffolk County Attorney General, along with the New

England FBI and State Police, for involvement in drug and firearm running in the street organization, the Almighty Latin King/Queen Nation Street Gang, also known as the "Latin Kings." According to the indictment, Mojica, whose nickname was "House," "is alleged to be a former Suffolk County Sheriff." He was charged with "conspiracy to distribute at least 5 grams of cocaine base and distribution of at least 5 grams of cocaine base" See FBI Boston Field Office (2013).

14. McDonald 2009.
15. Herman (1992).
16. Najavits (2002a).
17. Zlotnick et al. (2003.)
18. Sweeney (2010: 95).
19. Including groups such as African Americans, Holocaust survivors, Native Americans, and many different communities suffering complex and historical trauma: see Vogt, King, and King (2007); Courtois and Ford (2009); Kroll (2003); Morgan and Freeman (2009); Langer (1991).
20. Spinaris, Denhof, and Kellaway (2012).
21. Fassin and Rechtman (2009:21).
22. Young (1995).
23. Carr (2010:5).

5. WHERE MEDICINE IS CONTRABAND

1. Goodenough and Zezima (2011).
2. Curran (2016); Deehan (2015); Irons (2013).
3. Metzl (2003).
4. McHugh et al. (2013).
5. Centers for Disease Control (2013).
6. Good et al. (1992); Jackson (2011).
7. See work by Chutuape et al. (2001) on the relapse rates after short-term detoxification programs for opioid use disorder.
8. It is a commonly held belief that people can more quickly metabolize drugs present in their system by drinking large quantities of water or other fluids in order to "pass" a urine toxicology drug screen despite there being no evidence this is the case.
9. MacNeill (2018); Linton (2018).
10. Khantzian (2011).
11. O'Neill (2014).
12. Guenther (2013: xiii).
13. Schuman-Olivier et al. (2010).
14. Kakko et al. (2003).
15. Sordo et al. (2017); Marsden et al. (2017); Green et al. (2018)
16. Han (2012); Garcia (2010), Bourgois and Schonberg (2009).
17. Spencer (2013b: 14).
18. Sered (2013).
19. Casedino (2017).
20. Spencer (2013b).

21. Douglas (1966).
22. Massachusetts Department of Correction (2013: 12).
23. Massachusetts Department of Correction (2013: 16). Of note the Massachusetts Department of Correction states that the cost of the urine drug screening is $6, not, as Brittany stated, $140.
24. *Oxford English Dictionary* (2014).
25. Foucault (1995: 104).
26. Becker (2017).
27. The role of pharmaceutical marketing and manipulation of the American public and doctors alike has been well-detailed by many journalists and reporters: see Eban (2011); Meier 2003, 2007, 2013); Massachusetts OxyContin and Heroin Commission (2009); Van Zee (2009); Macy (2018).
28. Volkow and McLellan (2011).
29. Moran-Thomas and Biehl (2009); Kimberly and McLellan (2006).
30. Campbell (2007: 76).
31. Hornblum (1998).
32. Molotsky (1984).
33. Sinclair (2001).
34. Thomas et al. (2003).
35. Volkow (2010).
36. Pops 2016.
37. Krupitsky et al. (2011).
38. Gibson and Degenhardt (2005); Wolfe et al. (2011).
39. See Farrell et al. (1994) for a study of methadone's benefits. See Nolan et al. (2001), McLaughlin (2013) for more about drug courts and judges ordering patients onto medication.
40. Dubber (2001).
41. Vrecko (2010).
42. Sufrin (2017)
43. Massachusetts Department of Public Health (2017).
44. McKim and Burrell (2018); also see work on what kind of individuals are more predisposed to harmful behaviors while incarcerated: Tartaro and Lester (2010).
45. Stevenson (2012).
46. Oviedo-Joekes et al. (2009).
47. Rolles and Eastwood (2012).

6. RECOVERY IS MY JOB NOW

1. Gans writes of the excluded poor to emphasize "their being virtually completely left out of the formal economy and therefore out of the polity and mainstream society as well" (2009:80); he uses the term *blamed poor* also, "for they are often condemned for their own poverty and exclusion by failing to follow the rules of mainstream American culture" (2009:81). Michael Katz writes that the "deserving poor" include "children, widows, and a few others whose lack of responsibility for their condition could not be denied," while the "undeserving poor" are those who "have been thought to have brought their poverty on themselves" (2013:3).

2. Uggen (1999); Sampson (1993).
3. Rose et al. (2008).
4. Pager (2003).
5. Decker et al. (2013); see also Mallik-Kane and Visher (2008), whose research showed that in a poll of post-incarcerated people in Washington, D.C., one year after release, half the men had jobs versus one-third of women.
6. UN General Assembly (1948).
7. Wacquant (2010: 83).
8. Fraser and Gordon (1994).
9. Smith (2009: 67).
10. Narcotics Anonymous (1991: 74).
11. Contreras (2013); Bourgois 2001.
12. "Governor's Budget FY 2018: MA Department of Correction Budget." http://budget.digital.mass.gov/bb/h1/fy18h1/brec_18/dpt_18/hdoc.htm, Accessed November 12, 2018.

7. LIFE AND DEATH AFTER JAIL

1. Wong et al. (2003); Kaul et al. (1997).
2. American Hospital Association (2013).
3. Sociologist Margrit Shildrick argues that Levinas's notion of vulnerability is part of our hesitant response to the suffering, possibly monstrous, other: "Although it is initially the other who is vulnerable, who is figured as homeless, poor, widowed, orphaned, and whose suffering humanity invokes response, that response itself—or rather the irresistibility of the call—pitches me also into vulnerability. . . . It is my moral subjection to the other, my vulnerability in exposure to her vulnerability, that instantiates me as a subject" (2002: 92).
4. Like the people who experience strokes in Becker and Kaufman's study, Lydia experiences the effects of "the inherent tension in American society between a cultural ethos that espouses productivity and individual responsibility and shapes policy to that end, and the vicissitudes of illness that interfere with those cultural goals" (1995: 182).
5. Many in the substance-use treatment community have denounced using phrases like "substance abuse" or "substance abuser." See Kelly and Westerhoff (2010); Kelly, Dow, and Westerhoff (2010). As Lawrence Yang and epidemiological and medical anthropology colleagues have written about stigma, "In addition to compounding the experience of illness, stigma can intensify the sense that life is uncertain, dangerous, and hazardous" (Yang et al. 2007: 1528).
6. Smith (2009).
7. See work by historians of incarceration: Gottschalk (2006), Mancini (1996); Hirsh (1992); Thompson (2010); Meranze (1996). The sociologist Orlando Patterson (1982) has argued that slavery is a form of social death, literally enacting a relationship of domination that psychologically and physiologically altered the enslaved and their communities. He has controversially argued that the widespread psychological and civil disavowal of entire peoples during slavery has had measurable and ongoing effects on the relationships within contemporary black families and their communities.

8. Herzfeld (1992).

9. Binswanger et al. (2007). This research was supported by work conducted by Anne Spaulding and her colleagues that showed that long-term mortality was significantly increased among men who had been incarcerated fifteen years earlier. See Spaulding et al. (2011). There was also increased risk of infectious diseases such as HIV and Hepatitis C. See Hammett, Harmon, and Rhodes (2002) and Spaulding et al. (2009).

10. Patterson (2010): 593.

11. Sered and Norton-Hawk (2013).

12. MacDonald (1999).

13. Rich, Wakeman, and Dickman (2011).

14. van der Zanden et al. (2007); Martin Killias et al. (2009); Ferri et al. (2011).

15. Foucault 1997: 73.

16. Foucault 2003: 241.

17. Rose (2006: 24).

18. Campbell (2000); Lee (2010); McGreevy and Willon (2013).

19. Roberts (1991, 1997); Ettore (2007).

20. Foucault 1978: 173.

21. Foucault 2003: 256.

22. As Foucault (1980: 169) writes: "This analysis has at its practical objective at best to make poverty useful by fixing it to the apparatus of production, at worst to lighten as much as possible the burden it imposes on the rest of society. The problem is to set the 'able-bodied' poor to work and transform them into a useful labour force, but it is also to assure the self-financing by the poor themselves of the cost of their sickness and temporary or permanent incapacitation, and further to render profitable in the short or long term the educating of orphans and foundlings."

23. See work by Wilson (2007).

24. Foucault (2003: 239).

25. Richie (2012).

8. CONCLUSION: BREAKING "WICKED BAD HABITS"

1. Farmer and Gutierrez (2013).

2. Guattari (2003).

3. Davis and Dent (2001)

4. Chandler (2010: 332).

5. Nadelmann (1989); Gordon (1994).

6. Bachuber, Saloner and Cunningham (2014).

7. Kleinman (1999).

8. Loury (2007).

References

Acker, Caroline. 1997. The Early Years of the PHS Narcotic Hospital at Lexington, Kentucky. *PHS Chronicles* 112: 245–47.

———. 2002. *Creating the American Junkie: Addiction Research in the Classic Era of Narcotic Control*. Baltimore: Johns Hopkins University Press.

Alexander, Michelle. 2010. *The New Jim Crow: Mass Incarceration in an Age of Colorblindness*. New York: The New Press.

American Bar Association and American Medical Association. 1961. *Drug Addiction, Crime or Disease?* Interim and Final Reports of the Joint Committee of the American Bar Association and the American Medical Association on Narcotic Drugs. Bloomington: Indiana University Press.

American Civil Liberties Union. 2013. *The War on Marijuana in Black and White*. New York: ACLU.

American Hospital Association. 2013. "State Health Facts: Hospital Adjusted Expenses per Inpatient Day." Kaiser Family Foundation. Accessed November 25, 2013. http://kff.org/other/state-indicator/expenses-per-inpatient-day/.

Anslinger, Harry, and William Tompkins. 1953. *The Traffic in Narcotics*. New York: Funk and Wagnalls.

Bachuber, Marcus, Brendan Saloner, Chinazo Cunningham, and Colleen L. Barry. 2014. "Medical Cannabis Laws and Opioid Analgesic Overdose Mortality in the United States, 1999–2010." *JAMA Internal Medicine* 174 (10): 1668–73.

Baillargeon, Jacques, Ingrid Binswanger, Joseph Penn, Brie Williams, and Owen Murray. 2009. "Psychiatric Disorders and Repeat Incarcerations: The Revolving Prison Door." *American Journal of Psychiatry* 166 (1): 103–9. http://www.ncbi.nlm.nih.gov/pubmed/19047321.

Becker, Deborah. 2017. "Case Asks If It's Constitutional to Require Someone on Probation to Remain Drug-Free." WBUR.org. September 25, 2017.

Accessed 12 November 2018. http://www.wbur.org/news/2017/09/24/pro bation-drug-test-sjc.

Becker, Gay, and Sharon Kaufman. 1995. "Managing an Uncertain Illness Trajectory in Old Age: Patients' and Physicians' Views of Stroke." *Medical Anthropology Quarterly* 9 (2): 165–87. http://www.ncbi.nlm.nih.gov/pub med/7671113.

Beletsky, Leo, Elisabeth Ryan, and Wendy Parmet. 2018. "Involuntary Treatment for Substance Use Disorder: A Misguided Response to the Opioid Crisis." *Harvard Health Blog*, January 24, 2018. https://www.health.harvard .edu/blog/involuntary-treatment-sud-misguided-response-2018012413180.

Benson, Peter. 2009. *Tobacco Capitalism: Growers, Migrant Workers, and the Changing Face of a Global Industry.* Princeton, NJ: Princeton University Press.

Binswanger, Ingrid, Marc Stern, Richard Deyo, Patrick Heagerty, Allen Cheadle, Joann Elmore, Thomas Koepsell. 2007. "Release from Prison: A High Risk of Death for Former Inmates." *New England Journal of Medicine* 356(2): 157–65. http://www.pubmedcentral.nih.gov/articlerender.fcgi?artid =2836121&tool=pmcentrez&rendertype=abstract.

Blake, Andrew. 1970. "Boston's Problem with Heroin Spreading in Middle Class Areas." *Boston Globe*, March 5, 1.

Bloom, Barbara, Barbara Owen, and Stephanie Covington. 2003. *Gender-Responsive Strategies: Research, Practice, and Guiding Principles for Women Offenders.* Washington DC: National Institute of Corrections.

Bobo, Lawrence D., and Victor Thompson. 2006. "Unfair by Design: The War on Drugs, Race, and the Legitimacy of the Criminal Justice System." *Social Research* 72 (2): 445–72.

Boston Globe Editorial Board 1980. "The Affluent Addict: A Treatment Dilemma." *Boston Globe*, February 24, 1.

Boston Globe Spotlight Team. 1979. "Bay State Ponders Fixed Prison Sentences." *Boston Globe*, April 5: 17.

———. 2002. "The Geoghan Case." *Boston Globe.* http://www.boston.com /globe/spotlight/abuse/geoghan/.

———. 2007. "The Prison Suicide Crisis: A System Strains, and Inmates Die." *Boston Globe.* December 9, 2007.

Bourdieu, Pierre. 2000. *Pascalian Medititations.* Stanford, CA: Stanford University Press.

Bourgois, Philippe. 2001. *In Search of Respect: Selling Crack in El Barrio.* New York: Cambridge University Press.

Bourgois, Philippe, and Jeff Schonberg. 2009. *Righteous Dopefiend.* Berkeley: University of California Press.

Brandt, Allan. 2009. *The Cigarette Century: The Rise, Fall, and Deadly Persistence of the Product That Defined America.* New York: Basic Books.

Campbell, Nancy. 2000. *Using Women: Gender, Drug Policy and Social Justice.* New York: Routledge.

———. 2007. *Discovering Addiction.* Ann Arbor: University of Michigan Press.

Campbell, Nancy, J.P. Olsen, and Luke Walden. 2008. *The Narcotic Farm.* New York: Abrams.

Carr, E. Summerson. 2010. *Scripting Addiction: The Politics of Therapeutic Talk and American Sobriety*. Princeton, NJ: Princeton University Press.

Casedino, Alex. 2017. "Convicts without Care: How the Privatization of Healthcare in the U.S. Prison System Fails to Protect Inmates' Health." *Berkely Political Review*, January 28. Accessed 16 April 2018. https://bpr .berkeley.edu/2017/01/28/convicts-without-care-how-the-privatization-of -healthcare-in-the-u-s-prison-system-fails-to-protect-inmates-health/.

Centers for Disease Control. 2013. "Vital Signs: Overdoses of Prescription Opi- oid Pain Relievers and Other Drugs among Women—United States, 1999– 2010." *Morbidity and Mortality Weekly Report* 62 (26): 537–42. http:// www.cdc.gov/mmwr/preview/mmwrhtml/mm6226a3.htm.

Chandler, Cynthia. 2010. "The Gender-Responsive Prison Expansion Move- ment." In *Interrupted Life: Experiences of Incarcerated Women in the United States*, edited by Ricky Solinger, Paula Johnson, Martha Raimon, Tina Reynolds, and Ruby Tapia, 332–37. Berkeley: University of California Press.

Chinlund, Christine, and Dick Lehr. 1987. "Women Alcohlics Get Jail, Not Treatment Officials Say Law Ordering Special Care Is Not Being Carried Out." *Boston Globe*, January 18: 1.

Chutuape, Mary Ann, Donald Jasinski, Michael Fingerhood, and Maxine Stitzer. 2001. One-, Three-, and Six-Month Outcomes after Brief Inpatient Opioid Detoxification." *American Journal of Drug and Alcohol Abuse* 27 (1):19–44.

Ciechanowski, Paul, and Wayne Katon. 2012. "Posttraumatic Stress Disorder: Epidemiology, Pathophysiology, Clinical Manifestations, and Diagnosis." UpToDate. uptodate.com.

Clark, H. Westley, and Kathryn Power. 2005. "Women, Co-occurring Disor- ders, and Violence Study: A Case for Trauma-Informed Care." *Journal of Substance Abuse Treatment* 28 (2): 145–46. Accessed October 2, 2013. http://www.ncbi.nlm.nih.gov/pubmed/15780543.

Clark, Janet. 1961. *The Fantastic Lodge: The Autobiography of a Girl Drug Addict*. Boston: Houghton Mifflin.

Coakley, Martha. 2012. "Commonwealth's Statement of the Case Versus Annie Dookhan." https://archive.org/stream/563115-statement-of-the-case-dookh an/563115-statement-of-the-case-dookhan_djvu.txt.

Comfort, Megan. 2007. "Punishment beyond the Legal Offender." *Annual Review of Law and Social Science* 3 (1): 271–96. Accessed September 9, 2012. http://www.annualreviews.org/doi/abs/10.1146/annurev.lawsocsci .3.081806.112829.

Commonwealth of Massachusetts. 2016. General Laws, Part I, Title XVII, Chapter 123, Section 35: Commitment of Alcoholics or Substance Abusers. https://malegislature.gov/Laws/GeneralLaws/PartI/TitleXVII/Chapter123 /Section35

Contreras, Randol. 2013. *The Stickup Kids: Race, Drugs, Violence and the American Dream*. Berkeley: University of California Press.

Coughlin, William. 1987. "Drug, Alcohol Program at Prison to End." *Boston Globe*, May 3: 48.

Courtois, Christine, and Julian Ford, eds. 2009. *Treating Complex Traumatic Stress Disorders: An Evidence-Based Guide*. New York: Guilford.

Courtwright, David. 2001. *Dark Paradise: A History of Opiate Addiction in America*. Cambridge, MA: Harvard University Press.

———. 2004. "The Controlled Substances Act: How a "Big Tent" Reform Became a Punitive Drug Law." *Drug and Alcohol Dependence* 76: 9–15.

Curran, Kathy. 2016. "5 Investigates on Suboxone—The New Jailhouse Drug of Choice: Prescription Opiates Smuggled into Jails and Prisons." WCBV5, September 23. https://www.wcvb.com/article/5-investigates-on-suboxone-the-new-jailhouse-drug-of-choice/8248284.

Cuskey, Walter, Arthur Moffett, and Happa Clifford. 1971. "Comparison of Female Opiate Addicts Admitted to Lexington Hospital in 1961 and 1967." *HSMHA Health Reports*: 332–40.

Davis, Angela, and Gina Dent. 2001. "Prisons as Border: A Conversation on Gender, Globalization, and Punishment." *Signs: Journal of Women in Culture and Society* 26 (4): 1235–41.

Decker, Scott, Cassia Spohn, and Natalie Ortiz. 2013. "Criminal Stigma, Race, Gender, and Employment: An Expanded Assessment of the Consequences of Imprisonment for Employment: Final Report to National Institute of Justice." Phoeniz: Arizona State University. Accessed November 1, 2018. http://thecrimereport.s3.amazonaws.com/2/fb/e/2362/criminal_stigma_race_crime_and_unemployment.pdf.

Deehan, Peter. 2015. "Sheriff Warns That New White House Drug Policy Could Be Boon to Prison Suboxone Smuggling." *WGBH News*, November 9, 2015. https://news.wgbh.org/post/sheriff-warns-new-white-house-drug-policy-could-be-boon-prison-suboxone-smuggling.

DeLeon, George, and George Beschner. 1977. *The Therapeutic Community: Proceedings of Therapeutic Communities of America Planning Conference, January 29–30, 1977*. Washington DC: Department of Health, Education and Welfare and the National Institute on Drug Abuse.

Dennehy, Kathleen. 2005. *Governor's Commission on Corrections Reform: Major Recommendation #13—Dedicated External Female Offender Review*. Boston: Commonwealth of Massachusetts Executive Office of Public Safety Department of Correction.

Densen-Gerber, Judianne. 1973. *We Mainline Dreams*. Graden City, NY: Doubleday.

Depew, Bekka, Chuka Esiobu, et al. 2014. "Involuntary Commitment for Substance Abuse Treatment in Massachusetts: Problems and Proposed Solutions." Harvard Institute of Politics. http://www.iop.harvard.edu/sites/default/files_new/research-policy-papers/Section35HealthcarePolicyPaper.pdf.

Dietz, Jean. 1980. "Hub Alters Policy on Drug Care." *Boston Globe*, April 23: 1.

Dodge, L. Mara. 2002. *"Whores and Thieves of the Worst Kind": A Study of Women, Crime, and Prisons, 1835–2000*. Dekalb: Northern Illinois University Press.

Douglas, Mary. 1966. *Purity and Danger: An Analysis of Concepts of Pollution and Taboo*. New York: Ark Paperbacks.

Dubber, Markus Dirk. 2001. "Policing Possession: The War on Crime and the End of Criminal Law." *Journal of Criminal Law & Criminology* 91 (4): 1–151.

Eban, Katherine. 2011. "OxyContin: Purdue Pharma's Painful Medicine." *Fortune*. November, 9, 2011.

Elliott, Denise, Paula Bjelajac, Roger Fallot, Laurie Markoff, and Beth Glover Reed. 2005. "Trauma-Informed or Trauma-Denied: Principles and Implementation of Trauma-Informed Services for Women." *Journal of Community Psychology* 33 (4): 461–77. Accessed September 29, 2013. http://doi.wiley.com/10.1002/jcop.20063.

Estes, Andrea. 2012. "Indicted Drug Analyst Annie Dookhan's E-Mails Reveal Her Close Personal Ties to Prosecutors." *Boston Globe*, December 20.

Ettorre, Elizabeth. 2007. *Revisioning Women and Drug Use: Gender, Power and the Body*. New York: Palgrave Macmillan.

Everitt, Barry, and Trevor Robbins. 2005. "Neural Systems of Reinforcement for Drug Addiction: From Actions to Habits to Compulsion." *Nature Neuroscience* 8: 1481–89.

Fairbanks, Robert. 2009. *How It Works: Recovering Citizens in Post-Welfare Philadelphia*. Chicago: University of Chicago Press.

Farmer, Paul, Bruce Nizeye, Sara Stulac, and Salmaan Keshavjee. 2006. "Structural Violence and Clinical Medicine." *PLoS Medicine* 3 (10): e449. http://www.pubmedcentral.nih.gov/articlerender.fcgi?artid=1621099&tool=pmcentrez&rendertype=abstract, accessed June 13, 2011.

Farmer, Paul, and Gustavo Gutierrez. 2013. *In the Company of the Poor*. Maryknoll, NY: Orbis Books.

Farragher, Thomas. 2003. "In Death, Geoghan Triggers Another Crisis." *Boston Globe*, November 30.

Farrell, Michael, Jeff Ward, Richard Mattick, Wayne Hall, Gerry Stimson, Don des Jarlais, Michael Gossop, and John Strange. "Methadone Maintenance Treatment on Opiate Dependence: A Review." *British Medical Journal* 1994 (309): 997–1001.

Fassin, Didier, and Richard Rechtman. 2009. *The Empire of Trauma: An Inquiry into the Condition of Victimhood*. Princeton, NJ: Princeton University Press.

FBI Boston Field Office. 2013. "Eighteen Members of Almighty Latin King/Queen Nation Named in Federal and State Charges." Boston, MA.

Feldman, Nina. 2018. "Many 'Recovery Houses' Won't Let Residents Use Medicines to Quit Opioids." *NPR Shots*. Accessed October 16, 2018. https://www.npr.org/sections/health-shots/2018/09/12/644685850/many-recovery-houses-wont-let-residents-use-medicine-to-quit-opioids.

Ferguson, James. 2010. "The Uses of Neoliberalism." *Antipode* 41: 166–84. Accessed July 18, 2012. http://doi.wiley.com/10.1111/j.1467-8330.2009.00721.x.

Ferri, Marica, Marina Davoli, and Carlo Perucci. 2011. "Heroin Maintenance for Chronic Heroin-Dependent Individuals." *Cochrane Database Syst Rev*, no. 12. https://www.cochranelibrary.com/cdsr/doi/10.1002/14651858.CD003410.pub4/full.

Foucault, Michel. 1978. *The History of Sexuality*. New York: Pantheon Books.

———. 1980. "The Politics of Health in the Eighteenth Century." In *Power/ Knowledge: Selected Interviews and Other Writings 1972–1977*, edited by Colin Gordon, 166–82. New York: Pantheon Books.

———. 1995. *Discipline and Punish: The Birth of the Prison*. New York: Vintage Books.

———. 1997. "Security, Territory, Population." In *Michel Foucault: Ehtics, Subjectivity and Truth*, edited by Paul Rabinow, 67–80. New York: New Press.

———. 2003. "Society Must Be Defended." In *Society Must Be Defended: Lectures at the College de France, 1975–76*, 239–64. New York: Picador.

Fraser, James. 1997. "Methadone Clinic Culture: The Everyday Realities of Female Methadone Clients." *Qualitative Health Research* 7:121–39.

Fraser, Nancy, and Linda Gordon. 1994. "A Genealogy of Dependency: Tracing a Keyword of the U.S. Welfare State." *Signs* 19 (2): 309–36.

Freedman, Estelle. 1996. *Maternal Justice: Miriam Van Waters and the Female Reform Tradition*. Chicago: University of Chicago Press.

Fullilove, Mindy, Robert Fullilove, Michael Smith, Karen Winkle, Calvin Michael, Paula Panzer, and Rodrick Wallace. 1993. "Violence, Trauma, and Post-Traumatic Stress Disorder among Women Drug Users." *Journal of Traumatic Stress* 6: 533–43.

Gans, Herbert. 2009. "Antipoverty Policy for the Excluded Poor." *Challenge* 52: 79–95.

Garcia, Angela. 2010. *The Pastoral Clinic: Addiction and Dispossesion along the Rio Grande*. Berkeley: University of California Press.

Garriott, William. 2011. *Policing Methamphetamine: Narcopolitics in Rural America*. New York: New York University Press.

Gearing, Frances. 1971. "Evaluation of Methadone Maintenance Treatment Program." In *Methadone Maintenance*, edited by Stanley Einstein, 171–97. New York: Marcel Dekker.

Gibson, Amy, and Louisa Degenhardt. 2005. *Mortality Related to Naltrexone in the Treatment of Opioid Dependence: A Comparative Analysis*. Sydney, Australia: National Drug and Alcohol Research Centre.

Gilligan, Carol. 1993. *In a Different Voice*. Cambridge, MA: Harvard University Press.

Good, Mary-Jo Delvecchio, Paul Brodwin, Byron Good, and Arthur Kleinman. 1992. *Pain as Human Experience: An Anthropological Persective*. Berkeley: University of California Press.

Goodenough, Abby, and Katie Zezima. 2011. "When Children's Scribbles Hide a Prison Drug." *New York Times*, May 26, 2011.

Gordon, Diana. 1994. *The Return of the Dangerous Classes: Drug Prohibition and Policy Politics*. New York: Norton.

Gottschalk, Marie. 2006. *The Prison and the Gallows: The Politics of Mass Incarceration in America*. New York: Cambridge University Press.

Graham, A. W., and T. K. Shultz (eds.). 2003. *Principles of Addiction Medicine*. 3rd ed. Chevy Chase, MD: American Society of Addiction Medicine.

Green, Traci, Jennifer Clarke, and Lauren Brinkley-Rubenstein. 2018. "Postincarceration Fatal Overdoses after Implementating Medications for Addiction Treatment in a Statewide Correctional System." *JAMA Psychiatry* 75 (4): 405–7.

Greenfield, Lawrence, and Tracy Snell. 1999. *Women Offenders*. Special Report. Washington DC: Bureau of Justice Statistics.

Guattari, Felix. 2003. "Socially Significant Drugs." In *High Culture: Reflections on Addiction and Modernity*, edited by Anna Alex ander and Mark S. Roberts, 199–208. Albany: State University of New York Press.

Guenther, Lisa. 2013. *Solitary Confinement: Social Death and Its Afterlives*. Minneapolis: University of Minnesota Press.

Hammett, Theodore, Mary Harmon, and William Rhodes. 2002. "The Burden of Infectious Disease among Inmates of and Releasees from US Correctional Facilities, 1997." *American Journal of Public Health* 92 (11): 1789–94. http://www.pubmedcentral.nih.gov/articlerender.fcgi?artid=1447330&tool =pmcentrez&rendertype=abstract.

Han, Clara. 2012. *Life in Debt: Times of Care and Violence in Neoliberal Chile*. Berkeley: University of California Press.

Hansen, Helena. 2018. *Addicted to Christ*. Oakland: University of California Press.

Harvey, David. 2007. *A Brief History of Neoliberalism*. New York: Oxford University Press.

Harvey, Joseph M. 1970. "Police, Courts Seen Winking at Drug Laws: Bar Hits 'Harsh' Provision." *Boston Globe*, July 19, 1.

Hedegaard, Holly, Arialdi Minino, and Margaret Warner. 2018. "Drug Overdose Deaths in the United States, 1999–2017." NCHS Datea Brief No. 329. Centers for Disease Control/National Center on Health Statistics. https:// www.cdc.gov/nchs/data/databriefs/db329-h.pdf.

Herman, Judith. 1992. *Trauma and Recovery*. New York: Basic Books.

Herzfeld, Michael. 1992. *The Social Production of Indifference: Exploring the Symbolic Roots of Western Bureaucracy*. Oxford: Berg.

Hirsh, Adam. 1992. *The Rise of the Penitentiary Prisons and Punishment in Early America*. New Haven, CT: Yale University Press.

Holiday, Billie, and William Dufty. 1956. *Lady Sings the Blues*. New York: Lancer Books.

Hornblum, Allen. 1998. *Acres of Skin: Human Experiments at Holmesburg Prison*. New York: Routledge.

Hser, Yih-Ing, Valerie Hoffman, Christine Grella, and M. Douglas Anglin. 2001. "A 33-Year Follow-up of Narcotics Addicts." *Archives General Psychiatry* 58 (5): 503–8. https://jamanetwork.com/journals/jamapsychiatry /fullarticle/481765.

Humphries, Drew. 1999. *Crack Mothers: Pregnancy, Drugs and the Media*. Columbus: Ohio State University Press.

Hunt, Halsley, and Maurice Odoroff. 1962. "Follow-Up Study of Narcotic Drug Addiction after Hospitalization." *Public Health Reports* 77 (1): 41–54.

Irons, Meghan. 2013. "Prison Visitors Irate about Plan for Drug-Sniffing Dogs." *Boston Globe*, March 23.

James, William. 1914. *Habit*. New York: Henry Holt and Company.

Kajstura, Aleks. 2018. *States of Women's Incarceration: The Global Context 2018*. Northampton, MA: Prison Policy Initiative. https://www.prisonpolicy .org/global/women/2018.html.

Kakko, Johan, Kerstin Svanborg, Mary Jeanne Kreek, and Markus Heilig. 2003. "1-Year Retention and Social Function after Buprenorphine-Assisted Relapse Prevention Treatment for Heroin Dependence in Sweden: A Randomised, Placebo-Controlled Trial." *Lancet* (361): 662–98.

Kandall, Stephen. 1999. *Substance and Shadow*. Cambridge, MA: Harvard University Press.

Katz, Michael. 2013. *The Undeserving Poor: America's Enduring Confrontation with Poverty*, 2nd edition. New York: Oxford University Press.

Kaul, Rupert, Allison McGeer, Donald Low, Karen Green, and Benjamin Schwartz. 1997. "Population-Based Surveillance for Group A Streptococcal Necrotizing Fasciitis: Clinical Features, Prognostic Indicators, and Microbiologic Analysis of Seventy-Seven Cases." *American Journal of Medicine* 103: 18–24.

Kelly, John, and Cara Westerhoff. 2010. "Does It Matter How We Refer to Individuals with Substance-Related Problems? A Randomized Study with Two Commonly Used Terms." *International Journal Drug Policy* 21: 202–7.

Kelly, John, Sarah Dow, and Cara Westerhoff. 2010. "Does Our Choice of Substance-Related Terms Influence Perceptions of Treatment Need? An Empirical Investigation with Two Commonly Used Terms." *Journal of Drug Issues* 40: 805–18.

Kessler, Ronald, Amanda Sonnega, Evelyn Bromet, Michael Hughes, and Christopher Nelson. 1995. "Posttraumatic Stress Disorder in the National Comorbidity Survey." *Archives of General Psychiatry* 52: 1048–60.

Khantzian, Edward J. 2011. "The Capacity for Self-Care and Addiction." *Counselor Magazine* 12: 36–40.

Killias, Martin, Marcelo Aebi, Miriam Pina, Nicole Egli, and Pernille Skovbo Christensen. 2009. "Effects of Drug Substition Programs on Offending among Drug Addicts." *Campbell Systematic Reviews* 5 (August 27). https:// campbellcollaboration.org/library/drug-substitution-programmes-offending -drug-addicts.html.

Kimberly, John, and Thomas McLellan. 2006. "The Business of Addiction Treatment: A Research Agenda." *Journal of Substance Abuse Treatment* 31 (3): 213–19. Accessed September 13, 2012. http://www.ncbi.nlm.nih.gov /pubmed/16996384.

Kleinman, Arthur. 1999. *Experience and Its Moral Modes: Culture, Human Conditions, and Disorder*. The Tanner Lectures on Human Values. Delivered at Stanford University, April 13–19. https://tannerlectures.utah.edu /_documents/a-to-z/k/Kleinman99.pdf.

Kneeland, Paul. 1973. "Sheriff Says Jail Won't Help Junkies." *Boston Globe*, May 6, 10.

Kneeland, Paul, and Gregory McDonald. 1966. "The Combat Zone." *Boston Globe*, July 31, D6.

Kolb, Lawrence. 1925. "Types and Characteristics of Drug Addicts." *Mental Hygiene* 9: 301.

Koob, George, and Nora Volkow. 2010. "Neurocircuitry of Addiction." *Neuropsychopharmacology* 35 (1): 217–38.

Krawczyk, Noa, Caroline Picher, Kenneth Feder, and Brendan Saloner. 2017. "Only One in Twenty Justice-Referred Adults in Speciality Treatment for Opioid Use Receive Methadone or Buprenorphine." *Health Affairs* 36 (12): 2046–53.

Kroll, Jerome. 2003. "Posttraumatic Symptoms and the Complexity of Responses to Trauma." *JAMA* 290 (5): 667–70. http://www.ncbi.nlm.nih.gov/pubmed/12902373.

Krupitsky, Evgeny, Edward Nunes, Walter Ling, Ari Illeperuma, David Gastfriend, Bernard Silverman, et al. 2011. "Injectable Extended-Release Naltrexone for Opioid Dependence: A Double-Blind, Placebo-Controlled, Nulticentre Randomised Trial." *Lancet* 377: 1506–13.

Lajtha, Abel, and Henry Sershen. 2010. "Heterogeneity of Reward Mechanisms." *Neurochemical Research* 35: 851–67.

Langer, Lawrence. 1991. *Holocaust Testimonies*. New Haven, CT: Yale University Press.

Lansing, Sharon. 2012. *New York State COMPAS-Probation Risk and Need Assessment Study: Examining the Recidivism Scale's Effectiveness and Predictive Accuracy*. Albany, NY: Division of Criminal Justice Services Office of Justice Research and Performance.

Latour, Francie, and Thomas Farragher. 2001. "Sexual Abuse in Suffolk Prison: Pattern of Misconduct Raises Questions about Sheriff's Leadership." *Boston Globe*, May 23, A01.

Lee, William Adams. 2010. "Why Drug Addicts Are Getting Sterilized for Cash." *Time*, April 17. http://www.time.com/time/health/article/0,8599,198 1916,00.html#ixzz10NmaGMoo.

de Leon, George. 2000. *The Therapeutic Community: Theory, Model, and Method*. New York: Springer Publishing Company.

Leshner, Alan. 1997. "Addiction Is a Brain Disease, and It Matters." *Science* 278: 45–47.

Leukefeld, Carl, and Frank Tims. 1988. *NIDA Monograph 86: Compulsory Treatment of Drug Abuse: Research and Clinical Practice*. Rockville MD: US: National Institute on Drug Abuse.

———. 1993. "Drug Abuse Treatment in Prisons and Jails" *Journal of Substance Abuse Treatment* 10 (1): 77–84.

Linton, David. 2018. "Ex-Norfolk Prison Guard Gets Home Confinement, Probation." *Sun Chronicle*, September 17. http://www.thesunchronicle.com/news/local_news/ex-norfolk-prison-guard-gets-home-confinement-proba tion/article_714a40d0-9343-5686-94e6-324c4432639d.html.

Loury, Glenn. 2007. "Tanner Lectures Part I: Ghettos, Prisons and Racial Stigma." Delivered at Stanford University, Palo Alto, CA, April 4 and 5.

MacDonald, Michael. 1999. *All Souls: A Family Story from Southie*. New York: Ballantine.

Mack v. Suffolk County, 191 F.R.D. 16 (D.Mass.2000).

MacNeill, Arianna. 2018. "Authorities: Corrections Officer Charged after Attempted Suboxone Smuggling into Prison." *Boston.com*. November 19, 2018. https://www.boston.com/news/crime/2018/11/19/authorities-correc tions-officer-charged-after-attempted-suboxone-smuggling-into-prison.

Macy, Beth. 2018. *Dopesick*. New York: Little Brown and Company.

Mallik-Kane, Kamala, and Christy Visher. 2008. *Health and Prisoner Reentry: How Physical Mental, and Substance Abuse Conditions Shape the Process of Reintegration*. Washington, DC: The Urban Institute.

Mancini, Matthew. 1996. *One Dies, Get Another: Convict Leasing in the American South, 1866–1928*. Columbia: University of South Carolina Press.

Markel, Howard. 2011. *An Anatomy of Addiction: Sigmund Freud, William Halsted, and the Miracle Drug Cocaine*. New York: Pantheon.

Marsden, John, Garry Stillwell, Hayley Jones, Alisha Cooper, Brian Eastwood, Michael Farrell, Tim Lowden, Nino Maddalena, Chris Metcalfe, Jenny Shaw, and Matthew Hickman. "Does Exposure to Opioid Substition Therapy in Prison Reduce the Risk of Death after Release? A National Prospective Observational Study in England." *Addiction* 2017 (112): 1408–18.

Maskovsky, Jeff. 2005. "Do People Fail Drugs, or Do Drugs Fail People? The Discourse of Adherence." *Transforming Anthropology* 13 (2): 136–42.

Massachusetts Department of Correction. 2013. Massachusetts Department of Correction Inmate Substance Abuse Monitoring and Testing.

Massachusetts Department of Public Health. 2016. An Assessment of Opioid-Related Deaths in Massachusetts (2013–2014). https://www.mass.gov/files/documents/2016/09/pg/chapter-55-report.pdf.

———. 2017. "Data Brief: An Assessment of Opioid-Related Overdoses in Massachusetts 2010–2015." Released August 2017. https://www.mass.gov/files/documents/2017/08/31/data-brief-chapter-55-aug-2017.pdf.

Massachusetts Oxycontin and Heroin Commission. 2009. *Recommendations of the OxyContin and Heroin Commission. Boston*. Boston: Commonwealth of Massachusetts

Massachusetts Women's Justice Network. 2013. "Moving beyond Prisons: Creating Alternative Pathways for Women." Wellesley Centers for Women. https://www.wcwonline.org/pdf/ekates/CivilCommitmentsForWomenInMArev.pdf

Mbembe, Achille. 2003. "Necropolitics." *Public Culture* 15 (1): 11–40.

McDonald, Dan. 2009. "MCI-Framingham Suicide Prompts Discussion about Cuts to Mental Health Services." *MetroWest Daily News*, July 22.

McDowell, Elliott. 1950. The Commonwealth of Massachusetts Statistical Report of the Commissioner of Correction for the Year Ending December 31, 1949.

———. 1951. The Commonwealth of Massachusetts Statistical Report of the Commissioner of Correction for the Years Ending December 31, 1949, and December 31, 1950.

McGreevy, Patrick, and Phil Willon. 2013. "Female Inmate Surgery Broke Law." *Los Angeles Times*, July 14.

McHugh, R. Kathryn, Elise Devito, Dorian Dodd, et al. 2013. "Gender Differences in a Clinical Trial for Prescription Opioid Dependence." *Journal of Substance Abuse Treatment* 45: 38–43.

McHugo, Gregory, Nina Kammerer, Elizabeth Jackson, Laurie Markoff, Margaret Gatz, Mary Jo Larson, Ruta Mazelis, Karen Hennigan. 2005. "Women, Co-Occurring Disorders, and Violence Study: Evaluation Design and Study Population. *Journal of Substance Abuse Treatment* 28 (2): 91–107. Accessed October 2, 2013. http://www.ncbi.nlm.nih.gov/pubmed/15780539.

McKim, Jenifer, and Chris Burrell. 2018. "Lawsuits Add Up over Bristol County Jail Inmate Suicides." *Boston Globe*, March 9. https://www.boston globe.com/metro/2018/03/08/jailsuicides/EOyAfOw6RHUrjRWWHsY CuL/story.html.

McLaughlin, Sheila. 2013. "Ohio Judge Tries Drug to Rehabilitate Addicted Inmates." *Cincinnati Enquirer*, September 26.

McNamara, Eileen. 1992a. "Why Did Robin Peeler Die?" *Boston Globe*, June 7.

———. 1992b. "Paying Dearly for Privatization." *Boston Globe*, June 14, 14.

Meier, Barry. 2003. *Pain Killer: A "Wonder" Drug's Trail of Addiction and Death*. New York: Rodale.

———. 2007. "Narcotic Maker Guilty of Deceit over Marketing." *New York Times*, May 11.

Meranze, Michael. 1996. *Labortories of Virtue: Punishment, Revolution, and Authority*. Chapel Hill: University of North Carolina Press.

Merrall, Elizabeth, Azar Kariminia, Ingrid Binswanger, Michael Hobs, Michael Farrell, John Marsden, Sharon Hutchinson and Sheila Bird. 2010. "Meta-Analysis of Drug-Related Deaths Soon after Release from Prison." *Addiction* 105 (9):1545–54.

Metzl, Jonathan. 2003. "Mother"s Little Helper': The Crisis of Psychoanalysis and the Miltown Resolution. *Gender & History* 15: 240–67.

Metzl, Jonathan, and Helena Hansen. 2014. "Structural Competency: Theorizing a New Medical Engagement with Stigma and Inequality." *Social Science & Medicine* 103: 126–33.

Molotsky, Irvin. 1984. "FDA Announces New Drug to Block Cravings for Heroin." *New York Times*, November 29, 1984, 1. https://www.nytimes.com /1984/11/29/us/fda-announces-new-drug-to-block-craving-for-heroin.html.

Moran-Thomas, Amy, and Joao Biehl. 2009. "Symptom: Subjectivities, Social Ills, Technologies." *Annual Review of Anthropology* 38: 267–88.

Morgan, Robert, and Lyn Freeman. 2009. "The Healing of Our People: Substance Abuse and Historical Trauma. "*Substance Use & Misuse* 44: 84–98.

Morrissey, Joseph, Alan Ellis, Margaret Gatz, Hortensia Amaro, Beth Glover Reed, Andrea Savage, Norma Finkelstein, Ruta Mazelis, Vivian Brown, Elizabeth Jackson, Steven Banks. 2005. "Outcomes for Women with Co-occurring Disorders and Trauma: Program and Person-level Effects." *Journal of Substance Abuse Treatment* 28 (2): 121–33. Accessed October 2, 2013. http:// www.ncbi.nlm.nih.gov/pubmed/15780541.

Murphy, Sean, and Michael Rezendes. 2001. "Rouse Often an Absentee Sheriff." *Boston Globe*, May 25, A01.

Musto, David. 1999. *The American Disease: Origins of Narcotic Control*. 3rd edition. New York: Oxford University Press.

Nadelmann, Ethan. 1989. "Drug Prohibition in the United States: Costs, Consequences, and Alternatives." *Science* 245(4921): 939–47.

Najavits, Lisa. 2002a." 'Seeking Safety': Therapy for Trauma and Substance Abuse." *Corrections Today:* 136–41.

Narcotics Anonymous. 1991. "Getting Out of the Rut." *Just For Today: Daily Meditations for Recovering Addicts*, 74. Chatsworth, CA: Narcotics Anonymous World Service.

Narcotics Anonymous World Service. 1976. "Who, What, How, and Why?" https://www.na.org/admin/include/spaw2/uploads/pdf/litfiles/us_english/IP /EN3101.pdf.

Neiberg, Norm. 2012. Recorded interview by author. Newton, MA, November 9, 2012.

Neiberg, Norm, and Mary Clary. 1962. *The Commonwealth of Massachusetts Annual Report of the Commissioner of Correction Including Tables on Industries for the Year Ending Dec. 31, 1962*. Framingham: Massachusetts Department of Correction.

Newman, Robert. 1988. "New York City." In *Methadone in the Management of Opioid Dependence: Programs and Policies Around the World*, edited by Awni Arif and Joseph Westermeyer, 238–43. Geneva: World Health Organization.

Nolan, James. 2001. *Reinventing Justice: The American Drug Court Movement*. Princeton, NJ: Princeton University Press.

Nunn, Amy, Nickolas Zaller, Samuel Dickman, Catherine Trimbur, Ank Nijhawan, and Josiah Rich. 2009. "Methadone and Buprenorphine Prescribing and Referral Practices in US Prison Systems: Results from a Nationwide Survey." *Drug and Alcohol Dependence* 105(1–2): 83–88. Accessed September 9, 2012. http://www.pubmedcentral.nih.gov/articlerender.fcgi?artid=27437 49&tool=pmcentrez&rendertype=abstract.

O'Neill, Bruce. 2014. "Cast Aside: Boredom, Downward Mobility, and Homelessness in Post-Communist Bucharest." *Cultural Anthropology* 29, no. 1: 8–31.

O'Neill, Gerard, Dick Lehr, Bruce Butterfield, John Tlumacki, and Cindy Rodriguez. 1995. "Small-Timers Get Hard Time; Some Major Dealers Evade Stiff Sentences Others Can't Escape." *Boston Globe*, September 24, 1.

Ouimette, Paige, Rachel Kimerling, Jennifer Shaw, and Rudolf Moos. 2000. "Physical and Sexual Abuse among Women and Men with Substance Use Disorders." *Alcoholism Treatment Quarterly* 18: 7–17.

Oviedo-Joekes, Eugenia, Suzanne Brissette, David Marsh, Pierre Lauzon, Daphne Guh, Aslam Anis, and Martin Schechter. 2009. "Diacetylmorphine versus Methadone for the Treatment of Opioid Addiction." *New England Journal of Medicine* 361 (8): 777–86.

Oxford English Dictionary. 2014. S.v. "Contraband, n. and adj." OED Online. 2014. Accessed July 20, 2014. http://dictionary.oed.com..

Pager, Devah. 2003. "The Mark of a Criminal Record." *American Journal of Sociology* 108: 937–75.

Patterson, Evelyn. 2010. "Incarcerating Death: Mortality in U.S. State Correctional Facilities, 1985–1998." *Demography* 47 (3): 587–607. http://www.pubmedcentral.nih.gov/articlerender.fcgi?artid=3000056&tool=pmcentrez&rendertype=abstract.

Patterson, Orlando. 1982. *Slavery and Social Death: A Comparative Study.* Cambridge, MA: Harvard University Press.

Pellens, Mildred, and Charles Terry. Committee on Drug Addiction. 1928. *The Opium Problem.* New York: Bureau of Social Hygiene.

Pescor, M. J. 1941. Prognosis in Drug Addiction. *American Journal of Psychiatry* 97: 1419–33.

Pew Charitable Trusts. 2018. *Probation and Parole Systems Marked by High Stakes, Missed Opportunities.* https://www.pewtrusts.org/-/media/assets/2018/09/probation_and_parole_systems_marked_by_high_stakes_missed_opportunities_pew.pdf.

Pops, Richard. 2016. "Vivitrol in Focus: A Reconsideration of the Medical, Social, and Commercial Potential of an Important Medicine." September 26. Alkermes Analyst & Investor Event.

Rafter, Nicole. 1990. *Partial Justice: Women, Prisons, and Social Control.* New Brunswick, NJ: Transaction Publishers.

Raikhel, Eugene, and William Garriott. 2013. "Tracing New Paths in the Anthropology of Addiction: Introduction." In *Addiction Trajectories,* 1–35. Durham, NC: Duke University Press.

Rhodes, Lorna. 2004. *Total Confinement: Madness and Reason in the Maximum Security Prison.* Berkeley: University of California Press.

Rich, Josiah, Sarah Wakeman, and Samuel Dickman. 2011. "Medicine and the Epidemic of Incarceration in the United States." *New England Journal of Medicine* 364 (22): 2081–83.

Richie, Beth. 2012. *Arrested Justice: Black Women, Violence, and America's Prison Nation.* New York: New York University Press.

Roberts, Dorothy. 1991. "Punishing Drug Addicts Who Have Babies: Women of Color, Equality, and the Right of Privacy." *Harvard Law Review* 104 (7): 1419–82.

———. 1997. *Killing the Black Body: Race, Reproduction, and the Meaning of Liberty.* New York: Vintage.

Rolles, Steve and Nimah Eastwood. 2012. *Drug Decriminalisation Policies in Practice: A Global Summary.* Harm Reduction International. https://www.hri.global/files/2012/09/04/Chapter_3.4_drug-decriminalisation_.pdf.

Rose, Dina, Venezia Michalsen, Dawn Wiest, and Anupa Fabian. 2008. *Women, Re-entry and Everyday Life: Time to Work?* New York: The Women's Prison Association.

Rose, Nikolas. 2006. *The Politics of Life Itself.* Princeton, NJ: Princeton University Press.

Saia, Kelly, Davida Schiff, Elisha Wachman, Pooja Mehta, et al. 2016. "Caring for Pregnant Women with Opioid Use Disorder in the USA: Expanding and Improving Treatment." *Current Obstetric and Gynecology Reports* 5: 257–63.

Sampson, Robert, and John Laub. 1993. *Crime in the Making: Pathways and Turning Points through Life.* Cambridge, MA: Harvard University Press.

Sansone, Janet. 1980. "Retention Patterns in a Therapeutic Community for the Treatment of Drug Abuse." *International Journal of the Addictions* 15: 711–36.

Sawyer, Wendy. 2018. The Gender Divide: Tracking Women's State Prison Growth. Northampton, MA: Prison Policy Initiative. Available online: https://www.prisonpolicy.org/reports/women_overtime.html. Accessed 2019 April 30.

Schuman-Olivier, Zev, Mark Albanese, Sarah Nelson, Lolita Roland, Francyne Puopolo, Lauren Klinker, Howard Shaffer. 2010. "Self-Treatment: Illicit Buprenorphine Use by Opioid-Dependent Treatment Seekers." *Journal of Substance Abuse Treatment* 39 (1):41–50. doi:10.1016/j.jsat.2010.03.014.

Sered, Susan. 2013. "Our Prisons Are Drugging Women." *Salon*, August 8. Accessed August 30, 2013. http://www.salon.com/2013/08/08/are_americas_prisons_drugging_women.

Sered, Susan, and Maureen Norton-Hawk. 2013. "Criminalized Women and the Health Care System: The Case for Continuity of Services." *Journal of Correctional Health Care*: 19 (3): 164–77.

Shildrick, Magrit. 2002. *Embodying the Monster: Encounters with the Vulnerable Self*. London: Sage.

Sinclair, John David. 2001. "Evidence about the Use of Naltrexone and for Different Ways of Using It in the Treatment of Alcoholism." *Alcohol and Alcoholism* 36 (1): 2–10.

Singer, Merrill. 2005. *The Face of Social Suffering: Life History of a Street Drug Addiction*. Long Grove, IL: Waveland.

———. 2008. *Drugging the Poor*. Long Grove, IL: Waveland.

Smith, Betty. 1959. *Annual Report to the Commissioner of Correction*. Framingham: Massachusetts Department of Correction.

———. 1960. *Public Document No. 115 The Commonwealth of Massachusetts Annual Report of the Commissioner of Correction Including Tables on Industries for the Year Ending Dec 31, 1960*. Framingham: Massachusetts Department of Correction.

———. 1961. *Annual Report to the Commissioner of Correction*. Framingham: Massachusetts Department of Correction.

———. 1963. *Public Document No. 115 The Commonwealth of Massachusetts Annual Report of the Commissioner of Correction Including Tables on Industries for the Year Ending Dec. 31, 1963*. Framingham: Massachusetts Department of Correction.

Smith, Caleb. 2009. *The Prison and the American Imagination*. New Haven, CT: Yale University Press.

Soler, Esta, Laura Ponsor, and Jennifer Abod. 1976. "Women in Treatment: Client Self-Report." In *Women in Treatment: Issues and Approaches*, edited by A. Bauman. Arlington, VA: National Drug Abuse Center for Training and Resource Development.

Sordo, Luis, Gregorio Barrio, Maria Bravo, B. Inciar Indave, Louisa Degenhardt, Lucas Wiessing, Marica Ferri, and Roberto Pastor-Barriuso. 2017. "Mortality Risk during and after Opioid Substitution Treatment: Systematic Review and Meta-Analylsis of Cohort Studies." *British Medical Journal* 357: j1550.

Spaulding, Anne, Ryan Seals, Victoria McCallum, et al. 2011. "Prisoner Survival Inside and Outside of the Institution: Implications for Health-Care Planning." *American Journal of Epidemiology* 173 (5): 479–87. Accessed November 17, 2013. http://www.pubmedcentral.nih.gov/articlerender.fcgi?artid=3044840&tool=pmcentrez&rendertype=abstract.

Spaulding, Anne, Ryan Seals, Matthew Page, Amanda K. Brzozowski, William Rhodes, and Theodore M. Hammett. 2009. "HIV/AIDS among Inmates of and Releasees from US Correctional Facilities, 2006: Declining Share of Epidemic but Persistent Public Health Opportunity." *PloS One* 4 (11): e7558. Accessed November 17, 2013. http://www.pubmedcentral.nih.gov/articlerender.fcgi?artid=2771281&tool=pmcentrez&rendertype=abstract.

Spectrum Health Services. 2010. *Women's Recovery Academy: MADoc Participant Handbook.* Revised April 22. Worcester, MA: Spectrum Health Services.

Spencer, Luis. 2013a. *Massachusetts Department of Correction Program Description Booklet.* Boston: Massachusetts Department of Correction.

———. 2013b. *About the Use of Narcotic Detection Dogs.* Boston: Massachusetts Department of Correction.

Spinaris, Caterina, Michael Denhof, and Julie Kellaway. 2012. *Posttraumatic Stress Disorder in United States Corrections Professionals: Prevalence and Impact on Health and Functioning.* Florence, CO: Desert Waters Correctional Outreach.

Spurr, Lawrence. 1955. *Annual Report of the Commissioner of Correction Including Tables on Industries for the Year Ending December 31, 1955.*

Stein, Howard F. 1990. "In What Systems Do Alcohol/Chemical Addictions Make Sense? Clinical Ideologies and Practices as Cultural Metaphors." *Social Science & Medicine* 30 (9): 987–1000. http://www.ncbi.nlm.nih.gov/pubmed/2336576.

Stern, Donald, Mauricia Alvarez, Ralph Fine, et al. 2002. *Report of the Special Commission on the Suffolk County Sheriff's Department.* Boston: Commonwealth of Massachusetts. https://www.clearinghouse.net/chDocs/public/JC-MA-0012-0001.pdf.

Stevenson, Lisa. 2012. "The Psychic Life of Biopolitics: Survival, Cooperation, and Inuit Community." *American Ethnologist* 39 (3): 592–613. http://doi.wiley.com/10.1111/j.1548-1425.2012.01383.x, accessed November 7, 2013.

Strang, John, Jim McCambridge, David Best, Tracy Beswick, Jenny Bearn, Sian Rees, and Michael Gossop. 2003. "Loss of Tolerance and Overdose Mortality after Inpatient Opiate Detoxification: Follow-Up Study." *British Medical Journal* 326 (7396): 959–60.

Substance Abuse and Mental Health Services Administration. 2011. *Creating a Trauma-Informed Criminal Justice System for Women: Why and How.* Rockville, MD: SAMHSA.

———. 2018a. *Key Substance Use and Mental Health Indicators in the United States: Results from the 2017 National Survey on Drug Use and Health* (HHS Publication No. SMA 18-5068, NSDUH Series H-53). Rockville, MD: Center for Behavioral Health Statistics and Quality, Substance Abuse and Mental Health Services Administration. Retrieved from https://www.samhsa.gov/data/report/2017-nsduh-annual-national-report.

———. 2018b. *Clinical Guidance for Treating Pregnant and Parenting Women With Opioid Use Disorder and Their Infants.* HHS Publication No. (SMA) 18-5054. Rockville, MD: Substance Abuse and Mental Health Services Administration.

Sufrin, Carolyn. 2017. *Jailcare.* Oakland: University of California Press.

Sweeney, Megan. 2010. *Reading Is My Window: Books and the Art of Reading in Women's Prisons.* Chapel Hill: University of North Carolina Press.

Szalawitz, Maia. 2016. *Unbroken Brain: A Revolutionary New Way of Understanding Addiction.* New York: St. Martin's Press.

Tartaro, Christine, and David Lester. *Suicide and Self-Harm in Prisons and Jails.* Lanham, MD: Lexington Books, 2010.

Teplin, Linda, Karen Abram, and Gary McClelland. 1996. "Prevalence of Psychiatric Disorders among Incarcerated Women." *Archives of General Psychiatry* 53: 505–12.

Testa, Megan, and Sara West. 2010. "Civil Committment in the United States." *Psychiatry* 7(10): 30–40.

Thomas, Cindy Parks, Stanley Wallack, Sue Lee, Dennis McCarty, Robert Swift. 2003. "Research to Practice: Adoption of Naltrexone in Alcoholism Treatment." *Journal of Substance Abuse Treatment* 24 (1): 1–11.

Thompson, Heather Ann. 2010. "Why Mass Incarceration Matters: Rethinking Crisis, Decline, and Transformation in Postwar American History." *Journal of American History* 97 (3): 703–34.

Todd, Suzanne. 1975. *Methadone Maintenance Treatment in New York City.* New York: Committee on Youth and Correction, Department of Public Affairs.

Tompkins, Steve. 2004. "Press Release: Legislature Approves $2M Appropriation towards Strip Search Settlement."

Tracy, Sarah. 2005. *Alcoholism in America.* Baltimore: Johns Hopkins University Press.

Uggen, Christopher. 1999. "Ex-Offenders and the Conformist Alternative: A Job Quality Model of Work and Crime." *Social Problems* 46: 127–51.

United Nations General Assembly. 1948. *Universal Declaration of Human Rights.* http://www.un.org/en/documents/udhr/.

Valencia, Milton, and John Ellement. 2013. "Annie Dookhan Pleads Guilty in Drug Lab Scandal." *Boston Globe*, November 22.

Van der Zanden, Bart P., Marcel Dijkgraaf, Peter Blanken, Jan M. van Ree, and Wim van den Brink. 2007. "Patterns of Acquisitie Crime during Methadone Maintenance Treatment among Patients Elibile for Heroin Assisted Treattment." *Drug & Alcohol Dependence* (86:1): 84–90.

Van Waters, Miriam. 1957. *The Commonwealth of Massachusetts Statistical Report of the Commissioner of Correction for the Years Ending December 31, 1955 and December 31, 1956.* Framingham: Massachusetts Department of Correction.

Van Zee, Art. 2009. "The Promotion and Marketing of Oxycontin: Commercial Triumph, Public Health Tragedy." *American Journal of Public Health* 99(2): 221–7.

Vogt, Dawne, Daniel King, and Lynda King. 2007. "Risk Pathways for PTSD: Making Sense of the Literature." In *Handbook of PTSD: Science and*

Practice, edited by Matthew J. Friedman, Terence M. Keane, and Patricia A. Resick, 99–115. New York: Guilford Press.

Volkow, Nora. 2010. "Message from the Director: Important Treatment Advances for Addiction to Heroin and Other Opiates." *NIDA Blog*. https://archives.drugabuse.gov/directors-page-dr-nora-volkow-2004-present.

Volkow, Nora, and Thomas McLellan. 2011. "Curtailing Diversion and Abuse of Opioid Analgesics Without Jeopardizing Pain Treatment." *JAMA* 305: 1346–47.

Vrecko, Scott. 2010. "Birth of a Brain Disease: Science, The State and Addiction Neuropolitics." *History of the Human Sciences* 23 (4): 52–67. Accessed February 11, 2014. http://hhs.sagepub.com/cgi/doi/10.1177/0952695110371598.

Wacquant, Loïc. 2009. *Punishing the Poor: The Neoliberal Government of Social Insecurity*. Durham, NC: Duke University Press.

———. 2010. "Class, Race and Hyperincarceration in Revanchist America." *Daedalus*: 74–90.

Waldman, James. 2012. *Hound Pound Narrative: Sexual Offender Habilitation and the Anthropology of Therapeutic Intervention*. Berkeley: University of California Press.

Walsh, Kate, Valerie Gonsalves, Mario Scalora, Steve King, and Patricia Hardyman. 2012. "Child Maltreatment Histories among Female Inmates Reporting Inmate on Inmate Sexual Victimization in Prison: The Mediating Role of Emotional Dysregulation." *Journal of Interpersonal Violence* 27: 492–512.

Warren, James. 1953. *Statistical Reports of the Commissioner of Correction for the Year Ending Dec 31, 1953*. Framingham: Massachusetts Department of Correction.

Western, Bruce. 2006. *Punishment and Inequality in America*. New York, RSF.

Western, Bruce, and Becky Pettit. 2005. "Black-White Wage Inequality, Employment Rates, and Incarceration." *American Journal of Sociology* 111, no. 2: 553–78).

White, William L., and William R. Miller. 2007. "The Use of Confrontation in Addiction Treatment: History, Science, and Time for Change." *Counselor* 8 (4): 12–30.

Wilson, Ruth Gilmore. 2007. *Golden Gulag: Prisons, Surplus, Crisis, and Opposition in Globalizing California*. Berkeley: University of California Press.

Wilson, William Julius. 1987. *The Truly Disadvantaged: The Inner City, the Underclass, and Public Policy*. Chicago: University of Chicago.

Wolfe, Daniel, Patrizia Carrieri, Nabarun Dasgupta, Alex Wodak, Robert Newman, and R. Douglas Bruce. 2011. "Concerns about Injectable Naltrexone for Opioid Dependence." *Lancet* 377: 1468–70.

Wong, Chin-Ho, Haw-Chong Chang, Shanker Pasupathy, et al. 2003. "Necrotizing Fasciitis: Clinical Presentation, Microbiology, and Determinants of Mortality." *Journal of Bone & Joint Surgery* 85: 1454–60.

Yablonsky, Lewis. 1989. *The Therapeutic Community*. Bridgeport, CT: Gardner Press.

Yablonsky, Lewis, and Charles Dederich. 1965. "Synanon: An Analysis of Some Dimensions of the Social Structure of an Antiaddiction Society."

In *Narcotics*, edited by Daniel Wilner and Gene Kassebaum, 193–216. New York: McGraw-Hill.

Yang, Lawrence Hsin, Arthur Kleinman, Bruce Link, Sing Lee, and Byron Good. 2007. "Culture and Stigma: Adding Moral Experience to Stigma Theory." *Social Science & Medicine* 64 (7): 1524–35. Accessed August 23, 2011. http://www.ncbi.nlm.nih.gov/pubmed/17188411.

Young, Allan. 1995. *The Harmony of Illusions: Inventing Post-Traumatic Stress Disorder*. Princeton, NJ: Princeton University Press.

Zlotnick, Caron, Lisa Najavits, Damaris Rohsenow, and Dawn Johnson. 2003. "A Cognitive-Behavioral Treatment for Incarcerated Women with Substance Abuse Disorder and Posttraumatic Stress Disorder: Findings from a Pilot Study." *Journal of Substance Abuse Treatment* 25 (2): 99–105. Accessed August 7, 2013. http://linkinghub.elsevier.com/retrieve/pii/S074054720300 1065.

Index

abstinence-based programs: death risk and, 58, 134; harm reduction, philosophy of, 136; history of, 33, 43

ACT-UP, 197

addiction: addiction trajectories, 5–6; boredom, risks of, 160; changing definitions of, 19–21; community or prison debates, 44–46, 48, 49, 66; economic and sociological forces of, 79–83; gender differences in societal views of, 28–29; harm reduction, philosophy of, 136; Kolb's five types of addicts, 30; prison alternatives, history of, 42–44; prison-pharmaceutical nexus, 127–31; psychotherapy, history of prison treatments, 38–41; treatment of the "delicate female," 29–31; ubiquity of trauma in addicted persons, 89–92

Addiction Research Center, Lexington Prison-Hospital, 31–33

African Americans: civil commitments data, 56; drug use stigma and, 14; employment discrimination, 140–41; incarceration as common life phenomenon, 89; racial disparities in arrests and policing, 39, 56; relapse after treatment, 33; treatment providers, diversity among, 46

alcohol, 6; death rates after prison, 178; drug testing and, 125; history of women in prison, 27–29, 34, 35–36, 35fig, 37, 38–39, 41, 46, 58; involuntary commitment and, 51–52; medications given in prison, 60; naltrexone and, 127–28; therapeutic community treatment model, 43; War on Drugs and, 14; withdrawal from, 60

Alcoholics Anonymous (AA), 38–39, 43, 72, 78–79, 128–29

Alexis, 121, 124

Alice, 89–90

Alisha (Hayes), 84–89, 92, 97–103, 107, 108–9

Alkermes, 128, 129–30

alprazolam (Xanax), 57, 120, 133

American Bar Association: on alternatives to prison (1961), 42

American Medical Association: addiction, use of term, 20; on alternatives to prison (1961), 42

American Society of Addiction Medicine: addiction, use of term, 19–20

amphetamines, 6, 113

anger management classes, 97–98

architecture as means of control, 36

Ash Center for Democratic Governance and Innovation, 144

Ativan (lorazepam), 120

Auerbach, John, 16

Barbara McInnis House, 184

barbiturates, 113, 125

Bartley, David M., 45

Beaumont, Gustave de, 142

CALIFORNIA SERIES IN PUBLIC ANTHROPOLOGY

The California Series in Public Anthropology emphasizes the anthropologist's role as an engaged intellectual. It continues anthropology's commitment to being an ethnographic witness, to describing, in human terms, how life is lived beyond the borders of many readers' experiences. But it also adds a commitment, through ethnography, to reframing the terms of public debate—transforming received, accepted understandings of social issues with new insights, new framings.

Series Editor: Robert Borofsky (Hawaii Pacific University)

Contributing Editors: Philippe Bourgois (UCLA), Paul Farmer (Partners In Health), Alex Hinton (Rutgers University), Carolyn Nordstrom (University of Notre Dame), and Nancy Scheper-Hughes (UC Berkeley)

University of California Press Editor: Naomi Schneider

Founded in 1893,
UNIVERSITY OF CALIFORNIA PRESS
publishes bold, progressive books and journals
on topics in the arts, humanities, social sciences,
and natural sciences—with a focus on social
justice issues—that inspire thought and action
among readers worldwide.

The UC PRESS FOUNDATION
raises funds to uphold the press's vital role
as an independent, nonprofit publisher, and
receives philanthropic support from a wide
range of individuals and institutions—and from
committed readers like you. To learn more, visit
ucpress.edu/supportus.